Converting Old Buildings

Converting Old Buildings

Homes from barns, churches, warehouses,
stations, mills . . .

Alan Johnson

David & Charles

For my parents
James and Elfrida Johnson

British Library Cataloguing in Publication Data

Johnson, Alan, *1950–*
   Converting old buildings.
   1. Great Britain. Buildings. Conversion,
   extension & improvement
   I. Title
   690′.24

   ISBN 0–7153–8802–9

First published 1988
Reprinted 1991

© Alan Johnson 1988

Typeset by ABM Typographics Ltd Hull
Printed in Great Britain
by Redwood Press Ltd, Melksham, Wiltshire
for David & Charles
Brunel House Newton Abbot Devon

Contents

Foreword

This book has been written with the conviction that the expansion of home-ownership and the increasing enthusiasm for DIY is causing an enlarging group of discerning householders to seek greater individuality in their dwellings and more testing challenges in their DIY projects. This refinement in the taste of homeowners and prospective owner-occupiers is very clearly reflected in the change of policy of several of the major housebuilding companies who are now concentrating on the construction of speculatively built houses of pronounced 'personality' in contrast to the conspicuously standardised products of the recent past. It has long been recognised that there is no surer means of creating a home of clear character and individuality than by converting a non-domestic building into a house and early candidates for this treatment were the stables annexes of Victorian town mansions which we know today as 'mews houses'.

Present-day conditions provide an ever-wider range of specialised structures, retired from their original uses, which are suitable for conversion into dwellings. The continuing reduction in the number of manufacturing jobs and the increase in home-based commercial and administrative occupations guarantee that the process of redundancy of purpose-built work places will continue and intensify. The complementary decline in religious observance serves to add to the number of specialised buildings that are being released for conversion as churches and chapels fall into disuse.

A survey of owners and potential owners of period properties which was conducted in 1983 by the Historic Buildings Company showed that 60 per cent of those questioned expressed a preference for living in accommodation that had been converted from former agricultural or industrial uses.

However, that the policy of converting non-domestic buildings into dwellings will develop into a necessity rather than a fashionable whim or a 'sentimental' conservation measure is assured by the quickening pace of deterioration of the nation's housing stock and the continuing inability of the construction industry to build sufficient new houses to replace the life-expired dwellings.

Therefore, this book aims to give guidance to individuals and groups who are contemplating the adaptation of non-domestic buildings into dwellings, be they prospective owner-occupiers or tenants, firstly by outlining suitable approaches to such projects in the context of town planning and other statutory requirements, secondly by describing the constructional qualities and likely deficiencies of the types of buildings that can be considered for conversion, and lastly, by illustrating, through an analysis of more than a score of schemes, how these qualities may best be exploited, adapted and conserved. In this way, it is hoped that DIY enthusiasts undertaking conversions – and professionals working in the field – will be encouraged to enhance rather than erode the essential qualities of the 'recycled' buildings, thereby overturning the widespread opinion that 'conversions' necessarily detract from the qualities of the buildings they affect.

The book deals chiefly with *strategies* for building conversion. Though Chapters 3 and 4 describe the general 'anatomy' of traditionally constructed buildings and the more common building defects that can arise, there is not space to describe in detail all the constructional features that appear in a building of 'large domestic' scale as erected in the nineteenth or early twentieth centuries. For a detailed description of all these elements, readers are advised to consult my book *How to Restore and Improve*

Your Victorian House (David & Charles, 1984).

Although I have included some very large buildings, converted for multiple occupation, as well as much smaller buildings which have converted satisfactorily to provide only single dwellings, even the largest projects prove to be linked to the smaller buildings by a common thread of DIY endeavour. 'Direct labour' – ie the owner undertaking or managing the conversion work – has been the means by which an Oxfordshire barn has been renovated for use as a house (see page 74) and the method by which a vast, ruinous, neo-Gothic institute has been 're-cycled' as a complex of studio offices, workshops and flats (see page 190).

Almost all of the buildings considered were erected in the period 1850-1939, though photographs are included of a former primary school of 1970 (Plates 38 and 39) that has been converted, very successfully, into a sheltered housing scheme for elderly people, proving that even modern buildings of 'rationalised traditional' construction are not immune to being altered, by quite simple means, to evoke clear associations of 'home'.

Alan Johnson
Kingston upon Thames
1988

Acknowledgements

I am very grateful to Michael Mansell for drawing, very clearly, twelve of the figures that accompany the text and I am indebted to Anthony Lambert for suggesting the idea of a book on the subject of the conversion of non-domestic buildings into dwellings. Among many people who allowed me to visit buildings included, or considered for inclusion, in this book, patiently answered my many questions and generously loaned drawings or photographs which have been used to elucidate the text, I would particularly like to thank the following: William Assheton, Sheila Bates, Timothy Bruce-Dick, Steve Buckman, David Counsell, David Clarke, Angela Clemo, Mr and Mrs Flawn-Thomas, Michael Fullerlove, Tony Fretton, Mr and Mrs de Geus, Sue Goddard, Saskia Hallam, David Harrison, Rodney Heywood, Ged Lawrenson, Juliet Mann, Michael Manser, Angus Neil, Giles Quarme, Roy Toms, Roger Wagner, Tony West, John Wharton and Martin Wright.

Dr J. E. C. Peters' booklet *Discovering Traditional Farm Buildings* proved to be valuable in clarifying my thoughts about the characteristics of old farm buildings and the introductory section of Chapter 5 owes much to this highly informative pocket guide. Similarly, Clive Richardson's excellent series of articles on structural surveys which appeared in the *Architects Journal* in the summer of 1985 enlarged my appreciation of the small-scale repairs that can be made to rectify structural shortcomings in traditional buildings and has helped to make Chapter 4 a more comprehensive account of building defects and the related range of gentle remedies than would otherwise have appeared.

Lastly, but by no means least of all, my eternal thanks are due to my wife Liz for enduring so nobly my seemingly endless absences from the family hearth as the research, field work, illustration and writing of this book were conquered.

1 Finding and Funding Your Building

Householders and prospective purchasers who are contemplating the conversion of non-domestic buildings into dwellings will wonder how they can locate and identify the range of buildings available for conversion. In the purchase of conventional houses, the buyers contact estate agents in the area where they wish to buy, resulting in their names being added to the various agents' mailing lists. Details of appropriate properties are then despatched to the prospective purchasers as they become available. This mechanism may not be nearly so useful a means of unearthing non-domestic buildings as it is for locating houses and flats because vacant commercial premises, for instance, tend to be a secondary interest of the high street estate agent. Thus it is important that buyers seeking disused or redundant non-domestic buildings for conversion should be aware that there exist more specialised sources of information on the availability of such buildings.

First, the Society for the Protection of Ancient Buildings publishes a quarterly list of buildings of historical interest for sale, lease or auction, which concentrates on structures built before 1850 that are in need of repair or new uses. Domestic and non-domestic buildings are included in these lists. These lists are circulated only to members of the SPAB. It must be stressed that the terms of the manifesto which was the basis for the formation of the SPAB in 1877, and which remains the code to which all its members are expected to adhere, are quite clear in their condemnation of the over-zealous restoration of period buildings and, indeed, the destructive alteration or enlargement of old buildings for the purpose of putting them to new uses. Hence the SPAB tends to oppose the conversion of ancient rural barns into houses. It is also necessary to emphasise that buildings erected after 1850 – into which category fall the majority of properties considered in this book – are only occasionally included in these lists. Criteria for the inclusion of such late nineteenth-century buildings might include recognition that the authors of their designs were prominent Victorian architects and thus they might be considered inappropriate structures for conversion into dwellings. However, churches and chapels from all phases of the Victorian period appear regularly in the lists and by no means all the properties described represent the work of eminent architects.

Sister national amenity societies of the SPAB are the Ancient Monuments Society, the Georgian Group and the Victorian Society and the interests of the latter two societies broadly cover the eighteenth and nineteenth centuries respectively. Although neither group publishes lists of threatened buildings for sale, all cases of listed buildings from either period which are subject to proposals for their alteration or demolition are referred to them by the local planning authorities. Thus their respective caseworkers have a very wide and detailed knowledge of derelict, disused or otherwise redundant buildings which may be suitable for conversion as a means of preserving structures which would otherwise be lost. In the same way, the Ancient Monuments Society may be able to provide information on threatened buildings that might be salvaged through conversion to domestic use.

Another possible source of information on buildings suitable for conversion is the *Period Property Register* which is published by the Historic Buildings Company. Monthly lists are compiled from details of properties contributed by local authorities as well as estate agents and private vendors. Prospective purchasers receive copies of these lists following payment of an annual or half-annual subscription. This register of properties for sale appears at the beginning of each month; 200-300 properties are described and illustrated in each issue and over the six months of the minimum subscription period approximately one thousand buildings are illustrated and briefly described. Conventional houses clearly dominate the lists, although non-domestic buildings are not excluded.

Lastly, in some regions of Britain, official and semi-official bodies may be able to identify threatened buildings which might be suitable for conversion into dwellings as a way of saving them from destruction. In north-west England, the Civic Trust for the North West, based in Manchester, may be able to offer such information, while in Scotland, the Historic Buildings Bureau (Scotland), a branch of the Scottish Development Department, will answer enquiries related to historic buildings in that country, including those in jeopardy, for which alternative uses are sought.

Surveys

Once an appropriate building has been located, the prudent purchaser will consider commissioning a survey. In many ways this measure is identical to the policy that most buyers adopt in advance of purchasing a house. Just as the cautious buyer of a normal house may make an offer which, if it is accepted, remains 'subject to survey', so the wise purchaser of non-domestic premises will qualify his offer with the statement that the offer will hold good subject to receipt of a satisfactory structural survey report.

Structural Survey

While in the case of conventional houses it is reasonable to regard the structural survey commissioned by the prospective purchaser as an 'optional extra', chiefly calculated to bring peace of mind, an objective and thorough structural survey of non-domestic premises proposed for conversion is virtually essential. This applies because it should be clear that a good number of the many types of non-domestic buildings which may be considered for adaptation

into dwellings lack the staple qualities common to almost all conventional dwellings. For example, two properties of orthodox houses which are particularly apparent are the cellular plan and load-bearing masonry construction. A disused industrial or commercial building which it is intended to convert into dwellings may exhibit neither of these features. Thus the informed lay person's judgement, which may be a satisfactory assessment of the integrity and solidity of a modest conventional house, may be a wildly inaccurate appraisal of the soundness of a more specialised building. Expert advice may be required for the more practical reason that where funds must be borrowed to finance the purchase, it is likely that the lender or mortgagor will require the preparation of a professional, objective and satisfactory report of the building's condition before the loan is approved.

Where a structural survey is required – and it can be seen from the foregoing account that this is likely to be in almost all cases – it is strongly recommended that this investigation should be carried out by an architect, structural engineer or building surveyor who is well versed in the characteristics of the construction of old buildings of all types. A written report should result from a thorough inspection of the property and the worth of the report can be judged from the proportion of text which is taken up by qualifications, disclaimers and exclusion clauses. A preponderance of such clauses suggests that the inspection was superficial and may have been carried out by inexperienced or insufficiently knowledgeable staff. Clearly, a report which is riddled with disclaimers both fails properly to advise the purchaser of the suitability of the structure for adaptation to its new use and fails adequately to protect the buyer against the potentially serious consequences of making a purchase on poor advice. It is for this reason that it is suggested that inquiries concerning the preparation of structural surveys are confined to approaches to those members of the three building-related professions listed above who are noted for their knowledge of older buildings. In relation to the skills of architects in particular, it is useful to note that both the Clients Advisory

Service of the Royal Institute of British Architects and the Society for the Protection of Ancient Buildings can offer information on architects who specialise in the care and restoration of historic buildings.

Measured Survey

A structural survey, or survey of condition, should result in a comprehensive, descriptive and interpretative written report. It is unlikely that it will contain many, if any, drawings or sketches which can serve to confirm the purchaser's view of the suitability of the building for conversion. Where it is not readily apparent to the informed observer that a building will convert satisfactorily into a dwelling or a number of dwellings, it is strongly recommended that a measured survey of the building is commissioned. This is a service that a building surveyor is unlikely to be able to offer. Similarly, structural engineers are more used to restricting their investigation and recording procedure to the truly structural elements of buildings than they are to undertaking a comprehensive inspection of the complete fabric and producing the resultant detailed descriptive drawings. This task is best carried out by an architect. If the building being considered for purchase and conversion is of particular architectural or historic importance, it is possible that the purchaser or his architect may be able to interest students of the local school of architecture in organising a thorough measured survey. This invitation could result in the preparation of comprehensive and meticulous drawings of the building in the form of plans, elevations and sections which may be even more scrupulous than the products of a normal architect's service because they also rate as competitive submissions in a student project.

Clearly, the existence of comprehensive and highly accurate measured survey drawings – however they are obtained – greatly assists any architect in investigating the options for the conversion and in preparing drawings illustrating the general layout and details of the scheme.

Finance for Purchase and Development

The simplest means of procuring a non-domestic building for the purpose of converting it into a dwelling would be to purchase it outright for cash. As applies in the case of conventional house purchase, this option is unlikely to exist for most would-be owners of former watermills, churches or railway stations. Most will need to seek a loan or mortgage to finance, at least in part, their purchase of such buildings. Building societies, banks and local authorities are able to offer mortgages to finance freehold or leasehold owner-occupation. Freehold occupation places ownership in perpetuity in the hands of the owner-occupier and is the normal form of ownership of houses in Britain. For purpose-built flats or flats formed from the conversion of houses, leasehold ownership applies almost invariably. In the latter case, it is quite common for one of the flat-owners to hold the freehold too. The term of a lease is generally 99 years, although a 125-year term seems to be gaining in popularity (999 year leases which at one time applied to many houses in the north of England seem to have become rare and are, in any case, effectively the same as a freehold). Leasehold tenure is as suitable a condition for consideration for the offer of a mortgage as is freehold ownership, provided that a significant part of the lease term remains unexpired (eg, it may prove difficult to obtain a mortgage for purchase of a flat whose 99-year lease has only 50 years to run).

Building Society Mortgages

Until the late 1970s it was fairly unusual for a building society to offer mortages even for the purchase of conventional houses if they had been erected before 1919 – only more modern dwellings were felt to be acceptable risks. This rather rigid attitude has been relaxed in recent years, the societies have broadened their definitions of properties for the purchase of which they are prepared to offer mortgages, and it is now not only normal for building societies to invest in older houses, they are also prepared to consider making loans for the purchase and conversion of non-domestic buildings such as barns, churches and watermills. However, it needs to be stressed that this apparent willingness to consider providing finance for such projects may not apply in all cases. Building societies tend to wish to consider each case on its merits in the light of the likelihood of obtaining planning permission and the marketability of the dwelling, the latter quality being a factor which would be highlighted in the society's surveyor's report on the property. This report would refer to the work to be carried out on the property and would comment on the consequent suitability or otherwise of the project for mortgage assistance. It is almost certain that a mortgage which is offered in relation to a project involving the conversion of a non-domestic building into a dwelling following the submission of a favourable surveyor's report would not be advanced until the approved work needed to create the dwelling was complete. This condition could introduce a requirement for bridging finance (dealt with in the following section on Finance from Banks).

Where the conversion of a large building by a group of prospective owner-occupiers is contemplated, the possibility of obtaining a building society mortgage should not be discounted. In south-eastern England in the late 1980s the housing market witnessed such a steep rise in demand for dwellings that the consequent increase in house prices provoked an explosion in the number of house and flat-buying partnerships that were formed. In some cases houses purchased with building society finance were simply split into separate flats and there is no reason why a proposal for conversion of a non-domestic building should not be approached similarly. One large building society leaves space for four names in its mortgage application form and joint ownership of one property by a number of families is not an unusual arrangement. It is worth remembering that individual managers of building society branch offices are granted considerable discretion by the societies to offer mortgage finance to suitable applicants and that branches sited in cities or large towns are more likely to be willing to offer funds for unorthodox projects than are branches located in rural districts.

However, traditionally, it has been the role of building societies to provide finance for the purchase of dwellings for occupation by individuals and families solely, and a proposal involving the conversion of a non-domestic building into, say, two separate dwellings, one of which is for the use of the owner and the other of which is for letting to tenants is unlikely to win support from most of the main societies. Such schemes may obtain kinder treatment from certain small building societies or 'fringe' banks. It is also necessary to add that, under current law, not more than four persons may share a freehold.

Finance from Banks

At the present time prospective owner-occupiers are in the favoured position of having a range of financial institutions competing for the opportunity to provide mortgages – a condition which is in stark contrast to the 'mortgage famines' which prevailed periodically until little more than a decade ago. The high street banks are the main competitors of the building societies for this business, although certain fringe banks, whose titles are less familiar than those of the 'Big Four' are sometimes prepared to offer mortgages on less orthodox projects than the real estate which is purchased with finance from the building societies, clearing banks or local authorities.

If a mortgage is obtained from a bank, the mortgage interest relief against income tax which applies to mortgages obtained from building societies operates in exactly the same way. The mortgagee is asked to complete an application form requesting 'mortgage interest relief at source' (MIRAS) which the mortgagor then forwards to the Inland Revenue. The whole, or a significant proportion of subsequent mortgage repayments, depending upon the sum borrowed, is then viewed by the Inland Revenue as a tax-deductible charge on the owner-occupier and consequent repayments of the mortgage and interest are reduced below the gross amount which would otherwise be payable to the mortgagor.

The second role which a bank may need to perform in relation to the purchase of property is the provision of bridging finance. In the circumstance that a mortgage has been offered by a building society, but no part of the loan is to be released until all the work approved by the society's surveyor has been carried out, it is plain that the project cannot proceed in the absence of funds to 'bridge' the gap. Although the precise rate of interest on such a bridging loan may be at the discretion of the bank's branch manager, it is normal for the interest to be set at a rate at least 2 per cent above the bank's base lending rate.

Unlike long-term mortgages, the bank mortgage which is offered as bridging finance is not susceptible to mortgage interest relief at source because it should be needed only during the short period in which the approved work is implemented and accepted following the building society surveyor's reinspection of the premises. This acceptance triggers the award of the society's mortgage to which mortgage interest relief at source can apply. Thus it is advisable that the period of bridging finance is minimised if the mortgagee is not to suffer disproportionate expense in servicing this short-term loan. Yet there is a silver lining to this particular cloud. If a bridging mortgage is being used for the purpose of purchasing the mortgagee's sole or main residence, at the discretion of the Inland Revenue, it too may qualify for mortgage interest relief and this can be claimed retrospectively. Before the end of the tax year in which bridging finance has been employed, the bank provides a certificate stating the amount of interest paid. When this document is presented to the tax office an adjustment may be made to the mortgagee's tax-free allowance for the preceding tax year, resulting in a refund of a part of the income tax already paid.

Government Grants and Loans

Central government can play a role in providing funds to assist development through the mechanism of a City Grant. City Grant assistance applies to more than sixty local authority areas which lie largely in Inner London, the West Midlands, the North-West and the North-East – ie the depressed traditional industrial areas and the declining inner city commercial/residential areas of the capital.

City Grant is a mechanism which aims to promote the economic and physical regeneration of inner urban areas by encouraging private sector investment. It is available for capital investment projects which would not go ahead without some public sector assistance but which, with that assistance, are commercially viable and help to deal with urban deprivation. The common factors of schemes undertaken to date which succeeded in their applications for Urban Development Grants (the predecessor of City Grant) were substantial private sector capital investment and social benefits, such as new jobs, good quality housing or the reclamation of derelict sites or buildings. Thus, although developments such as the erection of new manufacturing or retail premises tend to be favoured for their capacity to generate increased employment, schemes involving only the creation of dwellings also qualify for consideration for award of City Grant. Environmental improvement – 'physical regeneration' – is seen as an aim second only to job creation. However, it must be appreciated that City Grant will never form the larger proportion of expenditure. The private sponsor is expected to meet the greater part of project costs, but if the value of the completed development would be insufficient to provide an adequate return on total project costs, City Grant is available to bridge the gap. The amount is decided after a detailed appraisal of the project, but proposals in which a large proportion of private finance is likely to be 'levered' into the scheme by a comparatively small public contribution in the form of City Grant are preferred. City Grant may be a grant or a loan or a combination of both. If the circumstances justify it, loan interest may be waived or a grant may be conditionally repayable. Most City Grant schemes are likely to be undertaken by companies, but partnerships, pension funds, charities or individuals may also apply for City Grant. It is central government's main requirement that the developer should have the expertise and financial resources to complete the project without further assistance from the public sector. Developers – who might, for example, include a group of prospective owner-occupiers hoping to obtain homes through the conversion of a disused commercial building and who believe that their project qualifies for City Grant – should first apply to their local regional office of the Department of the Environment for detailed guidance notes on the operation of this form of official help.

Because many projects for the conversion of non-domestic buildings into dwellings will involve the renovation of historic buildings, it is important to note that although City Grant may be payable to a project which is also receiving a grant from the Historic Buildings and Monuments Commission (see Chapter 2), the amount of City Grant offered will reflect the availability of this other central government assistance.

Alternative Forms of Tenure

Thus far, this survey of the means of funding the provision of dwellings through the conversion of buildings has assumed that freehold or leasehold ownership will be the form of tenure. However, there are alternative forms of tenure of dwellings despite the current concentration upon owner-occupation as the favoured option. Described below are other types of tenure which are particularly relevant to groups of people interested in solving their own housing problems or those of others.

Housing Associations

With the dramatic contraction of the private rented sector in the post-war period, a so-called 'third force' in housing provision has arisen behind the growing ranks of owner-occupiers and local authority tenants – the housing associations. This movement for the provision of housing through voluntary effort was greatly strengthened by the setting up in 1964 of the Housing Corporation, an agency of central government whose job it is to fund and to encourage the building of dwellings by housing associations. More than 2,500 housing associations are registered with the Housing Corporation. They are non-profit-making organisations run by committees of volunteers who give their time and energy to provide and manage housing for people who might otherwise be unable to buy or rent a suitable home. Some associations rely entirely on the work of volunteers while others employ staff. It can be seen, therefore, that housing associations are generally set up by concerned individuals in an attempt to solve other people's housing problems. People in housing need who collaborate in order to obtain and manage their own housing may decide to form a housing co-operative – another type of housing association which is described later.

While the purpose of a housing association may not seem pertinent to those who are considering the conversion of a non-domestic building to meet their own housing needs, for those who are approaching this condition from a different direction – namely, the task of rescuing and renovating a redundant building for residential use – the following brief account of housing association activities in the field of building rehabilitation may be relevant.

Through the agency of housing associations, many people who cannot afford to become owner-occupiers and who are not regarded as high priority cases on local authority housing waiting lists (eg, single people and small families) have been able to find suitable dwellings. Also, since 1980, the opportunities for people to buy dwellings built or refurbished by housing associations have increased through a variety of 'shared ownership' schemes. Shared ownership was introduced to help aspiring purchasers who cannot afford to buy a home outright. Prospective owner-occupiers may not be able to afford the full mortgage repayments, or the deposit, or both. Through shared ownership the purchaser buys a share of the property and pays rent on the remainder. Gradually, further shares may be purchased to progress to outright ownership. 'Pathfinder' is a shared ownership scheme which has been developed by a large West Midlands housing association in conjunction with a building society. The home buyers become members of a mutual housing association, jointly owned by its members, which has a 35-year index-linked mortgage on the rented share of the dwelling. They can sell at any time and retain all the growth in their share of the equity in the property after paying off the outstanding mortgage. Comparison with the repayments needed on a 100 per cent mortgage over a 25-year term shows this mechanism to be advantageous for home buyers with only small resources.

Also promoted since 1980 has been the Housing Corporation's scheme of Improvement for Sale. This policy involves the sale to first-time buyers of properties purchased and improved by a housing association. A central government grant covers any difference between the cost of purchase and improvement and the sale price (ie, to be affordable by the first-time buyer the purchase price is likely to have to be lower than the combined cost of purchase and improvement). It is not known how widespread has been the adoption of this policy, although the current volatility of the housing market suggests that it has been little used recently, the formerly rapid acceleration in the cost of dwellings making excessively large the government grant required for subsidising a sensible price to impecunious first-time buyers.

Although attitudes within the National Federation of Housing Associations are divided, some housing associations have recently been taking a more entrepreneurial stance than has been traditional in building and energetically marketing dwellings for sale. As applies in the above example of a shared ownership scheme, this approach has been aided by the use of funds stemming not only from central government via the Housing Corporation, but also from the private sector in the form of building society finance. The housing association which operates the 'Pathfinder' scheme also offers an 'Easy Start' option for the purchase of new homes which only requires a deposit of approximately 5 per cent, repayment of the mortgage being made over a 40-year term rather than the conventional 25-year period. Clearly, such an arrangement is attractive to those with a lower income and less capital than the typical young house buyer.

Formal or informal amenity groups who view the setting up of housing associations as a means of rescuing endangered buildings are likely to be advised by the Housing Corporation to work first of all with an existing local housing association to gain experience and build up a good track record before applying to register independently. This applies because the corporation must be confident that a registered association will be able to achieve its aims satisfactorily and that its committee has specialised experience and expertise as well as commitment and common sense. Also, an association will not be registered unless a local authority or the corporation can guarantee funding for the association's proposed housing scheme.

Probably the most promising course for the solution of the housing needs of a group of people who cannot afford, or do not wish, to become owner-occupiers, is the formation of a housing co-operative.

Housing Co-operatives

A housing co-operative is a type of housing association, although it differs from a conventional housing association in being a formally constituted group of people who together manage and control their own dwellings rather than those provided for others. Each person is a member of the co-operative and each has an equal say in management decisions and the opportunity to stand for election to any committees the co-operative may decide, by virtue of its size and work-load, to form to provide and run all the housing. No member individually owns their house or flat or makes a profit at the expense of another. The co-op owns, or holds a long lease on, the housing occupied by its members, but in the case of an approved project of a co-op registered with the Housing Corporation, most or all of the outlay for the purchase of the freehold or lease will be made either by the local authority or the corporation itself in the form of a loan. A calculation is then made to work out how much of this loan the co-op can afford to repay through the income obtained from members paying a fair rent for their homes. Where a co-op's members occupy buildings which have been renovated to provide dwellings, this sum is repaid by the co-op over 30 years. The remaining part of the loan is repaid, on completion of the building works, by central government subsidy administered by the Housing Corporation. This form of housing co-op is known as a 'fair rent co-operative' and the rent for each home is fixed by the local rent officer. It is reviewed every two years. Like the conventional housing associations which form the overwhelming majority of societies registered with the Housing Corporation, housing co-ops are continuously monitored by the corporation to help to ensure that good standards of management are maintained.

A co-operative can be formed by a group of people in housing need who wish to realise a proposal to buy and convert an existing building into dwellings. In order to borrow money and to enter into contracts with builders, etc, the co-operative needs to be legally established. Most housing co-ops do this by adopting rules which satisfy the requirements of the Industrial and Provident Societies Act and then paying a fee to register the co-op and its rules with the Registrar of Friendly Societies. Members of a co-op which is registered in this way have limited liability rather in the manner of a conventional commercial company. Such a co op must have at least seven members, all of whom purchase equal shares in the enterprise. The cost of these shares need only be minimal – perhaps as little as £1 each – but this very small financial stake is unlikely to be refundable to the member when he or she leaves the co-op. Most housing co-ops prefer to obtain a larger, but still modest, contribution from each member, which helps to cover costs incurred in administration etc. When the member leaves the co-op this sum is refunded and an equal contribution is expected from the replacement member. It is important to note that this share is not a share in the commercial sense. Because it is a principle of formal co-operation that no member shall profit at the expense of another, each member's share cannot gain in value. However, if the co-op operates so efficiently that savings are made, the members may decide to return this benefit to the co-op rather than banking it for future development, either by providing a new common amenity, or by reducing the weekly or monthly payments of all members. If the co-op wishes to qualify for government grants available to non-profit-making organisations which relieve housing stress, its rules must also satisfy the requirements of the Housing Act 1974 and it must be registered with the Housing Corporation. More information on the opportunities for forming housing co-operatives is available from the Housing Corporation (see Useful Addresses, p. 204).

Most homeless or potentially homeless people who believe that membership of a co-operative is likely to be the best way of solving their housing needs are unlikely to possess the wide range of skills necessary to manage the conversion and rehabilitation of buildings, even if they have been purchased by others. For this reason a system of 'secondary' housing co-ops exists. A secondary co-operative is a federation of primary co-operatives whose purpose is to provide services for its constituent members. Secondary housing co-operatives service the requirements of primary housing co-ops by providing the professional, technical, management, administrative and educational services which the individual members of a primary housing co-op may have neither the time nor the expertise to supply themselves. Acquiring the building for conversion, obtaining finance and subsidy as a housing association already registered with the Housing Corporation, contracting design and construction, are all tasks most efficiently undertaken by a secondary housing co-op or other sponsoring organisation. When the final account has been settled, ownership is transferred to the primary housing co-operative. The Housing Corporation publishes a list of secondary housing co-operatives and will advise aspiring co-operators of suitable organisations to approach for the provision of specialist services.

Self-build Co-operatives

A house-building co-operative is a co-operative in which members pool their labour and skills to build houses. The most common type of house-building co-operative in this country is the self-build co-operative of people organised as a co-op to build their own houses using their own labour. The usual size of a development carried out in this way is between ten and thirty dwellings. Upon completion, the houses are almost invariably transferred to the individual members who then become conventional owner-occupiers. Hence the co-operative lasts only as long as it takes to complete the project. In recent years around three hundred such short-life co-ops have been registered each year in

England and Wales.

This progress to individual home-owner-ship through group effort can be assisted by the Housing Corporation who can find loan finance and act as guarantor to help groups in genuine housing need who wish to form self-build housing associations. Also, self-build co-operatives are likely to obtain an increasingly sympathetic response from the private financial institutions which offer mortgages. A recently completed scheme of a self-build co-operative at Stirling in Scotland comprised thirty-six dwellings, twenty-seven of which were rehabilitated from a dilapidated nineteenth-century terrace, the remainder being new houses erected off concrete ground-floor slabs installed by a builder. The formation of the co-operative was backed by the local autho-rity, which also owns the site. Mortgages were provided by various building societies.

In countries other than the UK, it is common for self-build groups to occupy their completed scheme as a co-operative housing society. To try to encourage this arrangement, the Housing Corporation intends to fund a self-build pilot project in which a co-op will rehabilitate derelict dwellings, the members going on to occupy the flats either on a shared-ownership basis or as a conventional housing co-operative. The relevance of such an arrangement to the rescue and conversion to dwellings of a redundant non-domestic building by a group of impecunious and democratically minded self-builders is clear.

Use of Consultants

Although the main job of this chapter is to indicate the many ways in which buildings suitable for conversion into dwellings may be located and purchased, it is necessary to add a cautionary word about the adoption of an over-adventurous attitude towards build-ing conversion. Many unskilled or inexperi-enced people who launch themselves too enthusiastically into a substantial building or restoration project quickly find out that they have 'bitten off more than they can chew', with the eventual result that in-complete projects are offered for sale before (or after) family or marital relations are

seriously damaged. This step is sometimes a consequence of a shortage of funds to under-take further work, but equally it may be owed to the owner's incorrect assessment of his or her own ability to estimate accurately the extent of the work. In relation to the execution of the physical work, it is fairly easy for the owner with a realistic assess-ment of his DIY skills to estimate his ability to undertake the anticipated range of craft operations and to account for payments to tradesmen to cover the more onerous skilled tasks, but it is tempting to believe that economies can safely be made on the less tangible aspects of the project. Plainly, this area includes the employment of an archi-tect, building surveyor, quantity surveyor or even a structural engineer in the planning and realisation of the scheme. The involve-ment of such professionals can quickly come to be seen as a luxury rather than a necessity. It is possible that a multi-talented and very knowledgeable amateur with un-limited spare time may be able to plan and execute the work proficiently, in a logical sequence and to a prearranged programme, but such people are rare and most projects will require the input of expert advice at some stage.

Employing an architect can help in many ways. Even before the building has been purchased, the architect's skill of quickly visualising the possibilities for conversion inherent in existing buildings can help to confirm or modify the prospective owner's conversion proposals. Also, architects are trained to make measured surveys and to draw up, in a clear form, the results of such surveys. Architects who specialise in the restoration of old buildings are often expert in the diagnosis of defects in construction and building materials and the opinion of such a specialist on the condition of an existing building and its suitability for conversion can be invaluable. As well as providing a true-to-scale depiction of the general layout and structure of the existing building for the client's information and records, the architect's measured survey can also act as the basis for scheme drawings of the conversion and can help the architect and his client to better understand and graphically experiment with the conversion options. Drawings of the agreed scheme may then be modified and expanded to form the application documents for planning consent and building regulations permission. Architects are well acquainted with the process of consideration of such applications by planning officers and local authority building control officers and the involvement of an architect at this stage may save the average client much time and worry.

Similarly, employing an architect to organise other important pre-contract procedures, such as the selection of a builder through negotiation or competitive tendering, may pay dividends. Retention of his services for site supervision and the administration of the contract during the building operation may generate a cost-saving condition because the requirement that he should certify work as satisfactory before the builder receives payment is a valuable check on the stratagems of unscrupulous or greedy contractors. A well experienced building surveyor may be equally able to carry out many pre-contract functions and the contract administration, but very few surveyors will be able to visualise or convey to the client in drawings an imaginative and ingenious re-use of the space which is offered by the building selected for conversion.

In complicated projects the structural engineer is employed as a helpmate to the architect. Where the new structure – for instance, additional load-bearing walls, joisted floors and modified roofs – is straightforward and of traditional materials like brickwork, blockwork or timber, it may be well within the competence of the architect to determine the appropriate sizes and manner of assembly of such components and to provide the related simple calculations to satisfy the building control officer. If the scheme requires a complex structure including the use of steel, or reinforced concrete beams and columns, laminated timber beams or arches, or specialised forms of foundations, or proof is needed that an existing foundation or construction will accept considerable additional loads and stresses, then it is essential that a structural engineer is consulted.

Where the success of a scheme hinges upon an ingenious structural system (as might apply, for instance, in the conversion of a church interior) it is important that the structural engineer is introduced to the project at an early stage so that he may collaborate with the architect to produce a general layout of the scheme that is acceptable in both structural and architectural terms. Once this structural strategy has been integrated into the architecture and the necessary statutory consents have been obtained, the structural engineer's course through the contract runs parallel to that of the architect. He inspects the standard of the structural work executed by the builder and has the discretion to approve or reject the builder's related applications for payment by advising the architect of the suitability of this work. If the engineer condemns structural work, the architect may choose to make a proportionate deduction from his certificate which recommends payment of the builder by the client.

A similar peace of mind to that enjoyed by the client who employs a professional engineer to design and oversee a complicated restructuring of an existing building flows from the employment of a quantity surveyor on a project where a wide range of specialist activities or large amounts of diverse materials must be used. In projects where a complicated sequence of specialised jobs (eg, underpinning and the construction of basements) can be foreseen, there is a strong case for careful and thorough pre-planning of the construction operation by an independent consultant who can identify optimum contract arrangements and construction methods. Because of his close acquaintanceship with the project-planning methods and resources of contractors, a quantity surveyor may be able to give valuable advice at the very earliest stage of a project on the most cost-effective way of realising the scheme. Such advice may also be useful during the period of tender-offer analysis which follows the receipt of competitive tenders because it will assist the process of identifying the optimum offer.

Similarly, the value of the quantity surveyor's traditional 'building accountant' role as the quantifier of trade operations and materials must not be underrated. His compilation of a Bill of Quantities which acts as the basis for the preparation of competitive tenders and which operates as a check on the contractor's claims for payment during the building operation may be an indispensable service in complicated projects where careful cost control is essential.

2 Permissions and Building Procedures

Having found and purchased the building, it is necessary to give consideration to the statutory permissions which must be obtained before the physical work of conversion can proceed. The first such permission – which will approve or disapprove of the very strategy of change of use from former function to domestic use – is planning permission.

Planning Consent

Since 1947, development has been controlled under planning laws. This development control system exists in order to regulate in the public interest the development and the use of land. Therefore, a change of use – even though it may not involve building or other works – is regarded as development for planning purposes. Consideration of applications for planning permission and the resultant determination of these applications is undertaken by the local authorities who are also the local planning authorities. Districts and boroughs as well as county councils operate as local planning authorities, but this power is not granted to parish councils.

Several requirements must be fulfilled in making a planning application. First, application must be made on a particular form which is freely available from the local authority's planning department. This office will also define the number of copies of the form which must be completed (not more than four). Applicants may wish an agent, perhaps an architect or surveyor, to act for them, and such an agent can make the application on the owner's behalf. The form, which is not difficult to fill in, includes a set of standard questions which request information on the size and location of the site of the proposed development and the nature and purpose of the project. These must be

answered and it is a further requirement of the Town and Country Planning Act (1990) that a certificate is completed confirming the applicant's ownership of the site, or, in the case that the applicant is not the owner of the site, that permission to make the application has been given by the site owner.

Completion of the application form and the accompanying 'Section 66' certificate is clearly an inadequate explanation of most proposals and the inclusion of drawings illustrating the scheme is almost unavoidable. It is this circumstance which causes most applicants to seek expert advice and assistance. Application may be made for outline or detailed planning consent, although it is important to note that for the type of project which is the subject matter of this book – ie, involving a change of use – an outline application may not be submitted. Full, detailed particulars of such a proposal are required. The application documents must also be accompanied by a fee which is defined in the scale of charges that accompanies the application form. Once the local planning authority has received a valid planning application, it is required to determine the application within eight weeks. In the event that no decision is reached within this statutory period, the applicant has an automatic right of appeal to the Secretary of State for the Environment – a facility for which no charge is made.

In practice, it often takes longer than eight weeks for the local authority to transact any necessary consultations with the applicant, or other interested parties, and to obtain a decision from the planning committee of lay councillors. Most applicants steer the cautious course of patiently awaiting the council's decision. It is extremely unlikely that the time taken by a local planning authority to determine an application could equal the lengthy period which generally expires before an appeal decision is given.

Listed Building Consent

Many old commercial, industrial and ecclesiastical buildings are sufficiently noteworthy to qualify for listing as buildings of architectural or historic interest. Most buildings which were erected between 1700 and 1840 qualify for this status. For buildings put up after 1840, selection operates; only buildings of definite quality are on the list – a criterion that applies even more firmly to post-1914 buildings.

In the listed building system of England and Wales there are two main categories: Grade I and Grade II. A Grade I listed building is considered to be of exceptional importance and the opportunities for making substantial alterations to it are likely to be slight. Plainly, this limitation could apply equally to a proposal for change of use of a listed building even where the physical alterations proposed to make the building suitable for use as a dwelling are insignificant. The lesser grade of listed building is Grade II and the majority of listed buildings fall into this category which covers 'buildings of special interest which warrant every effort being made to preserve them'. The category Grade II* relates to 'buildings of particular importance and perhaps containing outstanding features . . .'; thus it is a more stringent category of listing than Grade II and it often applies to buildings which are generally of Grade II standard but which contain certain internal features of special interest. In these cases there is as strong a presumption against alterations to the interiors as there is to external changes and so such buildings may automatically disqualify themselves from consideration for change of use into dwellings. In Scotland the grades of listed building are A, B and C based on definitions very similar to those of the Grade I, Grade II* and Grade II classifications which apply in England and Wales.

The significance of this system to the building owner lies in the fact that those who wish to carry out substantial work to, or to demolish, a building that is on the statutory list of buildings, first have to make a special application to the local planning authority and obtain an approval known as Listed Building Consent. Like planning permission, this consent normally lasts for five years and if work has not started by then, the applicant must apply again. Application is made on a special form obtainable from the borough or district council planning department. It is a separate procedure from making a planning application because sometimes Listed Building Consent is required when an ordinary planning permission is not necessary. No fee is charged for consideration by a local planning authority of an application for Listed Building Consent. Where it is not clear that proposed alterations will be susceptible to official approval, building owners may be able to obtain advice from specialists, called conservation officers, employed by most local planning authorities. Government regulations require the local planning authority to advertise proposed alterations to a listed building for twenty-one days. The local authority also asks the Historic Buildings and Monuments Commission, local amenity societies and the national amenity societies, as appropriate, for their views only making its decision when it has considered all representations. Local authorities aim to complete this process within eight weeks – although in London, different consultations are undertaken and the procedures can take longer. Procedures are also slightly different in Scotland and Wales.

If work is carried out to a listed building without consent first being obtained, the penalties are heavy. On summary conviction an offender is liable to three months' imprisonment or a fine of up to £2,000 or both. Even if, following investigations, the work is considered reasonable, it is still an offence to carry out alterations to a listed building unless they have been authorised. The only mitigating circumstances that may be allowed are where the works are essential to preserve public safety. It is difficult to prove this condition in the absence of a Dangerous Structure Notice issued under the Public Health laws by the local authority, and even in this circumstance the owner must apply for Listed Building Consent before doing the work the notice requires. The owner of a listed building is also obliged to keep it in reasonable repair. If he does not do so, the local authority can serve a Repairs Notice. This specifies the work needed to bring the building up to a reasonable condition and gives a time limit for carrying it out. If the work is not implemented, the local authority can compulsorily purchase the building. Clearly, if the building has been deliberately neglected, a minimal purchase price will be paid. In some cases the council can have the basic repairs done without acquiring the building and then charge the cost to the owner.

Copies of all statutory lists are held at the local planning department where all the information on conservation areas is also kept. Purchasers of venerable non-domestic buildings who are uncertain of their official status will be reassured to learn that being on a list is a registered land charge and the information will appear on 'searches' of property carried out by solicitors acting on their behalf. Listed status may apply to the unconverted building or it may be conferred during or after the conversion process. The fact that a building is listed Grade II is not necessarily an obstacle to a proposal to convert it into a single home or several dwellings, provided the local planning authority can be persuaded that the scheme is not detrimental to those features of the building which qualified it for inclusion in the list. These qualities are more likely to be the general appearance or 'ambiance' of the building than particular details, and so conversion to a group of dwellings of, say, a large church with a noteworthy interior is likely to be regarded as a contentious proposal by the local planning authority because they will prefer to consider a new use which will keep the large internal volume as one undivided space. However, where the choice lies between conversion to dwellings and continuing dereliction which invites demolition of a structure that is a significant piece of the townscape, plainly the approval of any proposal for an uncontroversial new use is to be preferred to loss of the building. It is much less likely that such 'policy' objections to a proposal to convert a small listed building to domestic use will be encountered, although planning officers are likely to oppose insensitive additions to the exterior of a listed building which relies on its simple outline for its impact. This sensitivity may extend even to a proposal to insert an additional window in

a roof surface. Clearly, it is advisable to liaise closely with the local planning authority in order to establish exactly the acceptability of all proposed alterations, extensions or renovations which may not exactly reproduce the status quo.

Immunity from listing can be sought, and, if granted, will last for five years, but this procedure runs the risk of drawing public attention to the building. It is, in any case, debatable that the 'listing' of a building is a penalty which must be avoided at all costs. It seems that for the owners of many older houses, the conferment of listed building status on their properties is viewed as a distinction which enhances their value. Also, the fact that a building is listed places a duty upon the local authority to encourage its preservation and the recognition that this condition may be to the financial disadvantage of the owner has resulted in the creation of a range of opportunities for owners to apply for grants or loans to help pay for repairs and restoration. These facilities are described later. The fact that a building is listed may also show a financial advantage in relation to construction costs because radical alterations to a listed building (but not an unlisted building in a conservation area) may exempt the work from Value Added Tax. Although the tax position is extremely complicated, and owners are advised to obtain an expert opinion on each particular case, it appears that wholesale alterations (not maintenance or piecemeal modifications) to a listed building may exempt the work from the addition of VAT, which applies to all other construction work to existing buildings.

Conservation Areas

Since the passing of the Civic Amenities Act (1967), local planning authorities are empowered to designate conservation areas. They are areas of particular architectural quality where the grouping of all the buildings makes a significant contribution to the townscape. Local authorities have a duty to 'enhance' conservation areas and may do this by repairing buildings, creating vehicle-free zones, restoring street furniture, repaving in better materials and planting trees. In relation to this last activity, it should be noted that trees are protected in conservation areas – they are treated as if they have a Tree Preservation Order on them. Landowners who wish to fell or lop such a tree must notify the local planning authority who may require the planting of a replacement tree, while proposals for the demolition of unlisted buildings, or significant parts of such buildings (and this may include features such as garden walls) in conservation areas, require building owners to apply for Conservation Area Consent which operates in a similar way to the Listed Building Consent process described above.

Ecclesiastical Exemption

Anglican churches are not subject to the statutory Listed Building Consent procedure. Historic Anglican churches that continue to be used as places of worship have been exempted from the restrictions applied to secular buildings since the Ancient Monuments Act of 1913. This exemption means that a functioning Anglican church can be altered or even partially demolished in the absence of the approval granted by Listed Building Consent. Case law has subsequently established that the church buildings of all denominations are, while they continue to be used for worship, exempt from this control where partial demolition and alteration are planned.

However, the right to decide the future of their *redundant* churches without recourse to Listed Building Consent is a privilege enjoyed solely by the Church of England. Churches of other denominations are not exempt from the system so that, for instance, noteworthy former Methodist or Roman Catholic churches may qualify for listing while redundant Anglican churches of similar worth and date remain immune from such protection.

The Church of England operates its own structure of listing which is roughly the same as the classifications applied to historically or architecturally important secular buildings. The finest examples of its church architecture, including the ancient cathedrals, are listed 'Grade I' and a very large number of more modest churches are listed 'Grade II' but this internal system lacks the safeguards against ill-considered alteration and demolition which are built into the statutory system. Despite the Church of

England's readiness to hold public inquiries in relation to its proposals to demolish churches which are listed under its own system, such inquiries are non-statutory and the church authorities are not obliged to abide by the inspector's recommendations. Until recently the Anglican Church had complete freedom to deal with 'listed' ecclesiastical buildings in its ownership as it thought fit. This circumstance has now improved with the acceptance of the Church that it will take the advice of the Secretary of State for the Environment before effecting a proposal to demolish a 'listed' church building. The fact that no attempt to bring the protection of historic churches within the statutory system of listing has yet succeeded suggests that, for the foreseeable future, the Anglican Church will continue, almost independently, to determine the fate of the noteworthy religious buildings in its ownership. The usual nature of the recommendations for the re-use of redundant churches which are formulated by the Anglican Church may ensure that the stock of disused C of E churches available for conversion to domestic use will remain small for many years to come.

Building Regulations Permission

In parallel with the control of development through the planning laws runs the system of government control of public health and hygiene. Public Health legislation in England has existed since 1848 and in the 1870s its scope was extended to include standards of building construction and the layout of dwellings. In London, a building code had developed earlier in consequence of the Great Fire of 1666. This distinction between the system for the control of constructional standards in Inner London and that which applied in the rest of England and Wales lasted until 1986 when the Building (Inner London) Regulations (1985) were introduced as a version of the Building Regulations (1985) which operate outside the capital. There is now a uniform system of administration of building regulations throughout England and Wales, although the version of the regulations which applies in Inner

London retains certain standards which are unique to the capital. These requirements relate mainly to very large or high buildings, fire prevention and means of escape and the uniting of adjoining buildings through party walls. The law defining procedures for notifying adjoining owners of work to party walls in Inner London and the rights and obligations of adjoining owners has for long been distinct from the conditions which apply elsewhere in the UK, and these arrangements are not affected by the introduction of more standardised building regulations. Scotland has its own system of building regulations.

It is a principle of the Building Regulations (1985) that the control of constructional standards should not continue to be a monopoly of the local authorities. A system of 'self-certification' is approved by the controlling Building Act (1984) which allows certain organisations to operate as 'approved inspectors' of new construction. To date, only the National House Building Council (NHBC) has taken up this option, and then only in relation to new houses erected by some of its member companies. Thus it is very likely that owners who are engaged in advancing building conversion projects in the foreseeable future will continue to have to make application to the building control section of the local authority.

The Building Regulations (1985) define two ways of making an application. The owner, or his agent, may either submit a full application – which must include comprehensive drawings and specifications satisfying the relevant requirements of the regulations – or he may submit a Building Notice. The latter document, copies of which are freely available from the building control office of the local authority, notifies the building inspector of the owner's intention to undertake building work. The applicant is required to give brief details of the nature and extent of the work and assessment and approval of the quality of the building construction are effected through subsequent site visits of the building inspector. Perhaps it is apparent that the 'Building Notice' option is likely to be a riskier route to official approval than the pre-construction approval achievable through the full application, particularly in the case of a complicated conversion project. Where approval under the building regulations can be obtained prior to construction commencing, a clear picture is presented of arrangements and materials known to be acceptable to the building inspector and hence careful control of construction costs is possible. If the Building Notice procedure is adopted – perhaps because time is not available for a full application to be submitted and approved before building work must start – it is very unlikely that all the proposed layouts, details and materials will prove to be acceptable to the building control officer as he checks standards through site inspections, and consequent modifications to proposed* or already executed building construction may add considerable cost to the project.

Whether application for Building Regulations Permission is made through submission of a full application or a Building Notice, a fee is payable and the amount of this fee is defined by the scale of charges which the local authority sends with the application forms. For budgeting purposes, it is worth remembering that fees for the consideration of applications for building regulations permission and subsequent site inspections of the work are payable in two instalments. The 'plans fee' accompanies the application form, but the balance of the full fee is payable following the building inspector's first site visit and this charge is likely to be at least twice the plans fee.

Where a full application is made, the statutory period for consideration of a valid submission is five weeks, although this period may be extended to eight weeks by mutual agreement. However, few initial applications prove to be flawless so that most applicants will find that they receive from the local authority a letter identifying the unacceptable arrangements which also requests the submission of revised drawings. If this revised information arrives too late to be considered within the statutory period, a Notice of Rejection is likely to be issued in consequence of the lay committee's legal obligation to determine the application before time runs out, but the revised details are then checked and if they answer the shortcomings of the original submission, the applicant will subsequently receive a Notice of Approval.

There are two ways of providing information which complies with the requirements of the Building Regulations (1985). One way involves adopting the arrangements described in the 'Approved Documents' which are integral to the regulations and which offer 'ready-made' answers to the requirements. The other approach involves the satisfaction of the regulations by the adoption of materials and constructional arrangements which are approved by Codes of Practice and British Standards referred to in the regulations. This method makes much more work for the designer in justifying the 'unconventional' arrangements which are proposed, but it is likely to be an unavoidable course for the solution of some of the problems of the work which is controlled by the building regulations, particularly in the field of building conversion. This applies because a lack of space to incorporate 'Approved Document' arrangements, or the inescapable demand to use unconventional materials or an unconventional combination of materials, is much more likely to arise in work to an existing building.

Although the local building control officer has the authority to approve or disapprove of constructional arrangements, including internal and external drainage installations, there are other officials whose work relates to conditions within buildings who are his consultees. Prominent among the public servants who are likely to be consulted in relation to applications proposing the conversion of buildings to multiple occupation are the Environmental Health Officer and the local Fire Prevention Officer. The Environmental Health Officer has the power to approve or disapprove of proposed sanitary provision, related construction standards and means of ventilation in apartment buildings. Clearly, the conversion of, say, a large warehouse into many dwellings creates a new apartment building, and so the building inspector will seek this official's views. Consequently, the applicant may be required to complete additional forms which seek specific information on aspects which are the interest of the Environmental Health Officer. This official

also administers regulations set out by the Clean Air Act (1956), and in a development where, say, a single flue serves oil-fired boilers supplying heat to several dwellings, he will wish to be satisfied that the flue emissions will fall within the limits defined by that Act.

The local Fire Prevention Officer is empowered by the Fire Precautions Act (1971) to make recommendations for the provision of fire-resisting construction and fire-fighting equipment in 'designated' buildings. These include houses and flats more than three storeys high, so it can be seen that this description embraces conversions of high or multi-storey buildings into blocks of flats. It is plain that a lofty church interior might be high enough to accommodate four or five storeys of living space, resulting in a design proposal which would demand the involvement of the Fire Prevention Officer. The recommendations of this official may be obtained by sending duplicate copies of the layout drawings of the scheme with a covering letter requesting that one set of these documents is endorsed with his suggestions for the provision of fire-resisting construction (self-closing smoke-check doors, etc) and fire alarm and fire-fighting equipment. The standards for the provision of Means of Escape in Case of Fire are clearly defined in the mandatory rules which form part of the Building Regulations (1985) and schemes which fail to satisfy these requirements will not receive building regulations approval. The Fire Prevention Officer may be approached by the building inspector for his views on the adequacy of means of escape provision and he will add to this official's advice on the proper policy for escape routes by making recommendations for emergency lighting and fire-resisting construction associated with these features. Applicants are not under a legal obligation to install any of the features suggested by the Fire Prevention Officer in his recommendations, but a Fire Certificate must be obtained before beneficial use may be made of a 'designated' building and since the discretion to issue this document lies with this official, it can be seen that his 'recommendations' are more in the nature of mandatory requirements than airy aspirations which it is safe to ignore.

In the event that it appears impossible that the requirements of the building regulations can be satisfied in every respect, it is useful to be aware of the existence of the opportunity to install non-complying materials or construction where no sensible alternative exists. Where an approved solution to a constructional or planning problem cannot be found, and the sympathy of the building inspector can be enlisted, it is possible to apply for a 'waiver', or relaxation of the building regulations, to grant official approval to non-complying arrangements. It is, perhaps, a predictable penalty of this procedure that applicants may have to wait for many weeks before they learn of the success or otherwise of their waiver application.

Further Pre-contract Activities

Planning and building regulations permissions having been obtained, the way is clear for the building operation to proceed. However, it may be helpful to look at the possible range of other pre-contract activities.

Building owners who are contemplating a complicated conversion project will probably employ specialist consultants, among whom the architect is the key member. While it is wise to take his advice and that of the quantity surveyor, if such a specialist is also employed, on the optimum means of progressing the work, the following brief discussion of the comparative advantages and disadvantages of competitive tendering and negotiated contracts may help to clarify the main options for the realisation of the scheme.

Clearly, the best way to obtain a builder is through recommendation, and the building owner who employs an architect thereby enlarges his knowledge of the range of reliable and competent local contractors from which he may select names for inclusion on a tender list or with whom to negotiate a contract cost. As this statement suggests, from this point in the project, there are two basic ways of proceeding. Having identified apparently suitable and reputable firms, one very traditional approach finds the building owner negotiating a price with

the most suitable contractor.

The second approach, which is a conventional device for progressing large and middle-sized building projects, involves inviting several builders to compete for the work, the most favourable offer resulting from this tender competition being successful (it should be made clear at the time tenders are invited that there is no obligation on the part of the building owner to accept the lowest, or any, tender). The prime purpose of this procedure is, of course, to try to guarantee value for money by encouraging the submission of keen prices through competition. Yet many will realise that it is a danger of competitive tendering that it is tempting for a company which is desperate to obtain work to submit an artificially low offer in order to succeed in the competition, with the thought that profit can be regained during the contract period through claims relating to work which could not have been foreseen at the time of invitation of tenders. This condition is particularly common in the field of building conversion and the adoption of an unreasonable attitude by the builder in relation to the pricing of unavoidable additional work can lead to a very significant increase in contract costs. Although a Bill of Quantities can act as a check on such claims, it cannot hope to be a completely comprehensive document — there will always be 'grey' areas granting scope for argument over the interpretation of descriptions and the exact extent of the work.

The alternative course of negotiation with a single reputable builder may safeguard the building owner against the occurrence of this condition. Although the price which is agreed at contract commencement may seem high in comparison with a figure that could result from competitive tendering, it is less likely to be inflated by subsequent 'claims-consciousness' on the part of the builder. In any case, it is unwise to involve too many contractors in competitive tendering in an attempt to drive the cost down — better by far to restrict the tender list to a handful of reputable firms known to be well-experienced in conversion work.

Forms of Building Contract

The suggestion that the building work

should be undertaken under a contract begs a question about suitable forms of contract. In law, a contract exists where there is an offer, an acceptance and a consideration (ie, payment). Thus it can be seen that there is no necessity for a written agreement. The main advantage of adopting a standardised written contract is the wealth of case law related to its use which can be referred to if a dispute arises between the parties. The most commonly used building contracts are drawn up by the Joint Contracts Tribunal (JCT), a body formed from representatives of the main groups in the building industry which has inherited the role of publishing standard building contracts previously performed by the RIBA. There is a range of JCT contracts to suit projects of all sizes, but for the scale of project which represents the majority of schemes considered in this book, the JCT Form of Agreement for Minor Building Works, which was first published in 1980, may be the most appropriate document. Copies of this form can be purchased from the RIBA, (see Useful Addresses, p.204).

Another advantage of adopting one of the standard forms of building contract relates to the method of paying the builder. All the JCT forms refer to the system of 'interim certificates' which approve the making of stage payments to the builder. From the point of view of control of expenditure, obviously it is helpful to operate an arrangement in which payments for those parts of the work which have been carried out at particular points in the contract are made in related instalments. If such stage payments are tied to the issue of regular architect's certificates, then budgeting is made easier and the requirement that the architect should approve the quality of the related work before issuing his certificate is a valuable encouragement to the builder to adopt and maintain a conscientious attitude. Under the JCT contracts, the issue of these interim certificates is expected to be effected at approximately monthly intervals.

A further benefit of adherence to a standard form of contract relates to the terms for 'after service'. The JCT forms refer to and define the length of a 'Defects Liability Period' which runs from the point of completion of building work. Usually six months long, this is effectively a 'guarantee'

period during which the builder is expected to rectify, at no additional cost to the building owner, any work which is found to be defective. To encourage him to honour this obligation, a small proportion of the contract cost is retained after the work is complete and throughout the defects liability period. Only upon satisfactory correction of any defective items are these retention monies paid to the builder and the final certificate is issued. It may be difficult to agree equally satisfactory arrangements for the correction of building defects with the proposed contractor at the outset of the work if a JCT (or similar) standard form of contract is not employed.

Financial Aid for Repair and Restoration

Grants

Money may be available for the conservation of historic or architecturally important buildings from both central and local government sources. Under historic buildings legislation, grants for structural repairs are available for buildings of outstanding architectural or historic interest. Minor repairs, maintenance, alterations, improvements or redecoration are excluded. Owners have to show that they would not be able to complete the work without financial help and are usually asked to supply details of their assets and income to substantiate this. Unless the building has been empty for some time and cannot otherwise be brought back into use – and clearly this circumstance could apply to a redundant structure which is to be converted to domestic use – grants are not offered for recently purchased properties because the purchase price is assumed to reflect the state of repair. If the property is sold within ten years of the grant being made, some or all of the grant may have to be repaid. Normally the work must cost more than £10,000 and grant aid is usually less than 50 per cent of the full cost. Grant applications take some months to be processed and public access to the building – for at least twenty-eight days during the summer months – is usually required. These grants are administered by the Historic Buildings and Monuments Commission.

This agency may also help and give money to owners of all suitable buildings (whether listed or not) in conservation areas. These grants are normally up to 25 per cent of the cost of the eligible repair work to the main external structure and are available to local authorities, housing associations, voluntary organisations and private owners. Grant aid is given towards eligible items of expenditure which normally include structural repairs to the fabric of the building, repairs using traditional or natural materials such as stonework and restoration of features of historical or architectural interest. There are four categories of conservation area in which eligible buildings may be situated and the definition of these categories is intended to encourage local authorities, amenity societies, trusts and groups of private individuals to organise co-ordinated improvement schemes where they are most needed. Minor works or repair and restoration to individual buildings will not normally qualify for assistance. Grants are rarely given to commercial companies that can afford to pay the cost themselves, or to properties purchased within the previous four years. If the property is sold within a stated period, some or all of the grant may have to be repaid.

Owners of listed buildings in the Greater London area are eligible for grant aid for repair work which will protect and enhance a building's architectural interest and maintain its historic features. The maximum amount of grant available is 50 per cent of eligible project cost and each case is considered individually. Routine maintenance work is not eligible and work must not commence prior to application for the grant.

County and district councils and London borough councils are empowered to give money for the repair and maintenance of any building they believe to be historically significant, whether or not it is listed or situated in a conservation area. Alteration or improvement work and internal or external redecoration are not eligible. The cost of the work must be more than £500 and the decision lies with the authority not only on the amount which will be offered but also whether it will be in the form of a grant or a loan. Plainly, funds for such assistance are limited by annual budgets.

A dwelling lacking certain basic amenities may qualify under the Housing Acts for a home improvement grant from the district or borough council. An Intermediate Grant helps to install essential items such as an indoor WC and bath, and local councils are empowered to offer financial assistance where a property lacks these essential amenities and a valid application is made. However, improvement and intermediate grants can only be sought for houses built or converted before 1961, so this definition may disqualify new conversion projects. It may prove to be more fruitful to seek a Special Grant which can be awarded to assist the provision of homes by conversion, but such a grant is discretionary. Other forms of improvement grants – eg Repairs Grants – are also discretionary, and at the time of writing, available funds for such grants are low – very few are being awarded. Where there is some hope of funds from this source, extra money is available for improvement grants to historic buildings to ensure the repairs are carried out using the right materials. Like the standard Repairs Grant fund, this money is also limited by annual budgets.

It is also worthwhile considering an approach to charitable trusts, a significant number of which can make grants for the restoration and maintenance of historic buildings. A complete list of such trusts appears in the *Directory of Grant-making Trusts* which is published annually by the Charities Aid Foundation. A copy of this publication is kept in the reference section of most lending libraries. It is important to recognise that such grant aid is usually available only for the accurate restoration of historic buildings and a change of use of a non-domestic building into a dwelling, involving substantial alterations to appearance that erode evidence of its former use, is likely to disqualify a project from receiving grant aid from a private trust.

Loans

In parallel with the opportunities to obtain grants for the restoration of historic buildings lies the possibility of procuring low-cost loans to assist building purchase and renovation. The Architectural Heritage Fund, a revolving fund which is administered by the Civic Trust, can offer such loans to ease the cost of purchase, repair and preservation of historic buildings. These loans are available only to registered charitable trusts, and local historic buildings trusts have tended to predominate in the awards made to date. As they are not available to individuals or groups who would profit from the subsequent sale of the restored premises, this source of finance may be of more interest to amenity groups who wish to save an historic building by converting it to domestic use, than to those who wish to meet their own housing needs through such a project. To qualify for consideration for AHF assistance, the project must be financially viable and the maximum amount of loan is 50 per cent of project costs, the ceiling figure for this contribution being £150,000. The interest rate is currently 5 per cent per annum and normally the loan must be repaid within two years.

A wide range of loans at commercial rates is, of course, available to assist owner-occupiers in funding improvements to their dwellings. The clearing banks and the building societies will provide information on the general terms for such loans, although rates of interest are likely to exceed the banks' base lending rate by several percentage points.

3 Constructional Characteristics of Period Buildings

The modern large building usually incorporates a strong structural 'skeleton' on which, or within which, infilling construction to insulate and exclude the weather is installed. Georgian, Victorian and Edwardian buildings generally do not include such a discrete structure. The external and internal walls fulfil a major loadbearing and stabilising function. The majority of buildings were not designed in the sense that structural engineers would design a building structure today – by assessment of stresses and calculation of a suitable 'frame' to resist them – they were constructed with different degrees of understanding of traditional 'rules of thumb', leading to different structural forms and features in apparently similar buildings. Warehouse and mill buildings in particular often display a great variety of load-bearing floor constructions because the storage and machine loads they were required to resist differed in nature and were often of a very high order.

Where a discrete structural skeleton cannot be discerned, it is likely that all the elements of the building are acting together to prevent collapse. In relation to this arrangement, it is important to consider two factors when an old non-domestic building is being assessed for re-use as dwellings. First, many old buildings have been modified a number of times, often on a piecemeal basis, so that the combined effect on structural stability of original and later work can make further changes more difficult. Thus, an appreciation of the form and scale of the modifications is essential to the formulation of a rational conversion proposal. Secondly, all buildings are subject to gradual decay from deterioration of the materials used, or lack of preventative maintenance. The scale of the decay influences the scale of the renovation work and it determines how the life of the completed building may be extended.

FOUNDATIONS AND GROUND FLOORS

Many old buildings do not have foundations in the sense of a calculated, designed and carefully executed interface between the superstructure and the ground, yet they continue to resist loads from the building without apparent distress. Nowadays, even the most modest buildings on good ground tend to have mass-concrete strip footings beneath their walls in order to spread the loads. It does not follow that the means of founding older, and often more flexible, buildings were inadequate for the original uses of these buildings. Compatibility between the structure and the ground may have developed over a relatively slow process of construction and the long life of the building. Settlement is a time-dependent process, and if the building is sufficiently flexible to accommodate differential settlement over a long period, it is often reasonable to apply further loads which would have been unacceptable had all the loads been applied together at the outset. During an original construction period of perhaps two to three years in the case of a large building, there occurs all the movement that is likely to take place in gravel or sandy soils, and a considerable proportion of that which will occur in clay soil. The period of consolidation of clay soils can be considerable, and settlement or heave of the ground can also occur as a result of changes in the moisture content of the soil. Foundations on sandstone, limestone, or other rocks do not settle significantly, but foundations on chalk can behave like those resting on clay. Unsuitable ground materials which can cause continued movement are unconsolidated fill materials – such as might be found where the site of the building was formerly used as allotment gardens or as a rubbish tip

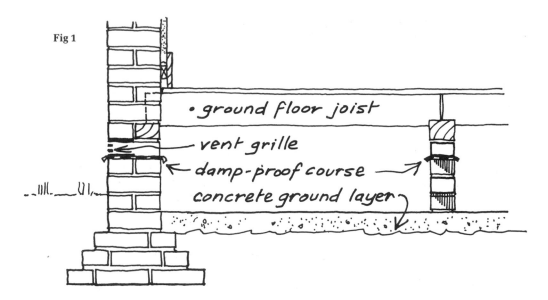

Fig 1

- peat and soft organic clays.

Old publications on building construction show a theoretical approach to foundation 'design' to the extent that the spreading of loads was recommended at the foot of a wall by means of 'corbelled' (ie, projecting) brickwork footings or wide mass-concrete strips or both. The spreading of concentrated loads was achieved with inverted arches, and very poor ground might demand the use of piled or raft foundations. In high quality buildings, where an architect was employed, and in industrial development and large-scale public works, where engineers were employed, foundations were usually reasonably well constructed. In contrast, speculative buildings of the eighteenth and nineteenth centuries were often erected using only a nominal spread-footing bearing, with the least amount of excavation in virgin ground. Any official rules concerning the width of foundations in relation to the thickness of the superincumbent wall were frequently applied as a maximum or norm rather than a minimum requirement.

Other than in industrial buildings where very heavy loads had to be catered for, the acknowledgement in traditional building construction of the difficulty of damp-proofing floors next to the ground led to the widespread adoption of timber for ground-floor structures, positioned over a layer of damp-resisting concrete with an air-space in between (Fig 1). This concrete ground layer was sometimes 150mm (6in) thick – although it was common to make it thinner – and the underside of the ground-floor joists was generally at least 300mm (12in) above its top surface. This applied because of the location of the damp-proof course; to ensure that rainwater splashing up around the building's perimeter did not penetrate the outer walls, the damp-proof course was ideally sited at least 150mm (6in) above the external ground level. As the air-space between the floor joists and the ground level had to be ventilated to prevent damp and a stagnant atmosphere congenial to dry rot, ventilation ducts installed in the external walls were located above the damp-proof course and below the timber wall-plate which supported the ends of the floor joists. This wall-plate was sometimes sited on a ledge on the inner surface of the external wall, making the construction at this low level half a brick thicker than the upper sections. Below floors of large rooms it was necessary to install intermediate supports for the joists at, say, 2m (6½ft) intervals, and these were provided in the form of single-skin, 'honeycomb' brickwork sleeper walls which allowed air movement through the whole of the underfloor void. In cheaply constructed buildings, it was often the practice to omit the concrete ground layer from the subfloor construction which meant that the sleeper walls were founded only on brick rubble. Provided the timber floor is raised sufficiently over generally dry ground, the absence of the concrete should not cause problems.

WALLS
Brickwork
DIFFERENT TYPES OF BRICK

Many different kinds of bricks were in use during the eighteenth and nineteenth centuries, ranging from strong and durable 'engineering' bricks produced in large kilns to 'common' bricks produced locally or even fired on the building site in 'clamps'.

Common bricks were made from local or readily available brick clays, little attention being devoted to evenness of firing or regularity of form. Such bricks were usually unsuitable for use as facing bricks but were strong and hard enough for general purposes. Since the inter-war period, this description has referred to the plain *Fletton* bricks which are used almost exclusively in work concealed by decorative finishes. They are named after the village near Peterborough where they were first produced in the 1880s and are machine-made bricks moulded from the Oxford clay of the Bedford, Buckingham and Northampton districts. Their normal colour is pink – usually patched where the bricks have been stacked on top of one another in the kiln. They are hard, regular-shaped bricks nowadays much used in load-bearing, non-facing construction.

Stock brick is a term which usually refers to bricks moulded by hand from southern English clay mixed with chimney ash, which were burnt in a *clamp* to produce the hard, durable yellow-brown bricks which are a familiar sight in many of the older buildings of London and the South East. A clamp is a large, elongated, flat-topped 'pyramid' of dried, unburnt bricks below which lies a shallow bed of coke which is ignited and allowed to burn for a period of ten to twelve weeks. The fire having died out, the clamp is dismantled and the fully burnt stock bricks are removed from its core. Stock bricks produced in this way were often used externally and were more suitable for this purpose than common bricks.

Place bricks are those which, having been furthest from the fire in the clamp or kiln, did not receive enough heat to burn them thoroughly. They are soft, uneven in texture and red in colour. At best, they were suitable only for use in non-load-bearing partitions. They readily deteriorate on being exposed to the weather.

Rubbers, Cutters or **Red Builders** are lightly burnt to be soft enough to cut or rub down very evenly and uniformly. They have no 'frog' (indentation in the top surface) and they were usually made oversize to allow for rubbing.

Engineering bricks are strong, dense, and smooth-faced. They are obtained by burning dried bricks to vitrification. Staffordshire blue bricks are the best known, although stronger red varieties were made at Accrington, Lancashire, Bristol and in parts of Yorkshire. Similar, though less strong, pressed bricks were made in Leicestershire and are termed 'Leicestershire Reds'. The use of all types developed from civil engineering applications in the mid-nineteenth century, particularly the construction of railway structures such as viaducts and overbridges.

Gault bricks are hard, close-textured, pale buff bricks manufactured from the chalky clay of the same name in Cambridge, Bedford, Essex and parts of Kent. Gaults were among the first bricks to be mass-produced by machine, and dense, precisely shaped varieties were available from the 1850s, although they are unobtainable today.

Concrete bricks are cast in moulds. They differ from the other forms of brick in that the aggregate is physically bound by cement rather than chemically combined with the other constituents. Concrete bricks were only produced in quantity after 1920.

The bricks used in many buildings of the eighteenth to early twentieth centuries are often of an assortment of qualities. Sound and regularly shaped bricks were the more expensive components and were used on the weathering faces of buildings, although the inner, concealed body of an external wall usually comprised softer and cheaper place bricks. Rubbers were frequently used to construct arches and decorative band courses.

The mixture of bricks employed in external wall construction can be clearly seen in many older London buildings. The well-burnt stock bricks assume the characteristic yellow-grey colour, but the place bricks remain pink. On stripping internal plaster off external walls of houses, it is usually found that the facing bricks are backed internally by pink place bricks. Party walls often comprise place bricks throughout, as do areas of external wall which are coated with stucco rendering.

TYPES OF MORTAR

The principal reason for laying bricks or stones in mortar is that bedding in mortar encourages a uniform transfer of load through elements whose irregularity or distorted forms might invite fractures, even under quite light pressures. The use of mortar also allows irregularities to be absorbed without variations in the coursing. It also acts as a gap filler to exclude the weather. Friction and adhesion between mortar and brick or stone prevents dislocation of the individual elements and it enhances the load-bearing qualities of the wall. All eighteenth and nineteenth century mortars were limestone or chalk based.

Lime-based mortars The understanding of 'slaked' burnt lime which was possessed by the Romans, disappeared with the decline of the Roman Empire. Lime manufacture became something of a matter of trial and error until the 1750s when the first formalised research into mortars took place. It was found that quicklime with cementitious qualities could be produced by heating limestone in a kiln to around 850°C (1,560°F). Chalk, which is a form of limestone, will produce pure or 'fat' limes. These are readily slaked with water, with the generation of considerable heat and a doubling of volume. They set or harden entirely by absorbing carbon dioxide from the atmosphere to form a soft crystalline carbonate of lime. The consequently slow gain in strength made mortars containing such limes unsuitable for rapid construction and the white 'lime putty' which results

from this ingredient was often reserved for essentially non-structural, semi-decorative work like the pointing of 'red rubber' brick arches. Limestones containing clay impurities can be burnt to form calcium silicates and aluminates. On the addition of water these so-called *hydraulic limes* set and harden chiefly by independent internal crystallisation. Any free lime present hardens by absorbing carbon dioxide. Generally speaking, the greater the clay impurity, the faster the setting time and the less carbon dioxide is required. Hydraulic limes are generally stronger than fat limes and they were used for structural purposes.

Lime was also a staple ingredient of plaster and both plastering and structural limes were normally mixed with sand (around 1:3 by volume) to increase the bulk of the material, to assist setting and to reduce drying shrinkage.

In performing one of the principal functions of a mortar – namely to act as a joint filler – lime mortars were found to be adequate because an external weathering surface (pointing) was provided. One of the chief advantages of lime mortars is that, being generally plastic rather than brittle, they are able to accept quite large deformations and distortions without the opening of brickwork bed joints or the splitting of bricks. This explains why any expansion of the bricks early in their life caused little visible cracking compared with the effects seen in modern masonry.

Portland cement mortar The manufacture of Portland cement in its modern form dates from 1824. Its basic ingredients are, again, limestone and clay in the proportion 2:1. These materials are ground together and the resulting powder is burnt in a kiln at between 1,200° and 1,400°C (2,190° and 2,550°F) to incipient vitrification to form clinkers. These clinkers are then ground to a fine powder which is the finished cement. The addition of water triggers a series of chemical reactions resulting in a dense and solid crystalline formation which seemed so similar to Portland stone that its inventor named the product 'Portland' cement.

Until about 1900, masonry was mainly constructed with lime mortars which thereafter slowly gave way to cement mortar. By the 1930s cement mortar had become the predominant material. Almost invariably such mortar contained a small proportion of lime to improve workability during construction (eg, 1:1:6, cement/lime/sand). Cement mortars are comparatively hard and brittle and they have higher crushing strengths than lime mortars. Consequently, walls built of cement mortar have a greater tendency to crack when subjected to distortion – either by brittle fracture of the mortar or, if the brick is the weaker material, by the snapping of bricks. Relatively small distortions can cause visible cracking. Lime mortars are more plastic and they can accommodate long-term movements.

BRICK BONDING

The art of bricklaying was well developed by the eighteenth century and the qualities of different brick bonds were understood. By far the most popular bonds were the 'English' and 'Flemish' bonds, of which the latter became the most widely used in eighteenth- and nineteenth-century house construction. In Flemish bond, each course comprises alternate 'header' bricks (ie, ends of bricks showing) and 'stretcher' bricks overlapping with alternate headers and stretchers in the course above and the course below (Fig 2). The headers were in-

Fig 2

tended as full bricks to bond the facing skin into the backing work, the latter usually being constructed from common bricks. Flemish bond was considered to give a more attractive appearance than English bond. Also popular was 'Flemish garden wall bond' in which headers were separated by three stretchers (Fig 3). This arrangement decreased the number of headers and re-

duced the bonding of the facing and common brickwork. English bond consists of alternate courses of headers and stretchers (Fig 4). It is

Fig 3

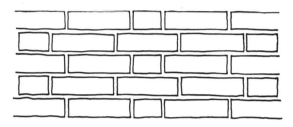

considered to be very strong because of the absence of straight joints within the wall, but it is more difficult to lay and is more

Fig 4

expensive than other bonds. Nevertheless, it was much used in civil engineering applications throughout the nineteenth and early twentieth centuries. 'English garden wall bond' uses either three or five courses of stretchers to one of headers, and it was one of the most popular of all brickwork bonds, particularly in the North and Midlands. Many other brick bonds were used with regional variations in their names.

BRICK JOINTING

The way the mortar joints between the bricks are formed may be as important for the appearance of the wall as the pattern of the bond. The completion of the partly filled joints of a new brick wall to give a neat mortar joint on, or close to, the face of the brickwork is termed pointing . The eventual replacement of this mortar surface is called repointing.

In the *flush* joint, the mortar is finished on

the same face as the brickwork and this treatment produces a very flat, undifferentiated surface, particularly where the bricks are of regular and precise shape. This type of joint is rarely suitable for repointing old brickwork because raking-out of the old mortar damages the corners of soft bricks and the wide joints which result from flush-pointing such damaged brickwork dominate unattractively the repointed surface. The *struck* or *weathered* joint is an alternative profile which is formed with the bricklayer's diamond trowel. It makes the brickwork appear 'stratified' because its sloping profile causes the horizontal joints to dominate the surface and the pleasing irregularities of old, oddly-shaped bricks are thereby obscured. However, it is an efficient shape of joint for throwing water off the wall and is much favoured for repointing work by bricklayers (Fig 5).

The most elaborate joint is produced by *tuck pointing*, which is a method for making

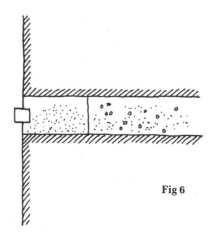

Fig 6

and tuck pointing was a way of making a surface look better-built than it was. Although workaday Victorian brickwork is likely to display the 10mm (⅜in) wide joints which characterise modern brick walls, good quality nineteenth-century facing brickwork may boast joints of only half this thickness. Where old brickwork is to be repointed and the expensive operation of repairing decayed tuck pointing is not necessitated, the *keyed* joint is likely to be the most suitable form of brick joint (Fig 7).

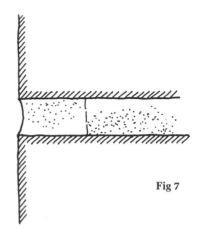

Fig 7

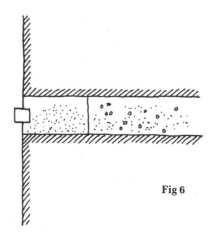

19mm

minimum depth of raking out for re-pointing

Fig 5

ancient brickwork look new, precise and regular. The original mortar having been raked out, the open joint is pointed up flush with a mortar which is coloured to match the general brickwork surface. Into this flush joint is inserted a thin, projecting and continuous square-section bead of white lime putty which contrasts strongly with the brick colour to suggest that the wall has been newly erected to fine tolerances (Fig 6). The thin putty bead of tuck pointing is easily explained; traditional builders equated thin brick joints with top-quality construction

It is obtained by running a short section of hosepipe or iron bucket-handle along the wet mortar to give a slightly recessed profile. This treatment restricts the joints to the gaps between corners of bricks and thus avoids the over-wide and visually dominant mortar joints which may result from the adoption of flush pointing in repointing work.

Stone Masonry

The erection of stone masonry requires greater skill than the construction of brickwork. Bricks, being all of the same size, are laid according to a regular pattern, whereas with each stone considerable judgement is required so that it may be laid in the best way.

Ashlar masonry is built with blocks of stone which have been very carefully made so that the joints do not exceed 3mm (⅛in) in thickness. It is the most expensive form of masonry and it depends for its strength on the size of the stones, the accuracy of the 'dressing' of the stones and the perfection of the bond, but hardly at all on the strength of the mortar. Because the joints are so thin, the mortar must be very fine and free from grit.

Coursed ashlar consists of blocks of stone the same height throughout each course with regular horizontal joints (Fig 8).

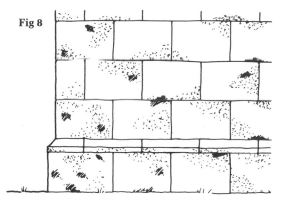

Fig 8

Random ashlar walls were built with rectangular blocks of all sizes and dimensions. It is a cheaper form of ashlar because it enabled a larger proportion of the stone to be used as it had been quarried.

Rubble masonry is built with roughly dressed blocks of stone. The bed joints and vertical joints in rubble work vary in thickness and the strength of the walling depends greatly on the mortar. It was conventional for masonry to consist of an ashlar or squared-rubble facing, bonded back into material of poorer quality (eg, random rubble or brickwork).

Another common form of construction comprised a facing skin of ashlar and a parallel backing-skin of brickwork or rubble masonry bonded together across an intervening cavity. This cavity was often filled with small loose stone chippings and broken blocks, frequently with little or no binding mortar. In later construction, some of the bonding problems were overcome by building the facing work independently of the backing but tied in with iron 'cramps' and dowels. Tongues, grooves and channels were incorporated in the stones to improve the bonding of individual blocks. These were designed both for direct interlocking of one stone with another and for indirect connections to backing masonry via tightly fitting plugs or loose-fitting dowels in slots sealed with lead or mortar. Rubble-filled walls, often with poor bonding between the facing and backing brickwork or stonework, were a feature of many, even multi-storey, buildings until the late nineteenth century.

Cavity Walls

The advantages of hollow or cavity walls began to be realised after the middle of the nineteenth century, presumably in parallel with a growing awareness of the causes of dampness in walls. The earliest examples of modern cavity construction treated the weatherproofing skin as an addition to the main structure of the wall. The normal wall thickness was maintained for the inner 'leaf', the cavity being enclosed by an extra facing leaf restrained by special ties built into the inner work. This form of wall construction was expensive to erect, and it is seldom found in buildings constructed before the twentieth century, except in highly specialised structures such as gunpowder stores (where it was important that the contents should be kept dry) or houses of the highest quality construction. Defects arising from 'optimistic' construction of vertically laminated masonry walls and old construction incorporating cavities and metal ties are described in the following chapter.

Arches

Arching is one of the oldest methods of bridging an opening. Arches are so arranged that an applied load forces one element against another as a wedge. Flat or shallow arches in brickwork are often found above window and door openings (Fig 9). The flat

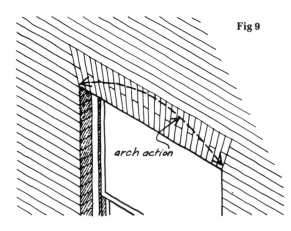

Fig 9

arch can resist loads because the line of thrust is contained within the arch and the tendency of the construction to spread is resisted by the buttressing action of the adjacent walls. *Relieving arches* in masonry were used to direct load away from built-in

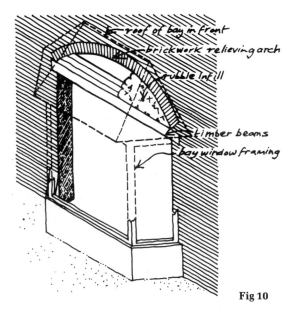

Fig 10

timber lintels. Such shallow timber beams may appear to support loads from above, but they are often relieved of a large part of this burden by arches built into the superincumbent masonry. These relieving arches were sometimes hidden by external features such as roofs over bay windows. It is unwise to attempt to remove the related lintels in the belief that the arches are transferring the entire load. The load resistance is a composite action, depending on the position of the arch in relation to the timber beam (Fig 10).

ROOFS, COLUMNS AND UPPER FLOORS

The pitched, or sloping roof was the form most commonly adopted in traditional buildings and, as applies in the majority of older houses, it was usually covered with a system of small overlap units – normally slates or tiles. Where very wide or intricately planned buildings dictated the use of large areas of flat roof, these structures were invariably covered with asphalt, although small areas of flat or awkwardly-shaped roof would be clad in sheet metal – either lead, copper or zinc. Roof structures would be formed from timber trusses, rafters, purlins and joists, or from metal trusses fabricated from light steel members, bearing on perimeter walls, massive intermediate walls or free-standing columns. Intermediate floors in lightly-loaded buildings were invariably of timber construction. Only in the later decades of the nineteenth century in multi-storey manufacturing and storage buildings which were required to resist very heavy loads did concrete slab or masonry jack-arched floors become common.

Timber Construction

The majority of constructions which survive from ancient times are of stone and because of this it is easy to overlook the equivalent tradition of timber construction. The use of timber in buildings has been a continuous process reflecting its availability, the relative costs of material and labour, developments in processing and distribution, and the growth in understanding of its structural behaviour and the problems of rot, insect attack and fire. The buildings considered in this book all date from a time when hardwoods had already become too scarce to be used on a large scale in building structures. The spread of fire between buildings and the long-term risks of rot and insect attack were often not fully considered. It is mainly these latter problems which affect the serviceability of timber structures and their distinguishing features and treatment are described in the following chapter.

TIMBER FLOORS

The layout of timber members in floors can differ considerably with the age of the building. In many larger buildings of the seventeenth and eighteenth centuries, heavy timber beams were used on to which joists were placed. These joists were often cut or 'cogged' on to the main beams to minimise the constructional depth of the floor. Consequently, the main beams were often the weakest elements and heavy loading of floors can result in considerable sagging of these members. This condition may not represent a worrying defect if the occupants

are prepared to 'live with' the constructional distortion. Timber floor joists were available in lengths far greater than could be easily obtained today and joists running from front to rear of large houses are quite common. This arrangement often allowed for the line of a load-bearing spine wall to be offset between one level and another. Thus it is unwise to dismiss too readily as inaccurate a measured survey which seems to show that very significant features do not occupy the same location on different floors. The discovery of this arrangement by accurate survey at an early date, may help to cancel out options for rebuilding which could prove to be very difficult and therefore highly expensive.

The span, direction and depth of floor joists can vary between apparently similar buildings and even within one building. In small Victorian buildings, floor joists were often 175-200mm (7-8in) deep. Areas where the floor framing system was modified were at fireplaces and bay windows. At fireplaces, a trimmer beam was used on which sat the brick arch of the hearth (often a stone

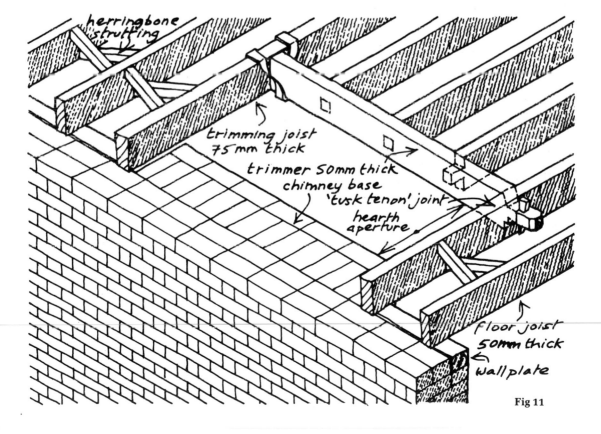

Fig 11

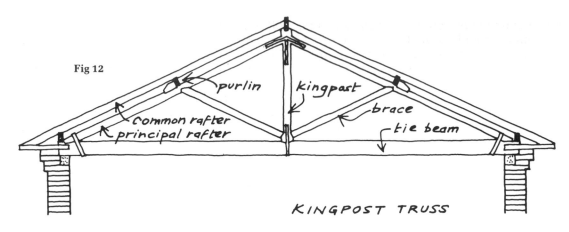

KINGPOST TRUSS

slab). The trimming joists which supported the trimmer were usually the same depth as the trimmer and common floor joists but thicker. Herringbone strutting was used to restrain the joists laterally at certain points and to distribute concentrated loads (Fig 11).

TIMBER TRUSSES
The high strength-to-weight ratio of timber when stressed parallel to its grain makes it an ideal material for the members of structural trusses and this fact was well appreciated by the traditional builders. The member sizes were usually governed by the design and detailing of the joints. Unlike steel roof trusses which use many small members and connections, older timber trusses usually consist of a small number of principal strut and tie members with inter-

locking timber and wrought-iron strap connections. Loads from substantial roof purlins were usually applied close to truss connection points (Fig 12). These trusses differ markedly from modern mass-produced and prefabricated softwood roof trusses which are sited at close centres in order to support the load imposed by the roof covering. In contrast to the substantial and widely spaced 'principals' of traditional purlin roofs, these 'trussed rafters' make use of many small-section bracing members connected together with thin-gauge metal 'nailing plates'.

TRUSSED PARTITIONS
Before the last two or three decades of the nineteenth century – ie, before wrought-iron or steel beams were readily available – it was usual for loads to be carried over large openings linking principal rooms by means of trusses built into partitions in the storey above (Fig 13). Even the simplest 'stud' wall without openings was usually braced by a diagonal strut. For this reason, many ordinary partitions between rooms may give the appearance of trusses when finishes have been stripped off and may therefore appear to have some load-carrying capacity. However, it is unlikely that any tying action exists where the partition runs across the floor joists and is perforated by original door openings.

TIMBER CONNECTIONS
In modern timber construction, all but the simplest joints are made with the aid of

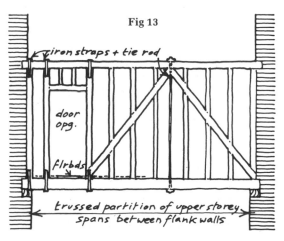

metal connectors: screws, framing anchors, joist-hangers and toothed-plate connectors. In earlier times, metal connectors were unusual except in elements like roof trusses, as described above. In most joints used in timber construction, the loads were transferred by direct timber-to-timber contact, the wood having first been formed into quite complicated shapes to very small tolerances. The assembled joint was often nailed or dowelled to prevent the pieces coming apart, but unlike modern truss construction, the nails do not directly contribute to the load-carrying capacity of the joint. A typically refined connection is the tenon and mortice joint (Fig 14). Once assembled,

Fig 14

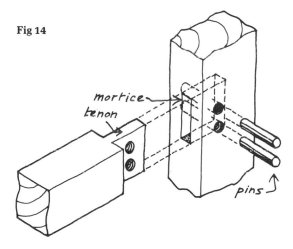

this type of joint conceals the true shape of the timber contact areas. A typical traditional floor-framing arrangement would include morticed or 'housed' joints between the joists which meet at right angles with no

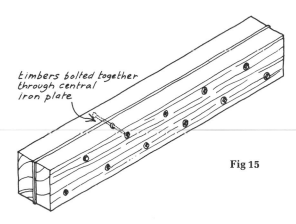

timbers bolted together through central iron plate

Fig 15

other form of fixing. 'Tusk tenon' joints may be found in the trimmer beams at fireplaces (Fig 11) where the integral hardwood 'key' was used to resist any tendency for the members to separate. Connections in substantial timber roof trusses were normally tenoned and dowelled, although the joints between strut and tie members would tend to separate if this were the only form of connection so that bolts through, or metal straps around, such joints were used to prevent separations.

COMPOSITE MEMBERS

Flitch beams are formed by taking a solid timber beam (usually about 300-400mm sq [12-16in sq]) and dividing it in half longitudinally. The two halves are then reversed and one section is turned 'upside down' before the two halves are reunited. The result of this is to ensure that any natural defect which may have occurred originally is divided and that it no longer dominates any one section. Thus higher strength may be achieved than was attainable with the unmodified timber. It was common for a steel or iron plate, of similar depth to the timber, to be sandwiched between the sections, and for the whole member to be bolted together (Fig 15). Other forms of internal strengthening or stiffening (eg, strips of hardwood or iron) may be hidden between the two sections of a flitch beam to create a trussed girder. This method may not contribute to a significant increase in strength, but it suggests an awareness on the part of the original builder of the need to maximise strength by eliminating naturally occurring weaknesses in materials. Such evidence of a careful approach suggests that the building construction is of good quality. Flitch beams were used in circumstances where it was believed that high strength was required. For example, to support a staircase bracketed off a flank wall, projecting flitch beams might be employed.

BRESSUMMERS

The term bressummer originally referred to the first-floor beam in an external wall which provided the bearing for the floor joists of a medieval timber-framed house, but later it came to mean any timber beam supporting masonry over a wide opening. Bressummers were often used in industrial buildings, Victorian and Edwardian houses where floor joists bear on a window wall, and above shop fronts. Serious problems may result in the latter case and are described in the following chapter.

Metal Structures

Cast and wrought iron were first used in buildings for decorative features, but their widespread use as structural materials arose as a consequence of the Industrial Revolution and ended with the general availability of steel. Early cotton mills with traditional timber structures suffered from frequent fires. 'Fireproof' (or, more accurately, non-combustible) construction was an important development of the early nineteenth century and used cast-iron pillars and beams to support brick jack-arch floors. These iron structural components came from the foundries which already produced castings for the mill machinery and the huge engines used to power them. One of the main uses of cast iron around 1840 was the construction of large dockside and railway warehouses. The manufacture of wrought iron expanded greatly to cater for the needs of railway construction and its development was encouraged by the need to build longer-span bridges and produce many miles of track. From the 1840s, the basic characteristics of the materials were established, although the quality of these products varied considerably. Wrought iron was initially quite expensive and cast iron had the advantage that it could be cast into decorative shapes. The constructional limitation of cast iron is its low strength-to-weight ratio which causes it to have low tensile strength. To overcome this problem, cast-iron beams were cast with wider or thicker bottom flanges than those found in wrought-iron components.

Wrought iron was produced by hammering and rolling profiles from solid billets of iron, the weight of which was generally limited by the practicalities of handling. This consideration tended to determine the maximum size and length of early wrought-iron members. To overcome this limitation, wrought-iron beams were also made up from plates, or they were made into trusses to cover longer spans, rivets being used to connect the parts. Attempts to make wrought iron economically in large quantities were extremely successful, but their success provoked a different development. The Bessemer process, patented in 1856, was intended to produce iron but instead produced steel six times as quickly as the iron puddling process. However, it was about twenty years before steel was produced in quantity to a reasonably reliable quality. One of the first major engineering achievements in steel was the Forth Bridge, completed in 1890. Steel found its first widespread use in the construction of the expanding railway system. The first rolled steel joists (RSJs) were produced in the 1880s and, from then on, this material gradually took over from cast and wrought iron so that it had entirely displaced the latter materials by the 1920s. Early samples of steel made by the Bessemer process were inconsistent and prone to failure, but the quality of this 'mild steel' soon improved and its strength was greater than wrought iron.

Between 1860 and 1890 all of the aforementioned materials were in use. Identification of a particular material is assisted by the different profiles which were particular to each. Cast-iron beams may be distinguished by their heavier bottom flanges and their shape was commonly determined by their function. 'Springing' members in the form of inverted 'T' or 'V' shapes were used to support masonry jack-arches. Cast-iron columns are usually of circular or cruciform shape in plan with different forms of head detail, marrying metal uprights to heavy timber beams in the warehouse structures of the South of England, and to iron beams in the northern textile mills. As this suggests, wrought-iron beams and large jack-arched or vaulted floors were more likely to be employed where heavier loads had to be supported or larger column-free spans were required.

Early examples of 'fireproof' floors included not only jack-arch constructions which could vary from ranges of long-span brick arches, perhaps 4.5m (15ft) wide between iron beams, to a 'ribbed' slab of

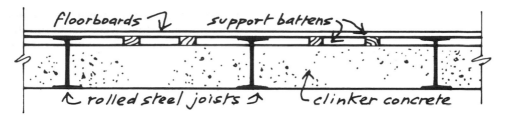

Fig 16

small-scale segmental arch profiles only about 1m (3ft) wide, cast in concrete between wrought iron 'tee' members, but also 'filler-joist' floors. This latter form of composite construction placed wrought-iron 'I' beams of shallow depth at not more than 1m (3ft) intervals; between these members, infilling clinker concrete was cast to give a continuous floor slab (Fig 16).

Common to both wrought-iron and steel members was the policy of riveting plates together to produce beams greater than about 300mm (1ft) deep. Thus it may be difficult to differentiate between wrought-iron and steel sections, apart from where the steel maker's name is embossed on the material. Wrought and cast iron, and, later, wrought iron and steel, may well be found in the same building, the more expensive wrought iron being used for slender, highly stressed members such as roof-truss components or tie rods.

Cast iron is a crystalline material, the main constituents of which are iron and carbon. It is the carbon which produces the characteristic brittleness and low tensile strength of cast iron. Modern cast iron is a much stronger and more ductile material than that encountered in old buildings. Imperfections in cast iron developed from the casting process rather than from the material itself. The iron often set with extraneous material or air voids within it. These were usually apparent as soon as the mould was broken and if such defects were too extensive, the member was recast. Minor defects were filled with molten lead. The iron entered the mould in a molten state and set as it cooled. Setting took place at very high temperatures so that any cast-iron member underwent a reduction in size after it had solidified and as it cooled to room temperature. For accurate casting, the mould pattern had to be

slightly oversize and the component had to be designed to avoid distinct changes in thickness. Internal right-angled corners were avoided by the adoption of rounded or splayed profiles. If these requirements were not met, the member cooled unevenly, which might produce cracking. The casting process made it possible to produce hollow members, notably hollow cylindrical columns. This was done by placing a separate core piece within the main mould, supported at its ends or at other points where holes could be permitted in the casting. This meant that the supports for the core had to be kept to a minimum. Sometimes insufficient support was provided and the core became displaced as the hot metal entered the mould, producing the variation in wall thickness which is typical of hollow cast-iron columns. In practice, where columns are not subject to significant eccentric loads, such inconsistencies are unlikely to result in serious structural weakness.

As the casting process itself placed no limit on the size of cast-iron members, the need for joints was dictated instead by the design and proposed construction sequence of the building. Joints occur most commonly at connections of beams and columns. Individual beams or columns were generally cast in one piece unless the weight of the component or the intricacy of its shape made this procedure impracticable. The most common type of beam and column connection transfers the load from the beam on to the column by direct bearing between one member and the other. Bolts or screws are incorporated to locate and stabilise the members, but they do not carry the principal loads.

Wrought iron, in contrast to the crystalline composition of cast iron, is a laminar or fibrous material, composed almost entirely of pure iron but containing impurities in the form of slag, which remains to give the layered character. Its constructional properties are improved by rolling, which tends to draw the laminar slag into fibres. The composition of wrought iron means that its strength is more variable than that of a more homogeneous material like steel. Unlike cast iron and because of its fibrous rather than crystalline composition, its compressive strength is slightly less than its tensile strength. This ability of wrought iron to resist tension, combined with the limitations on the maximum weight of any component, made mechanical connections in wrought iron much more important than those employed in cast-iron construction.

The process of heating and hammering together sections of iron was known as welding, but it has little similarity with the modern welding process and it was normally not considered to be a suitable means of forming structural connections. Wrought-iron structural components which could not be made by heating and hammering pieces of iron were formed by riveting. This process was also used to connect separate wrought-iron members, but riveting was primarily used to connect plates, angles and tee sections to form built-up stanchions, girders and trusses.

Mild steel came into general use in buildings after 1890. A catalogue of standard-size sections was first published in 1887 and the range of profiles was regularised into a national standard with the publication of British Standard No 4 in 1903. Usefully, the maker's name and the size of the member is often displayed on the web of each section in relief lettering. Mild steel is significantly stronger than wrought iron and is less variable, but it has a greater tendency to corrode. It is commonly found in joists, flat plates or rods, and, like wrought iron, in riveted plate girders or trusses. A comprehensive description of old joist sizes is available in a British Constructional Steelwork Association publication, entitled *Historical Struc-*

tural Steelwork Handbook (1984). Where site investigation and documentary information fail to confirm the identity of the material, a metallurgical test of a small sample will provide a quick and reliable result. It is worth noting that where there is evidence of welding of steelwork within a building dating from the late nineteenth or early twentieth century, it is likely that the steelwork was inserted into a pre-existing building rather than dating from the time of construction, because a reliable welding process by the electric arc method was not developed until World War II and early mild steel is likely to be incompatible with this method of welding.

Other Forms of Upper Floor Construction

The nature and possible problems of modern reinforced concrete introduce a very broad field which cannot be a concern of an account of the qualities of traditional building construction. Yet it is quite likely that concrete will be encountered in many buildings of the pre-1919 period, either as an element of the original construction, or, more probably, in additions to the fabric. The first fully-framed buildings in the UK date from around 1920. However, reinforced concrete was used in upper-floor construction and in internal columns within a structure of load-bearing brick perimeter walls from around 1900.

Apart from the use of concrete in the 'ribbed slab', jack-arch type and filler-joist floors described earlier, there were also numerous 'patent' floor systems, some using wrought-iron or steel plates acting compositely with the concrete. Some of the systems which were common in the USA around 1900 were also used in the UK. It may not prove possible to deduce that such systems are suitable for changed use except by excavating a section of floor to discover its exact composition and to check its structural adequacy.

4 Building Defects and Their Treatment

Although there are some advantageous features which result from the way older buildings were constructed – for instance, the ability of lime mortar brickwork to absorb differential settlement more successfully than cement mortar construction – in structural terms, most traditional buildings rely on gravity and friction to hold themselves together and have little tensile capacity. Thus, with thermal or ground

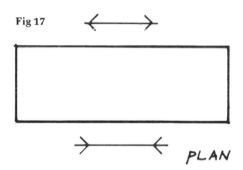

Fig 17

PLAN

movement they may come to lack 'togetherness'. A susceptibility to such problems can commence with as fundamental a factor as the shape of the building in plan. The build-

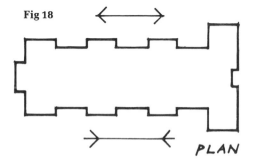

Fig 18

PLAN

ing fabric of a simple plan shape which is not roofed with a flat roof surrounded by a parapet (Fig 17) generally will be free from thermal or moisture movement cracks, while a corrugated plan may be able to absorb masonry movements like a bellows (Fig 18).

However, short 'returns' terminating long panels of brickwork are likely to develop cracks (Fig 19).

Probably the most variable building type in terms of constructional quality was the speculatively-built house as erected in the late eighteenth, nineteenth and early twentieth centuries. This book deals with more specialised structures, but the enormities practised in common speculative house construction are worth relating because many of these shortcomings are equally endemic to poorly built non-domestic structures. For instance, lack of care in brick-bonding was widespread and external

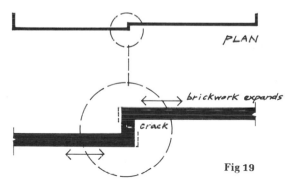

PLAN

brickwork expands

crack

Fig 19

rendering (the familiar 'stucco' of much nineteenth-century house construction) was often used to hide a poor quality building shell. The construction of industrial and commercial buildings often followed a different pattern because more pride was taken with the work and they were more likely to be carried out by large and experienced building companies. Mid-nineteenth century improvements in civil engineering construction spread into building construction and by the final decades of that century, all elements, from the foundations upwards, were likely to be carefully considered and well constructed.

It is important to recognise at the outset of

any inspection or assessment of a building for re-use that few older buildings retain the arrangement which was originally built. The quality of alterations can be poor. A well-conceived and competently built structure may have suffered from the subsequent actions of a small contractor who had far less structural knowledge than the original builder. In consequence, desperate structural problems may have been introduced which the alterations only served to conceal through replanning and redecoration.

Many of the defects in one building can be observed in contemporary structures and similar and neighbouring buildings. Traditional builders were conservative in their assessment of the load-bearing capacity of masonry or cast and wrought iron, but they were either highly optimistic or less concerned about the bearing capacity of foundations. Therefore, settlement often took place after construction. This is the principal cause of in-plane deformation of walls and most commonly arises from inadequate original sizing of footings, moisture changes in the soil, or as a result of altered patterns of loading. 'Ground heave' may also be a problem, particularly in clay subsoil where mature trees and their roots have been removed, causing the subsoil to expand and soften as its moisture content increases. Such movements result in particular crack patterns on wall surfaces which can provide a clue to the origin of the movement. Settlement cracking should not be confused with cracking resulting from thermal movement – ie, expansion and shrinkage. In-plane distortions are less serious than out-of-plane movement and they are commonly evidenced by sliding of panels of masonry and opening of cracks. Frequently, vertical loads retain a fairly clear line of support or 'load path' down to the ground and the existence of even quite large cracks, although detrimental to appearance and weather resistance, need not be structurally significant. In structural engineer's parlance, crack widths of less than 1mm ($1/16$in) are termed very slight and those less than 5mm ($3/16$in) are termed 'slight'. However, these classifications relate to the degree of damage and whether or not the movements are active.

The first step in assessing whether or not a wall which has been subject to out-of-plane deformations can be retained is to measure its deformation by carrying out a plumb-line survey. Wall deformations can be extremely deceptive to the eye and a visual assessment made from ground or roof level is often incorrect. In surveying an entire wall surface, not less than three plumb lines should be dropped, one each at the centre and close to the ends of the elevation. Extra lines should be dropped to enable any large but localised distortions to be measured. Offset readings should be taken at and between floor levels. It is most important to establish a base line from which the relative positions of all the plumb lines are measured, while in surveying a wall which is peppered with windows, the use of a theodolite or other optical method may show advantages over the use of plumb lines.

Many building defects respond best to a 'helping hand' rather than brutal surgery which can generate further problems. As in medicine, it is too easy to over-prescribe a remedy. The need to supply some tensile capacity to help to hold the building together can often be met by quite simple means, such as anchoring the floor structures more firmly to the walls with local ties. Stone masonry and brickwork are often weak and new steel ties are very strong, so it is preferable to provide wall restraint in small 'doses' rather than in concentrated areas.

Defects in existing buildings are often better understood if they can be monitored over a period of time. Out-of-plumb walls or cracking are natural candidates for such treatment. It is important to understand how any defects arose, whether they have reached a stable state and how they would be affected by the conversion work. Most defective old buildings give plenty of warning signs before they become dangerous. In this respect, many buildings which may appear to be unsafe continue to resist load without apparent distress.

Investigation, Repair and Upgrading of Foundations

The nature of the foundations of any old building is, of course, not as easily discovered as the general condition of the superstructure, but there is a practical procedure for investigation of this element which it is logical to adhere to. First, a visual inspection of the building and its neighbours should be made and any cracking or distortion should be noted. Secondly, where plans of the building exist either in the records of the previous owner or the local authority (drawings showing the general arrangements of proposed buildings in urban areas have been required by boroughs under public health legislation for more than a hundred years), these should be consulted together with any old maps of the locality which may show the nature and use of the land before it was developed (existing or former street names such as 'Marsh Lane' may give valuable clues to former land usage). The locations of trees and exposed or culverted watercourses may also be significant. Lastly, where there remains doubt and uncertainty about the cause of distortion, the substructure and foundations of the building should be exposed by the digging of trial pits adjacent to the external wall. In large buildings, foundation structures could include substantial brick corbels, inverted vaulting or timber piles linked by capping beams. Trial pits should be made close to, and down to, the existing foundation level, preferably both just outside and within the building. Alterations may have taken place and the danger of digging a single trial pit adjacent to an elevation and basing proposals for remedial work upon the condition of the revealed construction is that a local modification may be taken to be typical, with the consequence that the bearing capacity of the ground may be seriously over- or underestimated.

If it is concluded that upgrading or reinforcement of the foundations is necessary, a number of techniques are available. The choice is largely guided by the desire to avoid creating new problems during the remedial work. The main options in foundation upgrading are widening, to reduce bearing pressures, and deepening, to found the building on stronger ground or ground less affected by loads from adjacent buildings and seasonal movements. Many of the techniques can be carried out only by specialists, particularly the proprietary piling systems.

Much foundation strengthening is still carried out by traditional underpinning. Underpinning may be used to form deeper or wider foundations and it relies on adjacent excavations which need to be shored up and generous enough to allow access for concreting. It is installed by excavating short sections of ground below the footing in a sequence which ensures that adjoining sections are not excavated consecutively. Each excavation should expose no more than a 1.4m (4½ft) length of wall which should be capable of arching over the excavation. Where the quality of the brickwork is in question, this excavation width may need to be halved. Attention should be given to the position of openings, piers and crossbeams so that sections of the structure carrying heavy loads are not left unsupported. Underpinning of such elements without a special support system cannot be recommended.

The progression of underpinning along the wall is normally in groups of five short lengths which are excavated in the order 3, 1, 4, 2, 5 then 3, 1, 4, etc, where the first excavation is not at a sensitive part of the building. The trench is then dug and shored to the appropriate depth beneath the existing foundation and the underside of the footing is dug away and cleaned. Collapse of the soil behind the footing should be prevented by shoring up the side of the excavation. Any temporary shoring which, for reasons of convenience, is left permanently in place should not decay to leave voids in the ground. When the bearing stratum of the ground is reached, the concrete base is poured to within about 75mm (3in) of the underside of the footing. When the new base has hardened, the gap between the concrete and the footing is then packed with 'dry-pack' concrete (Fig 20). This concrete should consist of a 3:1 proportion of sand to cement mixed to a dry consistency and be well rammed into the void to limit further movement. In traditional underpinning, pieces of roofing slate were often used as wedges.

Where the ground quality does not improve significantly with depth, or where there are groundwater problems, widening rather than deepening the foundation may be more practical. Partial underpinning of a

Fig 20

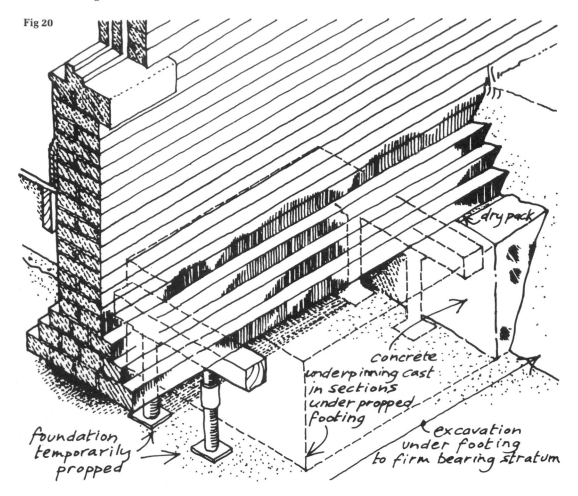

dry pack

concrete
underpinning cast
in sections
under propped
footing

excavation
under footing
to firm bearing stratum

foundation
temporarily
propped

wall may create further problems because masonry can crack if there is continued relative movement. For this reason, partial underpinning may not be the best way of correcting distortion of the superstructure that is owed to inadequate foundations.

There are various techniques for temporarily supporting structures to permit modification or strengthening with minimum disturbance. The technique of 'needling' involves cutting holes through a wall and inserting steel cross-beams or 'needles' so that the wall thrust is transmitted to vertical supports and their temporary foundations which are well clear of the foundation to be executed. Clearly, this technique relies upon easy access and the availability of adequate space on both sides of the wall.

The use of piles as a means of underpinning depends on acceptable cost, ready access, depth of existing foundation and

groundwater level, tolerance of noise and vibration and scope for extraction of the debris and soil. The simplest system is to form short bored piles using a hand- or machine-operated small-depth auger. The holes are then filled with concrete and reinforcement which can be tied into a concrete ground beam constructed at a later stage to support the wall. Such methods are necessarily implemented by specialists.

All underpinning operations carry the risk of minor movement of the superstructure as it adjusts to its new support. The use of cement grouting can act to underpin structures and upgrade foundations by filling voids in the ground and compacting loose, cohesionless soils. Such grouts can also be used to improve the integrity and capacity of existing masonry foundations. There are a variety of cementitious and chemical grouts which may be used in different cases depending on soil conditions, and advice on the suitability of such products for arresting movement in existing foundations should be sought from specialist contractors. A technique which has recently been improved is that of jacking-up foundations by pressure grouting. This result is brought about by compaction of a bulb of thick injected grout. The process demands that building movement is carefully monitored during injection of the grout and, similarly, it is a specialist operation.

Defects in Masonry

Improper Bonding of Brickwork

When front elevations were faced with rubbed bricks laid in thin 'putty' joints, the depth of individual facing courses was less than in the back-up common brickwork. The result was that only occasionally could the wall be bonded by the introduction of uncut headers from the facing skin into the back-up skin when the courses happened to fall evenly.

More common examples of the same weakness occur where facing-brick headers were deliberately cut in half ('snap headers'). Headers were provided only occasionally to give a nominal bond between facing and backing skins. In order quickly to achieve rooms shielded against the weather, it was common for the outer facing brickwork to be constructed later and the headers were often poorly bonded into pockets formed in the preceding work. This inner skin of poorer bricks, often containing built-in timbers (see later), might be carrying and be restrained by floor loads. Any compression or contraction of this inner brickwork may lead to shearing of the few headers, even if they are bonded, causing delamination of the outer skin which is then unrestrained. The collapse of such improperly bonded brickwork may be triggered by any disturbance during rebuilding operations.

Another example of lack of homogeneity in brickwork is found where party walls and external walls are improperly bonded together. Often party walls were erected in advance of the more visible and therefore neatly constructed front elevation, perhaps by unskilled or apprentice labour, while the 'face work' was constructed with greater care for appearance by more experienced hands. The party wall might be toothed to unite with the subsequent external wall construction, but the coursing of the two walls was rarely lined through so that most of the toothing was abandoned and the larger part of the junction was left unbonded. Sometimes a straight butt joint or a vertical slot was formed with no attempt at bonding at all. In both cases no effective restraint is given to the wall between floor levels and vertical or toothed cracks in the corners of such junctions are common.

Where the party wall and the outside wall are reasonably plumb at their junction and do not need to be rebuilt, the incorporation of stainless-steel wire ties is a practical means of preventing further dislocation of these elements. If such a junction is allowed to remain unbonded, the building will continue to lack the stability which may be needed to resist the action of extraordinarily high winds. The 'hairpin' ties are installed by drilling pairs of small holes through the bed joints of the external wall brickwork at vertical intervals not more than twice the thickness of that wall, each hole of each pair being roughly 20mm (¾in) inboard of each surface of the party wall. The short sections of joints between these holes are then raked out to a depth of 20mm (¾in) and grooves of identical depth are cut into the surfaces of the party wall to a length four times its thickness. Small-diameter 75mm (3in) deep holes are then drilled into both faces of the party wall at the end of each groove. 3mm (⅛in) diameter stainless steel wire bent into a 'U' shape is threaded through the outside wall and the legs of this 'hairpin' are laid in the party wall grooves, the ends of these legs being tucked into the party wall (Fig 21). To complete the installation, mortar pointing is applied over the wire and the gap between the party wall and the elevation which necessitated the work is dry-packed with 1:3 sand/cement mortar.

Faults and failures related to bonding within and between brick walls can equally well occur in stone construction. Where the masonry consists of an ashlar or squared rubble facing bonded back into poorer quality rubble or common brickwork, the coarser and more numerous joints in the

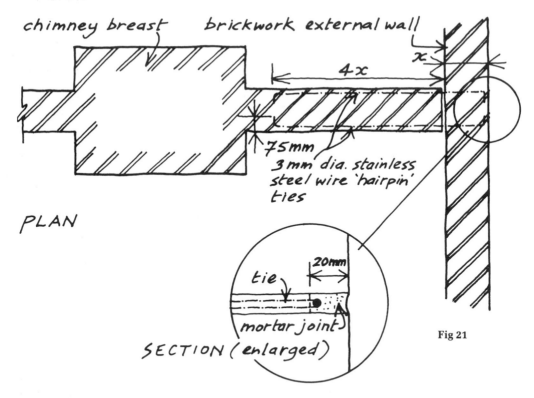

chimney breast brickwork external wall

$4x$

x

75mm
3 mm dia. stainless
steel wire 'hairpin'
ties

PLAN

20mm

tie

mortar joint

SECTION (enlarged)

Fig 21

backing may be more susceptible to compression than the fewer and finer joints in the ashlar, resulting in differential settlement or bulging. Localised bulging of a wall constructed in a similarly common way – namely where a facing skin of ashlar and a parallel backing skin of brickwork are bonded together across an intervening rubble-filled cavity – may indicate the emergence of a very serious problem because it suggests that delamination of this composite construction is occurring and the deformation is accelerating towards collapse under the surcharge imposed by the loose filling.

The twentieth-century enthusiasm for cavity walls as the means of ensuring dry conditions has resulted in a new range of building defects. Where the original construction was not carried out sufficiently carefully and the central cavity of brickwork external cavity-wall construction was not kept clean of mortar droppings as construction proceeded, mortar may have accumulated on the metal wall-ties which were used to connect the two leaves of masonry so that wind-blown rain which quickly saturates the thin external leaf is conveyed to the

internal leaf through this porous material, causing damp patches on internal finishes. The only remedy for this failure is the removal and replacement of the offending wall-ties.

Much more significant as a generic defect of the conventional cavity-wall construction which has dominated building in brickwork for the past sixty years is loss of integrity owed to the corrosion and snapping of cavity wall-ties. The form of cavity wall which was recommended from the mid-nineteenth century relied upon various patented types of stepped ceramic bonding bricks to tie the inner leaf of the wall to the outer skin. When the inevitable differential movement occurs between the two skins, it is common for rupturing of the bonding bricks to occur because they are brittle and possibly perforated to facilitate good drainage of the cavity. Differential movements between the facing and the backing brickwork can be better accommodated by the tolerance of bending or rotation which is a quality of the metal ties that were universally adopted when the shortcomings of bonding bricks became apparent. However, the type of tie which was almost invariably

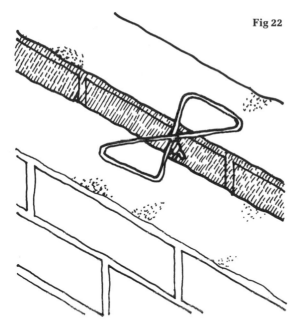

Fig 22

bricks should be used for all major walls, but the practice, particularly in speculative development, was the use of the best bricks where appearance mattered most and the employment of poorer and cheaper bricks where the work was concealed. From this policy arises the anomaly that the back-up brickwork, which tends to carry the most load from floors and beams, was constructed from the poorest bricks. Party walls and external stucco-finished walls were often constructed with poorer bricks throughout. It is logical that greater deformation under stress should be expected in the softer, underfired bricks. Where a wall is eccentrically loaded by upper floors and the roof, stresses on the inner face may be considerably greater than those on the outer face. A greater consolidation of 'lean' mortar (ie, mortar with inadequate cement content) is therefore to be expected near to the inner face of the wall, leading to bulging of the outer face (Fig 23).

If the sand used in the original mortar was not free of salts and other impurities, the presence of these ingredients might retard the setting of the lime or otherwise weaken the mortar. Although lime-based mortars can be hard and durable, it was common practice for builders to skimp on the lime

used – namely the galvanised steel wire 'butterfly' tie – is intrinsically flimsy and lacks the long-term corrosion resistance promised by its galvanised finish (Fig 22). Hence ties which it was believed would last for sixty years have rusted and snapped after only twenty years.

The consequent freeing of the facing skin is the worst defect that may be encountered in cavity construction. Fortunately, a few enterprising manufacturers have recognised the potentially very large market for simply installed and low-cost remedial devices which will rectify this condition and several types of supplementary cavity wall-ties-are available for insertion into holes drilled in the bed joints of the facing brickwork. Tightening captive nuts on the shanks of these fixings expands metal anchors in the wall's inner leaf and causes the ties to grip the outer leaf close to the external wall plane. The ends of these new metallic connections may then be concealed behind re-pointing of the affected mortar joints.

Problems with Materials

Bricks of the same composition and simultaneous firing can vary in quality depending on their position in the clamp or kiln and mortars may contain variable proportions of lime. The theory of traditional building construction was that sound, well-burnt

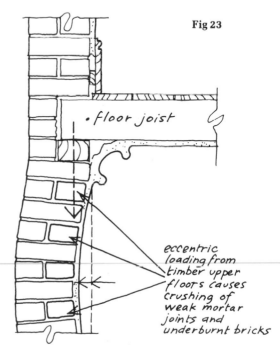

Fig 23

floor joist

eccentric loading from timber upper floors causes crushing of weak mortar joints and underburnt bricks

content of a mortar and to use unclean, poorly-graded sand. This shortcoming was most prevalent in speculative houses erected in London in the nineteenth century – and particularly during the building boom of the 1870s. Similarly, lime which was improperly slaked and which therefore contained particles of unslaked quicklime when built into the construction, can cause problems with the passing of time because these particles react with atmospheric moisture and 'blow' otherwise cohesive mortar joints. The identical defect in lime-based stucco rendering can have disastrous consequences for appearance and weather-tightness.

Before Portland cement was cheaply and readily available, other materials with cementitious qualities were used to make mortars with strengths greater than lime mortar. One of the principal alternative materials was the ash from coal-burning operations in industry. This 'flyash' was very variable in quality and because of its high sulphur content it was acidic in contrast to alkaline lime. Thus, metallic items tend to corrode in flyash mortar which is usually distinguished by its dark appearance. It was used throughout the nineteenth century and as late as the 1930s in some industrial areas. Owing to its widespread use in South Wales, the corrosion of metal wall ties in cavity-wall constructions in that region is a serious problem.

A common cause of deterioration of Portland cement mortar leading to structural instability is the presence of soluble sulphates in brickwork or in groundwater. These salts slowly attack the cement under continuously wet conditions, resulting in expansion or softening of the mortar. In severe cases, complete disintegration of the mortar can occur. It follows that external rendering and other finishes which contain Portland cement are also susceptible to sulphate attack. This defect is most likely to materialise in superstructure brickwork when driving rain or moisture which is trapped under rendering saturates the bricks and transports soluble sulphates from the bricks to the mortar joints. With expansion of these joints, rendered surfaces crack horizontally and vertically in a pattern reflecting the brick courses behind. A chimney stack which has been built or repointed in cement mortar may begin to lean because its windward face is more prone to sulphate attack and consequent expansion of the mortar than is the lee side (Fig 24). Thus, bulging walls, curving

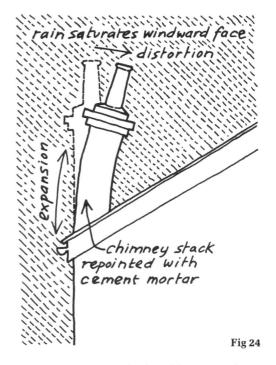

Fig 24

chimney stacks, cracked and loose rendering and friable mortar joints can all be symptoms of sulphate attack.

Mortar deterioration owed to sulphate attack is an irreversible process which can only be stopped by eliminating the sources of water. In cases of severe damage where water cannot be prevented from saturating the walls and the brickwork or the adjacent ground has a high sulphate content, demolition and rebuilding of the walls with bricks of special quality and mortar containing sulphate-resisting cement may be the only solution.

Fortunately, deterioration of mortar through sulphate attack is unlikely to pose serious problems for most traditionally constructed older buildings for the simple reason that lime mortar was used in the construction of their walls. The manufacture of building limes is carried out at lower temperatures than the processes used in cement production. This results in a different chemical structure from essentially

identical ingredients. The sulphate-suscep-
tible compounds which are relatively
abundant in Portland cement are scarce in
limes, so that sulphate attack is less of a
problem in lime mortar. Therefore, it is
often a mistake to attribute bulging of
exposed walls containing lime mortar to
sulphate attack. Such deformations are
more likely to be related to premature
loading of the brickwork when it was new, a
lack of lateral restraint, or non-uniform
construction of the wall in cross-section (eg,
the use of 'snap headers' as described
earlier).

Built-in Timbers

Deformations in masonry may be exacerbated
by the presence of built-in timber. 'Bonding'
or 'coursing' timbers were often used
behind the facing skin of brickwork or in
internal walls as a means of improving the
bond between otherwise almost independent masonry elements and to spread out
loads from higher panels of brickwork on
the slow-setting weak lime mortar of the
earlier construction. Sometimes such
timbers were built-in to provide joinery
fixings, while wall-plates set into the brickwork were used to support the floor joists.
The natural cross-grain shrinkage or compression of bonding timbers can result in
wall movements, particularly bulges in
external walls.

More serious is the risk of timber decay
from rot or insect attack which can cause
serious structural problems, particularly in
narrow and heavily loaded panels such as
may be found between closely spaced window openings. Not only is the effective
section of the brickwork reduced, but it is
also subject to eccentric loading (Fig 25).
This type of masonry pier, located between
sash windows in an eighteenth- or nineteenth-century house — and workshops,
schoolrooms and station buildings were all
constructed similarly — may have a substantial part of its area taken up by the
weights boxes of the windows and the
shutter recesses. It may also have built into
it the main timber floor beams as well as
wall-plates and bonding timbers holding
poor quality masonry together. Once the
facing skin has started to move away from
the backing, there is little that can be done to
save it. The use of modern replacement
cavity-wall ties is not effective because most
walls were built with lime mortar which has
lost its adhesive qualities through becoming
dry and friable. Stripping and rebuilding of
the facing skin is also not generally successful. The backing skin is so weak that it may
collapse while the outer skin is removed.
The only cost-effective remedy may be to
rebuild the wall. Where rotting of bonding
timbers can be deduced from the interior
following stripping of the corroded plaster,
but this defect has not yet affected the
verticality of external wall surfaces, it is
possible to prop temporarily the superincumbent brickwork and to remove the
timber, filling the masonry void with new
brickwork and dense mortar dry-pack to
replace the decaying wood. Where such
timber members provided a bearing for floor
joists, this can be restored by installing a
continuous steel angle support, fixed to the
face of the wall with chemical anchors and
providing a ledge on which bear the joist-
ends (Fig 26).

Another problem which may result from
the combination of timber with masonry is
the deformation of brick arches owed to
failure of their wooden backing lintels. This
condition may be deduced from diagonal
cracks in the facing brickwork above the

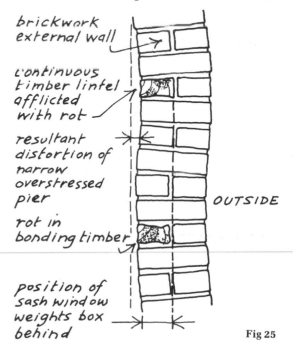

brickwork
external wall

continuous
timber lintel
afflicted
with rot

resultant
distortion of
narrow
overstressed
pier

rot in
bonding timber

OUTSIDE

position of
sash window
weights box
behind

Fig 25

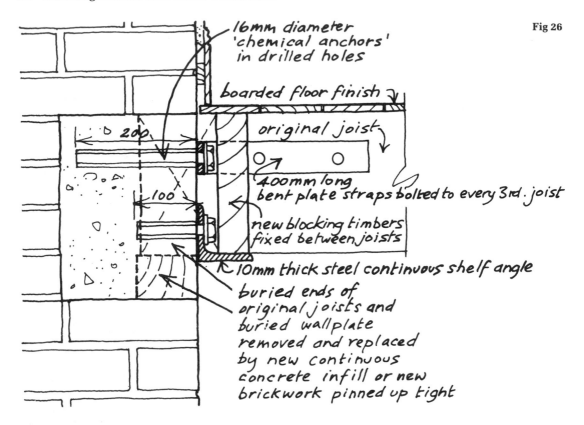

Fig 26

16mm diameter 'chemical anchors' in drilled holes

boarded floor finish

original joist

200

100

400mm long bent plate straps bolted to every 3rd. joist

new blocking timbers fixed between joists

10mm thick steel continuous shelf angle

buried ends of original joists and buried wallplate removed and replaced by new continuous concrete infill or new brickwork pinned up tight

arched opening and sagging in the centre of the arch or the arch bulging outwards. In contrast, loose arch bricks and vertical cracks in the brickwork above and below the opening are likely to be signs of failure of the surrounding structure rather than the arch itself. The former types of deformation are brought about by sagging of the backing lintel due to rot. Thus more load is thrown on to the slender 'soldier course' brick arch. The arch may be caused to buckle and bulge outwards. Alternatively, the top of the arch compresses and sags, allowing the superincumbent brickwork to crack and drop. This condition can be rectified by propping the structure, needling the wall above the opening and carefully numbering and dismantling the arch bricks for re-use.

The timber backing lintel is removed and the arch is reset in mortar on timber centering with stainless steel butterfly wall ties projecting from the rear of the radial joints. While the mortar is still green the centering is eased down to allow the arch to tighten under its own weight and a reinforced concrete backing lintel is cast in situ

against the ties and brickwork (Fig 27). Finally, the joint of the head of the arch and lintel with the supported brickwork is

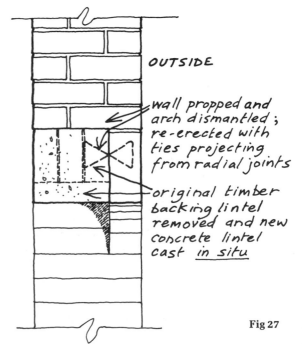

OUTSIDE

wall propped and arch dismantled; re-erected with ties projecting from radial joints

original timber backing lintel removed and new concrete lintel cast in situ

Fig 27

packed tightly with dry mortar and slates and the needles and props are removed.

Deformation of Untied Flank Walls

Perceptible bulging of an entire wall plane, where the largest deformation is at mid-height and there are gaps between the wall and adjoining floors and partitions, may be as attributable to an original lack of 'to-getherness' in the structure as to short-comings in the materials or the combination of materials. This judgement applies par-ticularly to flank walls which run parallel to the floor joists.

The condition is most noticeable in tradi-tional detached or semi-detached house construction where the timber floors span from front to rear and do not restrain the external flank walls because they do not bear on them. Even when the floors do span on to the flank wall, there is often a staircase running up inside the wall that eliminates floor restraint over a significant section of the wall. Over many years, this effectively free-standing wall bulges outwards in the vertical plane between the restraint afforded by the ground and the roof structure and in the horizontal plane between the front and rear corners (Fig 28). This bulging is caused by the imposition of load from the roof timbers, wind suction, thermal movement, etc.

Provided the wall has not bulged out-wards by more than a sixth of its thickness, it can be restrained against further deforma-tion by the insertion of stainless steel straps at each floor level and by bracing the floors with plywood decking to deliver the re-straining force back to load-bearing walls at right-angles (Fig 29). If the wall is not restrained, the out-of-plumb forces of the bulged wall will make it bulge further until it collapses. The stainless steel straps used to reinforce the construction consist of 30 x 5mm (1¼ x ¼in) bars, 1,200mm (48in) long with one end bent over. They are fed through a bed joint of the brickwork from the outside of the wall and then fixed on to the notched top surfaces of the first three floor-joists with three No 12 countersunk-head woodscrews. Either 50 x 50mm (2 x 2in) herringbone strutting or solid blocking is fitted between the first three joists and the whole assembly is tightened with folding

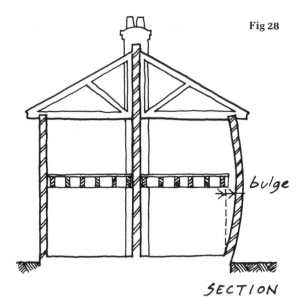

Fig 28

SECTION

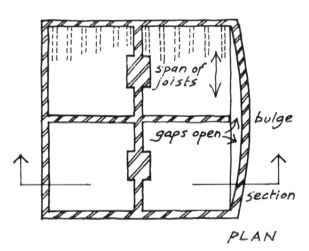

PLAN

wedges nailed into place.

Sometimes there have been previous attempts to restrain bulging walls, and the existence of cast-iron bosses, cruciform or 'S'-shaped steel plates on wall surfaces provides evidence of built-in tie-rods which may simply anchor back a bowing external wall to the opposite wall. If these connec-tions are insufficient to restrain the wall, in time they pull the opposite wall out-of-plumb. To obtain stability, all forces must be opposed by equal and opposite forces. As the object of restraining a bulging wall is to stop it moving further, tie bars must be anchored to something stiff like a wall corner. Thus it may be possible to rearrange restraint straps so that they are anchored to

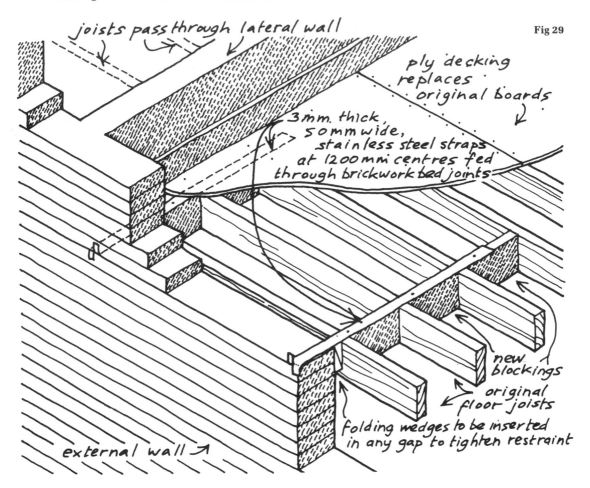

Fig 29

joists pass through lateral wall

ply decking replaces original boards

3 mm. thick, 50 mm wide, stainless steel straps at 1200 mm centres fed through brickwork bed joints

new blockings

original floor joists

folding wedges to be inserted in any gap to tighten restraint

external wall →

masonry walls running at right angles to the bulged walls. This can be achieved either by creating a 'diaphragm floor' with plywood sheets screwed to the joists, or by running steel straps diagonally across the tops of joists, anchored to the corners of the opposite wall (Fig 30). This rearrangement depends upon side walls not having been weakened too much by window openings. Alternatively, it may be possible for existing

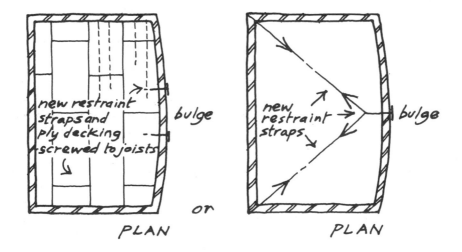

new restraint straps and ply decking screwed to joists

bulge

PLAN

or

new restraint straps

bulge

PLAN

Fig 30

ties to be replaced with the less conspicuous stainless steel straps described earlier.

Damp Penetration

As porous materials, brickwork and stonework may be subject to decay from proximity to permanently damp ground, or where they occupy locations highly exposed to the elements. Underburnt or 'place' bricks which can usually be recognised by their lighter colour may be prone to early deterioration, particularly if they are sited at or near to external ground level or used as copings on garden walls, chimney stacks or parapets. In such exposed positions, underburnt bricks are easily saturated by driving rain even if the mortar joints are sound and a subsequent frost will cause the bricks to 'burst' or delaminate as the entrapped water expands upon freezing. Bricks which lose their durable outer surface in this way will quite quickly deteriorate as their softer clay cores are exposed to the weather. A long-term repair of such damage demands the cutting out of the affected bricks and their replacement with new or good quality salvaged bricks. This defect may be more conspicuous at the foot of yard and garden walls than it is in the main walls of a building for two reasons. First, from around the middle of the nineteenth century it was normal to incorporate a damp-proof course close to ground level in external wall construction and secondly, because it was recognised that the inclusion of a dpc could concentrate rising dampness from the ground in the lowest courses of the wall, care was taken to use hard bricks or bricks of special quality in this area. Such measures were not taken in the construction of free-standing walls for fear that the inclusion of a low-level dpc could create a 'slip plane', allowing the upper brickwork to slide on the plinth below the dpc, with a consequent loss of stability, and the effects of rising damp upon these structures were tolerated.

Quite often in industrial buildings a damp-proof zone was created at the base of the buildings by constructing the footings and a low plinth to the external walls in impervious blue engineering brick. Clearly, this form of construction may continue indefinitely to resist damp penetration from the ground, but in the majority of buildings which originally incorporated only an asphalt, lead sheet or tarred hemp dpc, it is likely that this barrier will have broken down under the weight of the structure or through brittleness which increases with time. Evidence of an outworn dpc is provided by decaying plasterwork at low level on internal surfaces of the main walls.

The classical procedure for renewing a dpc is to shore up the wall and then to remove alternate sections of the lowest brick courses. These shallow panels of masonry are subsequently rebuilt with a damp-proof course of slate or similar impervious material incorporated in the new structure. When these renewed sections are complete, the retained sections are demolished and rebuilt, thus completing the continuous damp-proof course. This operation is very expensive and in recent years other methods have been developed in order to achieve an almost equally effective result.

A modern method of inserting a new physical dpc uses a special chain-saw to cut a continuous slot in a low-level bed joint of the affected wall, into which a new polyethylene dpc is fitted in a series of 1m (3ft) lengths. Care is taken to overlap generously the adjacent sections of dpc which are wedged in place with pieces of slate, and that part of the slot not filled by the impervious material is filled with 1:3 cement/sand dry-pack mortar. Where it is not practical to make the cut below the internal ground-floor level, the shallow strip of internal wall-face left below the dpc and above the floor surface should be treated with at least two coats of bituminous paint to resist dampness, and any related timber skirtings should be replaced with more durable trim such as profiled quarry tiles which do not require fixings that could penetrate the wall sealant. The specialist contractors who install such damp-proof courses normally insist that any adjacent plasterwork which may have been affected by dampness is hacked off the masonry and the wholesale removal of a continuous 1m (3ft) deep band of plaster from the foot of the affected wall is standard procedure. Following the insertion of the dpc, the denuded masonry is given some time to dry out before new plaster comprising a sand/cement base coat incorporating a water-repellent ingredient and a hard plaster finishing coat is applied.

Clearly, the sawing of a wall for the insertion of a damp-proof course is an effective and practical treatment for rising damp in a detached building, but where a structure shares a wall with adjoining premises in a separate ownership, this method is unlikely to be acceptable. In this circumstance, impregnation of the lowest courses of the wall with a water-repellent fluid containing silicone can help to keep rising damp at bay. To be most effective, such an injected chemical dpc, like any new physical barrier, requires the removal of a 1m (3ft) depth of plaster from the foot of the internal surface of any affected wall. Small-diameter holes at 150mm (6in) intervals in a horizontal row are then drilled down into the heart of the wall and the proprietary liquid is poured into these openings or injected under pressure until the foot of the wall is saturated with the water-repellent mixture. Just as the plaster which is applied after the installation of a physical dpc must include a water-repellent additive, so the plaster which recoats a wall that has been impregnated with a chemical dpc must be equally damp-resisting if the installer's guarantee is to hold good.

The history of chemical damp-proof courses extends back only to the late 1940s and their general application to renovation work is of even more recent date, so there is, as yet, little evidence to show that they are reliable in the long term. The replacement of an outworn dpc by insertion is recommended in preference to chemical injection where ready access to the affected area makes practical such treatment.

In addition to these radical techniques for the prevention of rising damp, there exist various patent methods and materials designed to alleviate or conceal small areas of dampness, including a system in which small-diameter porous ceramic tubes are inserted in external walls in order to 'vent away' the dampness. Such a system, together with the several forms of 'dry-lining' damp-concealment construction which are available, is best reserved for the treatment of only very slight occurrences of damp penetration.

Decay and Repair of Timber

It is mainly rot or insect attack which affects the serviceability of timber structures. When an attack is found, it is advisable to obtain the view of a specialist who will be able to identify the type of decay and advise on the treatment of the timber, including designating any parts that should be removed. Where fungal decay is found, this expert should specify the cause and suggest measures for its elimination. Clearly, the existence of timber decay is likely to be related to other shortcomings in the condition of the building and these faults may require rectification in addition to treatment of the timber. Problems may have been built into the original design through the inadequate protection of timber from ground moisture, lack of ventilation or roof-slopes which were insufficiently steep to drain away all rainwater. Equally, defects may be owed to some earlier modification of the original arrangement or construction and these changes need to be identified and corrected. This circumstance could include the bridging of an original dpc by 'remedial' rendering applied over insufficiently weather-tight brickwork. More probably, decay and deterioration of materials and installations is the result of lack of maintenance, the results of which may include blocked or broken rainwater drains, displaced roof tiles or peeling paint finishes, all of which can lead to timber decay.

Rot in Timber

Timber decay which is not owed to insect action is normally the result of fungal attack. It aids understanding of these phenomena to recognise that the function of all timber pests is to break down and convert dead trees into soil, allowing new trees unimpeded growth. The fact that the dead wood has been shaped for use as a building material is of no consequence to a fungus or a beetle.

The fungi are parasitical and can only live by feeding on organic matter, including wood and leaves. In contrast to most plants, they breathe in oxygen and give out carbon dioxide. All fungi require about 20 per cent moisture content in the host wood to germinate and although in new buildings the moisture content of the timber may be as high as 18 per cent, this is soon reduced to about 12-14 per cent by heating and ventilation of the enclosed spaces. Therefore, in a sound, dry building there is no need to fear fungal attack.

The most serious and devastating wood fungus and the species most frequently found in old buildings is dry rot or *Serpula lachrymans*. Having established itself in damp timber, this infection can spread to dry wood and brickwork. Its life-cycle starts with a spore, of which there are countless millions in the atmosphere. These spores are highly resistant to extremes of heat and humidity and are very long-lived. A spore which lands on wood with a moisture content of 20-25 per cent in a still and stuffy atmosphere where the temperature is between 7° and 27°C (44° and 80°F) can germinate and then throw out hollow strands known as hyphae . These initially hair-like fibres seek out and feed off the cellulose in the wood which is digested by the fungus to leave a dry, dessicated and fragile shell of wood-fibre or lignin which, in the absence of the cementitious cellulose, cannot continue to perform any structural role required of the timber. Having drawn the cellulose from one section of the wood, the hyphae reach on to adjacent sections of timber to continue the process, while the strands of the initial attack unite into an equally fast-spreading cotton-wool-like growth known as mycelium . In the later stages of an attack, strands called rhizomorphs develop from the mycelium to convey moisture from the decomposing wood to sound timber many feet away, weeping 'tears' on to it until it, too, is subjugated and ripe for attack. When this action is well established, the fungus will produce a sporophore, or fruiting body, which produces millions of spores. The sporophore is at first a whitish-grey, unpleasant-looking fleshy growth and gradually becomes more leathery and dewy. It bursts at intervals to release into the atmosphere an enormous number of rusty-red spores which are carried on the breeze to germinate in distant damp timber, starting the process afresh.

Dry rot exhibits an almost uncanny knowledge of the presence of timber and is able to thrust through brickwork mortar joints and to travel across brickwork behind plaster over great distances in its search for fresh food. In this respect, it is quite capable of spreading from one building to another through a thick party wall. Evidence of the existence of dry rot may be found in a musty smell pervading a suspect space; the presence of a whitish cotton-wool-like fungal growth on timber; cracking and bulging of joinery mouldings such as skirtings and door linings owed to the shrinkage of hidden fixing timber which has been attacked by the fungus; and readily apparent ravaged timber showing deep cracks across the grain, giving a 'cubed' appearance. Once dry rot has been discovered, the only remedy is extermination of the fungus together with the rectification of the unhealthy conditions which invited the attack. The fungus has no heart nor 'Achilles' heel' and unless it is completely destroyed to its limits, it will develop fresh strength and start again to devour the timberwork.

There are two possible strategies for the treatment of an attack of dry rot. The building owner may either employ a builder to carry out the work of opening up and eradication, or he may call in one of the numerous specialist firms to deal with the attack. If a builder is entrusted with the work, it must be ensured through a full briefing and careful supervision that only conscientious, knowledgeable and skilled tradesmen are employed who are able to give rational advice on the proper nature and extent of the remedial treatment if the initial assessment of the degree of damage proves to be inaccurate. The advantage of employing a specialist firm is that its tradesmen are more likely to be well trained and experienced in this field of building preservation, with a thorough and successful job being a more certain result. However, it should be clear that any firm which issues a guarantee must inevitably err on the side of over-zealousness, which will add to expense.

The first step in eradicating dry rot is to find the heart of the outbreak and to trace its extent with great care and thoroughness. Each branch of the fungus must be traced from its source to the growing tip, and finishes should be opened up to reveal timber ½m (1½ft) beyond the affected material. Floorboards, plaster, timber trim, including architraves and skirting boards, and other finishes (including apparently impenetrable tiling) must be removed from timber and masonry if the slightest suspicion exists that the fungus has reached beneath or behind them. When the full extent of the attack is known, treatment can begin.

If fruiting bodies are present, these should be treated with fungicide to prevent the spread of air-borne spores. Then all infected timber is cut out so that all affected wood, including apparently sound wood up to ½m (1½ft) away from the visible extremities of the attack, is removed. Where important structural timbers are infected but have not been weakened by the fungus, it may be practical to treat them with fungicide and to retain them. All fungus-infected timber which has been removed should be burned immediately together with any shavings or sawdust from the infected area. Brickwork into which the mycelium has spread and any masonry which adjoins an outbreak must be similarly poisoned. If a structural wall is too thick to absorb the fungicide to its core, it must be drilled with a series of holes into which the liquid is injected in order to permeate the entire thickness. Wherever possible, walls should be treated from both sides. Leaking gutters and roofs, defective rainwater downpipes, mounding of adjacent soil which bridges the dpc and all other sources of dampness must be removed. Poorly ventilated and stagnant spaces must be opened up to a constant current of air by the introduction of new ventilation openings as even a vigorous attack of dry rot can be arrested (but not reduced) by exposure to fresh air.

New timbers inserted as replacements should be thoroughly treated from every face against infection. Common chemical treatments include pressure impregnation with copper, chrome or arsenic salts. These are industrial processes carried out only to order unless the use of 'treated' timber in the rebuilding is specified from the outset. The chemicals are water-borne and the timber takes a long time to dry out. Even though these treatments drive the chemicals into the timber to a much greater depth than surface application by spray or brush, the wood may not be completely impregnated, particularly in the heartwood, so that notches and ends cut on site after treatment must be dipped in preservative or touched up with a brush. If this is not done, the protection is bypassed.

Other forms of fungal decay of timber in buildings are relatively unimportant because they are not able to spread to sound wood. However, they do indicate the existence of unhealthy conditions in which more serious trouble could develop. As this observation suggests, combined or separate attacks from dry rot and other less voracious fungi are common in neglected and decaying buildings. These minor fungi are generally termed wet rot. *Coniophora cerebella*, or the cellar fungus, is the most common. It cannot live on timber with a moisture content of less than 25 per cent and thus is usually found in situations too damp for dry rot. The fungus can be identified by its fine dark brown or black strands and its green and leathery fruiting body. A paper-thin shell of sound wood is left on the surface of the infected timber which shows deep cracks along the grain but rarely across it as may result from dry rot. Eradication of the less serious fungi is usually a simple matter of cutting out and burning the infected timber. However, it is wise to treat the area with fungicide as a precaution against any subsequent outbreak of dry rot which could be encouraged as the construction dries out.

Insect Action on Timber

The destructive action of beetles on timber is rarely as serious as fungal attack because an infected section is only weakened by the combined cross-sectional area of the tunnels it contains – the strength of the surrounding wood remains unimpaired. Beetle attack which has ceased requires little attention except for any necessary repairs to the damaged timbers. In contrast, an active attack should not be left unattended and can be identified by the clean appearance of the 'flight holes' and the little patches and piles of fresh bore dust which fall from them.

The main insect enemies of timber in buildings are the death-watch beetle and the common furniture beetle and the two are often found together. It is at the larva stage of their development when boring and feeding of the grubs takes place that the damage is caused because the adult beetles do not eat and they live only for a short time. The different species can be identified by the different sizes of their flight holes and sometimes by the type of wood attacked. In early summer, the beetles themselves may also be found.

The death-watch beetle has a life cycle of three to ten years depending upon the nature of the timber it inhabits. It lays its eggs in any cracks or crevices in suitable timber – hardwood is preferred, particularly the outer and softer layers of sapwood. Timber which has already been affected by fungus or decay offers a special attraction. The attack is usually concentrated in damp and more easily edible wood such as built-in bonding timbers, the eaves ends of rafters and the bearing ends of beams and trusses. After the grubs have eaten extensive 'galleries' in the wood over a period of years, with the resultant dust being emitted in bun-shaped pellets, the larva enters a pupal stage lasting three to six weeks and emerges as a fully grown beetle. It remains in its pupal chamber until the following spring and emerges in April, May or June to seek a mate. It is at this time that the characteristic tapping sound which gives the beetle its name can be heard. The flight holes are about 3mm (1/8in) in diameter. An attack may die out if the timber becomes hard and unpalatable to the beetle with age and correct maintenance.

The common furniture beetle can be found in both hardwood and softwood, chiefly in the sapwood from close to the bark. Therefore, it is a more serious pest in the lighter construction adopted in post-medieval buildings where the proportion of sapwood is high. Although, as is apparent in 'woodworm' damage to furniture, flight holes frequently appear in polished surfaces, the eggs are laid in cracks, joints and unvarnished recesses. They hatch out in 3-4 weeks and the larvae bore into the wood. After a period of 12-36 months, the last 2-3 weeks of which are spent in a pupal stage near the surface, the grub becomes a fully grown beetle. It immediately finds its way to the surface and emerges to mate in the months of June, July or August. The flight holes of the furniture beetle are smaller than those of the death-watch beetle and are about 1.5mm (1/16in) in diameter. Wet or damaged timber is the most appetising food for the insect but apparently sound wood may be equally badly afflicted.

The house longhorn beetle is another insect pest which seems to be confined to parts of Hampshire and south-west Surrey. It is found mainly in timbers less than fifty years old and is a much larger insect than the furniture beetle. Its larvae bore voraciously to and fro along the grain of the wood, generally under a thin, intact surface. The beetle emerges in June or August via few and scattered flight holes about 6-12mm (1/4-1/2in) long which inadequately represent the true extent of the unseen damage. Only fresh, sound wood is affected.

As applies in the treatment of fungal attack, in the eradication of insect pests it is necessary to identify the unhealthy conditions which have invited the attack, and to cure them at source. Dampness and lack of ventilation are as welcoming to insects as they are to wood fungi and once these conditions are rectified the beetles will feel less inclined to stay. All local dust, dirt and rubbish should be cleared away, partly to remove conditions congenial to the beetles but also to facilitate treatment with insecticide. The full extent of the attack must be discovered in order to assess its severity. It is important to differentiate between timbers which have been so badly eaten that their strength has been reduced, necessitating replacement, and those which, though damaged, still contain enough sound wood to continue their original jobs. Timber which is so severely honeycombed that it is virtually useless – termed 'frass' – is likely to coincide with the sapwood content of structural timber. Thus some affected beams which are riddled with holes and appear to be useless, may be found, on investigation, to contain solid heartwood quite adequate to perform their structural roles.

The most extensive and expensive part of the work in some cases is the initial removal of wholly infested wood and beetle-riddled frass. The latter can be removed by scraping or wire-brushing. All infested wood must be cleared away and burnt and related constructional cavities must be cleaned out carefully. When the sound timber is clean and readily accessible it can be treated with insecticide. The methods of application are brushing, spraying and injection. The technique in brush application should be to spread the liquid generously over the surface and into cracks. Spraying is carried out with a coarse spray at low pressure. Where the bearings of timbers are inaccessible, it may be necessary to drill deep holes for saturation of the buried beams' ends by injection. Because flight holes connect with sub-surface galleries bored by the insects, injection into these cavities is also a good means of impregnating hidden material with insecticide. Generally, sound timbers, such as wall-plates and lintels which are built into masonry and which show only one or two surfaces to the building interior, may be treated by coating their exposed faces with a thick 'mayonnaise' preservative paste.

The success of the treatment depends very much on the skill and intelligence of the operatives and careful supervision to ensure that attention is given to the full extent of affected areas. Plainly, this process is facilitated if the working areas are readily accessible, well lit and well ventilated.

Any new timber which is introduced into the treated areas in repair or replacement work should also be treated with preservative containing an insecticide. In practice, the proprietary liquids which are used in the pressure-vacuum impregnation of timber against fungal attack also contain insecticides and effectively identical products are available through builders' merchants and DIY outlets for brush and spray application on site.

In-situ Repair of Timber

In addition to rot and insect attack which may be regarded as defects intrinsic to timber, problems also arise from the way timber elements of traditional buildings were assembled. Frequent use was made of the bressummer arrangement described in the preceding chapter for the introduction of large openings, such as shopfronts, into pre-existing buildings. Many such heavy timber beams supporting the joists of the first floor were inserted into existing buildings in such a way that their ends may have had an inadequate bearing on to slender timber 'storey posts' installed adjacent to the party walls. Intermediate storey posts were sometimes added to support these bressummers and the wall above. Problems often develop where bressummers and storey posts were installed in an existing building because of progressive sagging of the timber as well as the crushing effect of the superincumbent masonry and the onset of rot. In later Victorian buildings, iron beams and columns replaced timber in this arrangement. Where these members were built into the original construction, such problems would be less likely, but the causes of defects and deterioration associated with bressummers should be identified, particularly if it is the intention to increase loads upon these elements. Conspicuous distortion of a broad opening spanned by a bressummer may call for the insertion of diagonal steel bracing, brick piers to stiffen flank walls and new intermediate supports.

A more common problem in timber upper floors and suspended ground floors is the rotting of joist-ends above built-in wall-plates. When 'untreated' timber (ie, wood which has not been impregnated with pre-

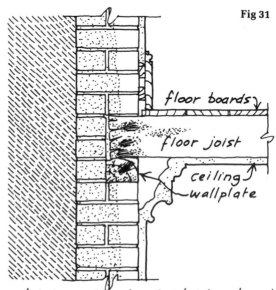

Fig 31

floor boards

floor joist

ceiling

wallplate

driving rain saturates brickwork and rots joist ends and wallplate concealed by finishes

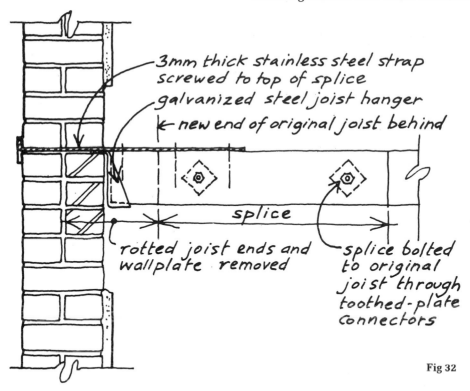

3mm thick stainless steel strap screwed to top of splice

galvanized steel joist hanger

new end of original joist behind

splice

rotted joist ends and wallplate removed

splice bolted to original joist through toothed-plate connectors

Fig 32

servative) is built into solid walls, it has no protection from dampness in the wall and it is common for joist-ends to be shielded by a skin of brickwork only half-a-brick thick (Fig 31). Such joist-ends will decay if their moisture content remains over 20 per cent for long periods. Unfortunately, there are usually no signs of an impending problem before structural failure occurs. Moss growth on an external solid wall may suggest that the wall and its built-in joist-ends have been subjected to damp. This condition can be corrected by temporarily propping the floor, cutting out the rotten joist-ends, treating the sound timber to be retained with preservative and restoring support to the joists through a bracket or joist-hangers (Fig 32). The wall-plate, which is likely to be decayed, should also be removed. Where decay has advanced along the joist into the building interior, it may be necessary to splice on a new timber end to the member, carried on a joist-hanger. The length of this splice and the size of the bolt for making the connection depends upon floor span, loading, spacing of joists and distance of the splice from the support, but for a 4m (13ft) span in domestic-type work,

with joists at 400mm (16in) centres, the splice would be 610mm (24in) long with two 12mm (½in) diameter bolts installed 400mm (16in) apart over 75mm (3in) square toothed-plate connectors. To ensure that the wall retains adequate lateral restraint after the joists have been rehung, stainless steel straps at about 1,200mm (48in) centres should be installed. In some circumstances, it may prove more economical to replace complete joists.

Overloaded or lightly structured timber floors are also likely to deflect or sag, producing a dished or sloping floor surface. This condition is worsened by the cutting of notches in the joists to house sub-floor services like heating pipes. Consequently, excessive deflection, or, in extreme cases, collapse, can occur. It is often possible to fill these notches with hardwood wedges. This measure does not correct the existing deflection but it stiffens the floor to imposed load. Where it is not possible to strengthen a sagging floor by the addition of secondary timbers relieving the overloaded joists, it may be feasible to strengthen any integral timber beams by inserting steel flitch plates into slots formed in these members (Fig 33).

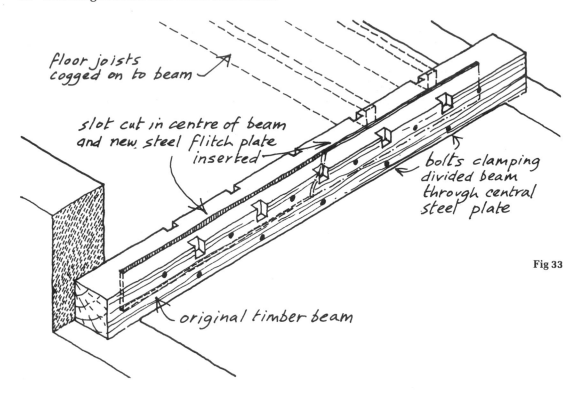

floor joists
cogged on to beam

slot cut in centre of beam
and new steel flitch plate
inserted

bolts clamping
divided beam
through central
steel plate

Fig 33

original timber beam

Alternatively, where access is available, steel strengthening plates can be added to a beam's top and bottom surfaces to form flanges. These two techniques, and the addition of steel side or cross-rods respectively to strengthen individual beams or entire joisted floors at mid-span, all involve the substitution of metal for overstressed wood in the part of the member that is subject to tensile stress.

Roof trusses, as well as timber floors, can fail in a variety of ways, and failure by crushing at the joint of the principal rafter with the tie is assisted by any decay which affects this area. As this joint is usually close to the bearing of the truss, it may be possible to repair a truss comprising small timber members with plywood gusset plates (Fig 34). There also exists a range of specialised repair methods which use epoxy resins. These substances are able to permeate and saturate partly decayed timber. On hardening, the resin/timber combination acquires high strength and rigidity more akin to the cured resin than to timber. This material will also bond well to stainless steel rods so that badly decayed timber can be drilled, stitched and glued to achieve higher strengths than the original construction. However, this is a very expensive process which is usually reserved for repairs to failed joints in ancient timber-framed structures where the removal and replacement of individual members is impracticable.

Defects in Roof Coverings

Where a sloping roof was originally erected to the correct pitch (ie, the roof was not constructed at too shallow a slope, which would cause rain to penetrate its covering of slates or tiles) defects are invariably owed to the deterioration of the roof covering or the breakdown of joints between materials, which in roofs usually means outworn metal valley-gutters, dislodged hip and ridge cappings and deformed or poorly repaired flashings.

Slates eventually decay because of their reaction with weak acids formed from sulphur and other atmospheric pollutants dissolved in rainwater. The slates 'exfoliate' and begin to absorb, rather than resist, moisture. Slated urban roofs are likely to have reached this state after about eighty years. The 'grip' of the slate on its fixing nails is not assisted by this reduction in rigidity and dislodged slates seen on old roof-slopes may have slipped because decay has affected the parts of each slate closest to the fixing nails. A more usual reason for slipped slates is corrosion of the original iron fixing nails. The weight of a slate will eventually sever the rusted shanks of iron nails and high winds encourage such dislodged slates to slip further out of place. Where the general condition of a slated roof-slope is good, slipped slates may be resited by extracting the remains of the corroded fixings from beneath the overlapping course with a slater's ripper. The head of a narrow strip of lead, zinc or copper, which will form a clip or 'tingle', is then fixed to the sliver of batten accessible through the joint exposed

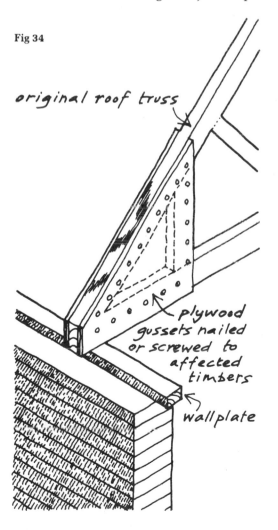

Fig 34

original roof truss

plywood gussets nailed or screwed to affected timbers

wallplate

by the extracted slate and the slate is slid back into place over this strip and secured by folding the free end of the metal over the lower edge of the slate (Fig 35). This clip fixing of slipped slates is merely an expedient which cannot forever put off the day when the permanent refixing or renewal of the entire roof covering is necessary.

There are two forms of sub-slate roof-deck construction favoured by the traditional builders which may store up serious problems for restorers of old buildings once a breach has occurred in the roof covering. The first potentially troublesome arrangement involved the nailing of the slates to timber battens in the conventional way, but these battens were first fixed to boarding or 'sarking' nailed to the top surfaces of the rafters. Even where a bituminous felt layer was laid on top of the boarding, this form of construction is likely to compound problems of rainwater penetration once a gap appears in the roof covering because the water which enters, instead of draining out of the construction at the eaves, settles on the upper edges of the local slate-fixing battens, inducing rot both in them and the boarding. Equally bad from the point of view of damp exclusion in the circumstance of a breach appearing in the roof surface, and even worse in terms of the restrictions it places on the opportunities for salvaging slates in any wholesale reconditioning of the roof covering, is the arrangement in which the slates are nailed directly to boarding, no fixing battens having been incorporated. If this form of construction cannot be identified from an inspection of voids in the roof surface made from the exterior, it may be possible to deduce whether or not it applies by noting the pattern of nails which have penetrated into the roof-space through the boarding. Such an inspection should also help to identify any dampness or rot which has affected the boarding. Where such decay is well advanced, complete replacement of the roof cladding with a boarded, counter-battened and battened construction, including underslating felt and a new slated surface, may be required.

Defective tiled roofs can produce problems identical to those posed by ageing slate roofs, but because clay plain tiles are necessarily hung on battens (not every tile is

Fig 35

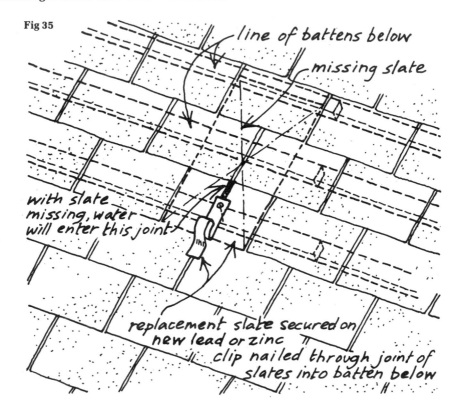

line of battens below

missing slate

with slate missing, water will enter this joint

replacement slate secured on new lead or zinc clip nailed through joint of slates into batten below

nailed except on very steeply pitched roofs) and it is not possible simply to apply tiles direct to a boarded surface as in the case of a slate covering, the problem of rotting roofing battens and sarking does not arise in connection with tiling. Much more common in tile roofing – as it was in the cheapest form of slated roof – was 'open batten' construction in which the tiles are hung on battens fixed directly to the top surfaces of the rafters without any intermediate boarding. It is in snowy weather that owners of buildings roofed in this way most regret this form of construction because wind-blown powdery snow easily enters narrow chinks in the roof surface, and where there is no underslating felt (as applies in most old constructions), the snow settles between the ceiling joists, later melting and saturating ceilings and other internal finishes. Tiles are less durable than slates, but good quality clay plain tiles can easily last for sixty years. Because the majority of tiles are simply hooked on to the battens, it is easier to replace a slipped or broken tile with a new unit than it is to replace a nail-fixed slate.

Owing in part to their lower cost, it has become popular in recent years to replace both clay plain tiles and slates with interlocking concrete tiles. This policy can produce further problems. Where roofspaces are not well ventilated (as occurs when a roof is reclad with a more windproof and watertight construction), the closetextured nature of the concrete tiles which contrasts with the relative porosity of clay tiles may encourage the formation of condensation on their undersides, encouraging dampness and rot in stagnant roof-spaces. More seriously, because the tiles are much heavier than either slates or clay tiles, the simple replacement of one of these traditional coverings with concrete units, where no steps have been taken to strengthen a lightly structured roof, is likely, at best, to result in deflection of the roof surface (sagging of concrete tile replacement roof surfaces is a common sight in older houses). At worst, collapse of the roof structure may result. Such a circumstance is far less likely to arise if defective slating is replaced either with a new natural slate roof or a surface of one of the several types of lightweight synthetic slate that are now obtainable.

A common weakness of the joint between materials in roofing results from the replacement of outworn lead flashings with a splayed mortar fillet at the junction of the roof surface with projecting chimney-stack or party-wall-parapet brickwork. Eventual breakdown of the bond between the mortar and the brickwork introduces an open joint which draws in moisture down the back of the small lead or zinc soakers which are incorporated to drain from the roof edge any moisture that penetrates the mortar (Fig 36). The only enduring solution to this problem is the replacement of the mortar fillet and soakers with a carefully installed sheet-lead stepped flashing.

Asphalt was often used as a flat-roof surface in older buildings in locations where it was appreciated that a sheet-metal covering would prove unsuitable because of the very large area of roof or where regular foot traffic was anticipated. It was also used as the finish for small or irregularly shaped subsidiary roofs over bays and porches, etc. Where it was used to coat a sloping surface, it is likely that defects will emerge, inviting water penetration, because the material tends to 'creep' under its self-weight. This property is intensified by the action of sunlight on the asphalt. As the material becomes hotter, it regains the capacity to flow which characterised its molten state at the time of its installation. Consequently, splits appear in the surface which will admit water. On flat surfaces this action is minimised by laying a carpet of light-reflective white limestone chippings on the asphalt, but this treatment cannot be extended to sloping sections or to roofs carrying regular foot-traffic. A special solar-reflective white paint may be applied to these panels which will increase the life-span of the surface. One great advantage of asphalt over other forms of sheet roof cover-

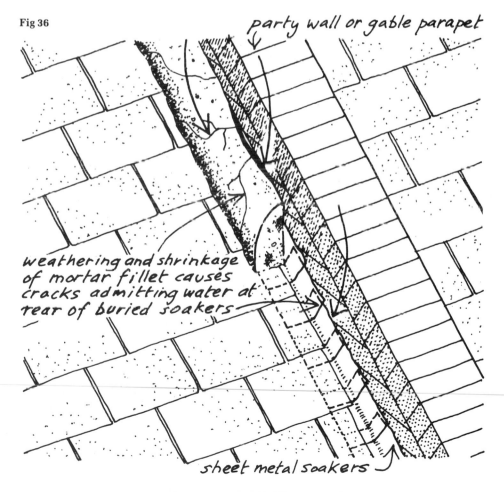

Fig 36

party wall or gable parapet

weathering and shrinkage of mortar fillet causes cracks admitting water at rear of buried soakers

sheet metal soakers

ing is its tolerance to being 'patched' in situ . Small repairs may be made to a damaged surface by flooding the affected area with molten asphalt after the defective section has been cut out. Eventual physical breakdown of the material is delayed by careful preparation of the substratum and it has always been safer to lay asphalt on concrete roof slabs than on timber boarding. Where a defective asphalt roof on boarding is to be renewed, the level boarded surface must be covered with bituminous felt before the asphalt is applied. The felt acts as a membrane which isolates movement in the boards from the asphalt, the natural elasticity of which may not be sufficient to absorb such movement.

Re-use of Metal Structures

The successful re-use of an existing iron structure depends on the quality of the original construction and whether it has been subjected to significant alterations. The opportunities for successfully re-using a structure to which it is necessary to make major modifications in order to suit it to its new task are small, even with ironwork of exceptionally good quality. This is because original structures tend to be fairly well matched to the original requirements for load-bearing.

Because iron structural members were used in circumstances where great strength was required, it is very unlikely that serious defects, such as could affect timber or masonry before they become unsafe, can arise without causing collapse. However, less significant defects are often readily identified. These include delamination of wrought iron which arises with corrosion, owed to the presence of slag in the material between layers of almost pure iron. Also, it should be noted that there were no satisfactory ways of forming structural connections in cast iron by any processes such as welding, brazing or soldering. If such techniques appear to have been used, the structure should be regarded as suspect, because all reputable Victorian engineers were aware of the risks of making connections by these methods.

Where there is no need for a retained iron structure to accept enlarged loads and it is apparent that the metal members are in good condition, not having been subjected to detrimental modifications, the chief consideration in re-using the installation is to achieve an acceptable standard of fire resistance. The building owner must establish whether the structure will provide an acceptable period of fire resistance in its unmodified state or if it can be simply modified to meet mandatory requirements. The performance of cast iron in fire is better than might be expected by those who have some knowledge of the dramatic reaction of steel structures to fire. It is possible for hot iron to crack under a stream of cold water (ie, from fire brigade emergency action), but cases where this circumstance has led to premature structural collapse are rare. Cast-iron members generally heat up more slowly than equivalent steel sections. The strength of cast iron also decreases less rapidly with temperature. Because of the original engineers' appreciation of its intrinsic brittleness, cast-iron members tend to be stressed to lower levels than steelwork and the way they were incorporated into buildings usually allows them to expand in a fire without generating increased stresses. Where cast-iron columns support timber beams, the exposed surfaces of the beams may char, but they do not expand and generate lateral movements on columns as might steel beams or iron beams. Thus there is every reason for building control officers, when assessing conversion proposals which rely on the re-use of aged iron structures, to consider the fire performance of each case on its own merits. Consequently, it is not unusual for a local authority to confer a fire resistance capacity of half an hour on an unprotected cast-iron structure. According to circumstances, the building inspector may be prepared to rate an unprotected cast-iron structure as one hour fire-resisting and where iron beams are partly embedded in brickwork or concrete (eg, in jack-arch and filler-joist floors) a greatly enhanced fire-resisting performance results from this partial protection.

Where the fire-resistance of a cast-iron member must be increased, it is no longer necessary to apply protective materials which conceal the shape and 'character' of the components. Various intumescent materials are available which can be sprayed on to the iron, after suitable cleaning and priming, to give a fire-insulating coating. There are 'thin film' and 'thick film' materials, the former being generally described as intumescent paint and the latter as intumescent mastics. Both types work on the principle of swelling up at high temperatures to produce a 'charred' foam coating which so insulates and protects the member from heat that the temperature of the metal remains well below that of the fire. The maintenance of structures with intumescent coatings should be carefully considered, particularly if there is a risk that the covering may be removed at some future time in the life of the building. Suitable products and the exact extent of their application should be agreed with the local authority's building control officer before the rebuilding work is commenced.

Where the surfaces of cast-iron columns and other compression members display cracks, these defects need not necessarily reduce the opportunities for re-use of these elements. Techniques exist for the 'stitching' of such fractures and they include a method in which groups of holes spaced at pre-defined centres are drilled across, and at right angles to each crack. The residual iron between these holes is then broken out and a 'multi-dumb-bell' shape metal 'key', pre-cast in a special alloy, is inserted tightly into each serrated aperture by gentle hammering. Many such keys are required to stitch together securely a significant crack. When sufficient keys have been installed, their projecting parts are ground down, the new metal and the iron local to the crack is sanded, and the surface may be repainted, producing a virtually invisible repair which restores most, if not all, of the strength of the original component.

5 Farm Buildings

The detailed design of farm buildings changed only gradually in the past, but the rate and type of change is now very much quicker as a result of the significant alterations in farming methods which have occurred since World War II – primarily greatly increased mechanisation. Consequently, the traditional buildings are generally becoming redundant. They may be modified, but often this is not feasible, causing new structures of a very different kind to be erected. The old buildings are then demolished or left to decay.

All farm buildings provide valuable evidence for agricultural history. The traditional buildings tend to reflect the considerable regional differences in types of farming and in the methods of housing and threshing the crops or housing and feeding the livestock. The old buildings that survive and can be preserved thus have a cultural significance as well as the functional potential for conversion to other uses. Hence there follows a full description of the origin and staple features of the constituent parts of the traditional farmstead because it is important that the untutored town dweller who is contemplating the purchase and conversion of an old farm building should recognise the different building types, understand the operational influences which shaped the form of each structure, and frame his or her ideas for the conversion so that any permanent evidence of agricultural history which the building provides is not erased.

As farming methods changed, so the designs of farm buildings may have been changed to adapt to the new ideas. The pace of change varied according to the region so that a building layout considered out of date in one area might still be fashionable in another. The design of farm buildings was also affected by the local building tradition. During the nineteenth century, with improvements in communications, these traditions were modified by the consequently increased sensitivity to changing preferences in architectural styles. The speed at which an awareness of national fashions in architecture grew varied from one area to another. Sometimes, quite independent of this influence, certain rural estates continued to practise their own distinctive styles of building.

A group of farm buildings, together with the farmhouse, forms the farmstead. Farmsteads are found in nucleated or closely grouped settlements (ie, villages and hamlets), in small groups of two or three farms, or they are isolated. The location of traditional farmsteads is the result of centuries of development and change. Those that remain in villages are the survivors of a larger number of such groupings which were much reduced by the policy of enclosing open fields which was pursued during the eighteenth and early nineteenth centuries. Thus a settlement of two or three farmsteads, or even an isolated one, could be the shrunken remains of a village or hamlet. The isolated farmstead may represent either the occupation of previously unfarmed land by a single farm or the movement of a farmstead out of a village following enclosure of the open fields.

Sometimes farm buildings were built away from the central farmstead. Generally, they did not form a fresh farmstead as they lacked some necessary buildings. The foremost non-farmstead building group and the type of most relevance to readers of this book who are seeking an old agricultural building to convert, is the *field barn*. It consisted of a threshing barn, often with an attached shed and foldyard for sheltering loose cattle. Field barns were built to serve land lying some distance from the farmstead, or which could only be reached from it by way of steep hills. They first appeared in the seventeenth century and ceased to be built after the middle of the nineteenth century, when the advent of portable threshing machines meant that ricks could be built and threshed in the fields and field barns were no longer needed. For this reason, many of these structures have disappeared.

The number and size of the buildings of the farmstead was affected not only by the size of the farm but also by the type of farming practised. On an arable farm with only a few cattle kept to make manure, little provision would be made for these animals, but there would be one or more barns, stables and shelters for carts. On a mixed farm, there would be a larger number of buildings for cattle, while on a pastoral farm the reduced need for waggon horses caused the stables to be small and there would be little accommodation for crops. It is interesting to note that sheep had almost no effect on the form of the farmstead as buildings were very rarely provided for them.

Where land was readily acquired so that the farmstead could be enlarged in a logical way, rather than the haphazard development which resulted from the erection of buildings on whatever sites became available, individual buildings within the grouping were sited so as to maximise efficiency. Threshed straw had to be taken from the barns to the cattle or the horses for use as feed or litter. Because the cattle were the principal users of straw, it was important to have them near the barn. Then the stable could be either beyond the cow-house or adjoin the barn on the other side. For economy in building costs, these three types of farm buildings were sometimes combined into a single building. The form most frequently found is the barn with lean-tos built against it to provide cow-houses, stables or cart-sheds. The cost of one wall was saved and because the buildings housing animals were close to the barn, they could be supplied more easily with straw. Another common composite building placed the cow-house, stable or cart-shed under part of the barn. The part of the barn sited on top of these areas thus became a loft raised above the threshing floor. In some cases, this arrangement was adopted to take advantage of sloping ground. However, the *bank barn* was a different response to a sloping site.

The barn was built parallel to the ridge of the bank, being entered at high level on the uphill side. On the downhill side the barn was thus at first-floor level with the cow-house, stable or cart-shed lying underneath. This type of building is almost unique to the Lake District of England.

Within the farmstead, the farmhouse might be attached to some, or all, of the other farm buildings. Where the barn adjoined the dwelling it is called a *laithe house*, and often the stable and cow-house were built beyond the barn as part of the same range. Such buildings can be found in the Pennine region of Yorkshire and the Lake District, although these combination buildings are not restricted to the north of England, similar types being found in the Westcountry. Close contact with animals and manure was not always desired, so an extreme solution was to move the farm buildings well away from the farmhouse — sometimes even out of sight of it. Where the farmstead is sited away from the house, a labourer's cottage might form part of the group, for security reasons.

Although former stables and cow-houses may offer opportunities for conversion into dwellings, it is often the case that they were too cheaply and impermanently built and are too small to provide a structure which is easily adapted into a house. This applies even where (as was usual) the stable incorporated a loft for the storage of hay so that this fodder could be pitched readily into the racks in the stalls below, because the loft exploited the roof space and was rarely built as a full-height upper storey. In contrast, stables attached to large town mansions in Central London convert very satisfactorily into 'mews houses' because living accommodation for the grooms and coachmen was originally provided in purpose-designed upper storeys.

Barns as Dwellings

More promising as a building type for conversion into living accommodation, as many people have recognised, is the barn. This is because the barn is often the largest of the non-domestic buildings of the farmstead and the large volume which it encloses

Plate 1 A traditional stone-built threshing barn; note the 'owl hole' sited high in the gable

offers many options for the creation of a comfortable and characterful dwelling. In most traditional farmsteads it was also the central point to which the other buildings related. A comprehensive account of the function and characteristic features of traditional barns follows, because it is apparent from even a brief tour of any rural district that the treatment meted out to many old barns in the course of their conversion into houses has been insensitive, or even atrocious, and these enormities have occurred despite their owners' clearly expressed intentions to preserve, rather than erase, the 'barn-like' qualities of the buildings. The encouragement of a more enlightened attitude in would-be converters of barns is crucial to the welfare of the architectural heritage of the countryside because the number of old barns converted to date may represent only the tip of the iceberg. It is estimated that seventy thousand old barns survive, many in poor condition. Most are ill-adapted to the demands of modern, mechanised agriculture and, unless converted to new uses, may well disappear. These buildings are now almost equally at risk from insensitive conversion as they are from demolition because a softening in the attitude of local planning authorities towards proposals for change of use of agricultural buildings has recently been encouraged by central government in an attempt to ameliorate the worsening financial circumstances

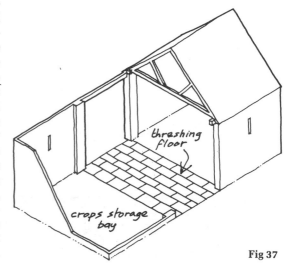

Fig 37

of farmers. Most farmers view old buildings as a liability and the relaxation of a planning authority's traditional strictness in assessing proposed changes of use of such structures enhances their development potential, makes them more marketable and encourages the owner to sell them and to put up cheaply built, impermanent and often ugly sheds for storage of crops and farm machinery.

Traditionally, the barn was a building for housing and threshing the corn and pulse crops grown on the farm, the former category comprising wheat, oats, barley and rye, and the latter including peas and beans. It could also house hay (cut grass) and threshed straw. Almost invariably, barns had one threshing floor, with bays for housing the crops opening off it (Fig 37 and Plate 1). The threshing floor, which was paved, probably in contrast to the floor surfaces of the bays to either side, always ran across the barn. The size of barns varied greatly, but there were nearly always only one or two threshing floors. The size of the farm was not the only factor affecting the size of its barn. The most important factor was whether all the crops were housed in the barn or whether some or all were kept in ricks in the fields, being moved to the barn for threshing. The practice in medieval times was to house all of the grain crops in the barn, using ricks as a last resort only when the barns were full. This procedure naturally produced very large barns. By the early eighteenth century in Scotland and Northumberland, the bulk of crops were housed in ricks, the barns consequently being small with space for housing only one rick at a time and a threshing floor. In contrast, the practice of storing all the crops in barns and so of erecting large buildings, continued well into the nineteenth century in the south of England and East Anglia. Contemporary reasons for continuing to build large barns included the view that grain was better housed in barns than in ricks and was always at hand to be threshed, while the cost of thatching ricks was avoided and savings were made by avoiding the double-handling generated by moving ricks to the barn for threshing.

The barn was filled with harvested crops,

Plate 2 The opposing waggon-door openings and the air vent slits show clearly in this side view of the barn

leaving only the threshing floor clear. The crops were stacked right up to the roof ridge, or close to it, so using almost all the roof space. Until the eighteenth century it was common to house two, three or more crops together in the barn, but a later development was the use of half the barn for threshed straw, filling only one side of the threshing floor with unthreshed corn, and the emergence of this practice may have accompanied the increased use of ricks for housing crops or faster threshing by machinery.

Apart from the general qualities of broad, plain, unperforated surfaces, simplicity of shape and an impression of massiveness (particularly in stone-built barns), several other features are characteristic of traditional barns. Perhaps the most conspicuous is the large *waggon door*. The most common type is the high, wide central doorway, closed by hinged double doors. This doorway was made high in order to permit laden waggons or carts to enter the barn and to unload from the threshing floor into the bays. Its height also admitted light to illuminate the threshing operation and air for winnowing the husks from the threshed grain. It was normal for pairs of waggon doors to face each other on opposite side walls of the barn (Plate 2), but in some barns the threshing floor could be approached only from one side, there being a blank wall opposite. This prevented the through draught which was valued for winnowing and meant that carts had to back out, so it was a less popular arrangement. High porches shielding the waggon doors are found in many surviving medieval barns and in some later examples, particularly in the South. They were useful for increasing the size of the threshing floor and in protecting crops on this surface during inclement weather. Laden wagons could shelter in such porches if the threshing floors were already occupied by other vehicles unloading. The porch could also be used as a cart-shed. Barn doors commonly stopped 305-610mm (1-2ft) above the ground with a separate panel of boards below. This was held in place by a groove in the bottom of the door jamb which projected slightly for the purpose. This 'lift', as it is called, enabled the foot of the doors to clear the manure in the yard and kept pigs off the threshing floor

when the doors were open. It would also catch grain bouncing off the floor with the force of flail threshing.

The second most characteristic external feature of many barns is the *pitching hole*, a window-like opening, covered by a wooden shutter, several of which might be provided in the side and end walls in order to pitch corn or hay into the barn from a cart standing outside. They also admitted light and air if the barn was not full. In shape, such apertures were roughly square, although circular openings began to appear in the early nineteenth century and are often a conspicuous feature of the brick-built Victorian estate barns of Cheshire.

Lastly, *air vents* were provided in the walls of barns to prevent the crops inside from becoming mouldy. Air vents in stone-built barns were normally slits or single holes, often widely spaced and sometimes arranged in rows. No special provision was needed in weatherboarded timber-framed barns because the boards did not fit closely together. The greatest range of types was found in brick-built barns owing to the ease with which patterns could be formed by omitting half-bricks or narrower units without affecting the structural stability of the walls. As in stone-built barns, slits were widely used in brick structures and they were generally arranged in rows. Half-brick-wide holes were easily arranged in rows and granted good overall ventilation. Geometric arrays of holes appeared in the mid-nineteenth century – probably in parallel with the Victorian enthusiasm for patterned 'polychromatic' brickwork – and seem to be the most widespread type. Not to be confused with air vents is the *owl-hole*, a nearly square or circular opening 150-230mm (6-9in) across, set high up in the gable of the barn. This feature was first introduced in the eighteenth century to let owls into the barn to catch vermin.

Barn interiors were generally open from end to end – there was no physical separation of the threshing floor from the bays. The commonest and oldest barn plan places the threshing floor in the middle. A barn with a central threshing floor would be at least three structural bays in length, each bay being perhaps 4.25-5.5m (about 14-18ft) long, although the distance between roof

trusses could be smaller (say, 3m (10ft)), the bays might be of different lengths and the simple triangular roof trusses might not span more than 5.5-6m (18-19½ft) (Plate 3). Barns were sometimes built with integral aisles, along the lines of a church. Clearly, such an arrangement necessitates the use of more elaborate and comprehensive timber framing than would be employed in a narrow barn where masonry walls provide all the support for the roof. The use of aisles permitted the erection of a much wider building than would otherwise have been possible. Aisled barns are of the order of 9-15m (29-49ft) wide; a simple triangular truss could be made to span a building 10m (33ft) wide, but most 'single-cell' barns were of the width defined above and would certainly not exceed 7.5m (24½ft) in width. Aisled barns are found in two main areas of England. Timber-framed examples have survived in an area extending from Wiltshire and Hampshire across to Suffolk and Kent. The other area is South Yorkshire and the Pennine district of Lancashire. In some of the barns in these latter areas, the aisles

Plate 3 Massive triangular timber trusses support the 'purlin roof' of the barn

were not used for storage but were shut off for some other purpose, such as housing the cattle. The quite complex structure of timber-framed aisled barns may present problems of maintenance and preservation, as well as constraints on flexibility of internal planning, for the would-be converter of such a building to domestic use. However, it is clear that an imaginative treatment of this form of interior could show off the texture and complexity of the original timber structure to dramatic effect.

Threshing machines were initially more used in the north than in the south of England, commencing in the early nineteenth century. At first, the machinery was fixed, standing within the barn. Naturally enough, the introduction of machinery led to a new plan in some contemporary barns. The threshing floor disappeared. One end of the barn was completely lofted, with the corn being fed into the building at first-floor level through pitching holes. The other part was a straw barn. Reliable portable threshing machines were a later development and were used much more in the south than in the north. The machine could either stand on the threshing floor of an orthodox flail-threshing barn, which provided shelter from the weather, or it could be taken to the ricks in the fields. The first practice probably encouraged the retention of many old and large flail-threshing barns which might otherwise have fallen into disuse, inviting demolition. Indeed, apparently traditional flail-threshing barns continued to be built throughout the nineteenth century because of their ability to house the threshing machine as well as the crops. In contrast, adoption of the second policy guaranteed the disappearance of many old barns because they bécame redundant unless they were retained as covered rick-houses or stores for straw. However, the protection of hay, straw or even unthreshed corn was more simply achieved by the erection of a more modest and inexpensive building than the traditional flail-threshing barn. This is the *hay barn* or *Dutch barn* which is completely open on one or more sides. Very old examples consist of brick or stone pillars supporting a pitched roof, but they were rarely built before the late nineteenth century as they were considered an extravagance. Their use increased considerably from the 1880s when the familiar skeletal iron-framed hay barn with a curved corrugated-iron roof began to appear in all parts of the country. It will be appreciated that these insubstantial structures cannot form as satisfactory a basis for conversion into dwellings as can the traditional masonry-built flail-threshing barn.

Rectory Farm Barn, Upper Heyford, Oxfordshire

As photographs of the original building show clearly (Plates 1-3), before conversion, this stone-built barn displayed many of the conventional features described in the foregoing account. It included large waggon door openings in the middle of each side elevation, with storage bays to either side of the central threshing floor to which these doors gave access. Ventilation was provided by slits sited high in its stone-built walls and the gables contained owl-holes close to the apex of the roof (Plate 1). Unfortunately, the roof surfaces had been reclad with corrugated iron when the original locally quarried stone slates became unserviceable. The barn was built in 1839 and was the largest structure in a range of buildings. When the present owner purchased it, the barn was part of a redundant farmyard in the centre of the small stone-built village of Upper Heyford. The required accommodation was a residence for a family of five and the new owner requested that the living accommodation should be on the first floor to take advantage of the splendid views to the west over the Cherwell Valley.

An attached shed to the south of the barn was demolished, and the architect, Timothy Bruce-Dick, decided to infill the gap between the barn and a range of cow-houses which existed to the north with a two-storey structure which would act as a covered link to this northern wing and provide a playroom over garages (Fig 38 and Plate 4).

As well as creating enlarged internal accommodation, this treatment also helped to form a sheltered eastern entrance courtyard, the other two sides being a grass bank on the east and a new stone wall to the south. The existing stone walling was retained and the original massiveness of the east elevation was preserved and even emphasised by retaining the high level ventilation slits and minimising the number of new windows on this sunless side. Bathrooms, a kitchen and a utility room, needing only small windows, were located behind this elevation (Fig 38).

The association with a traditional barn incorporating porches has been skilfully exploited in order to broaden the width of the building at its centre so that an enclosed entrance porch and a generous 'dog-leg' staircase, giving access to the first floor, could be included on one side, while the equivalent projection on the west side houses an oriel window serving the dining-room which gives a commanding view over the Cherwell Valley. Where these projections of the formerly open central bay of the building are not glazed, they are finished in dark-stained timber, a treatment that has

Plate 4 Rectory Farm Barn, Upper Heyford, Oxfordshire: the east elevation of the converted barn showing the new garage/playroom wing on the right

Plate 5 Rectory Farm Barn, Upper Heyford, Oxfordshire: the converted barn's west elevation overlooking the Cherwell Valley, showing the large oriel window of the first-floor dining room

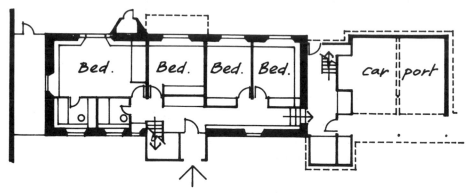

GROUND FLOOR PLAN

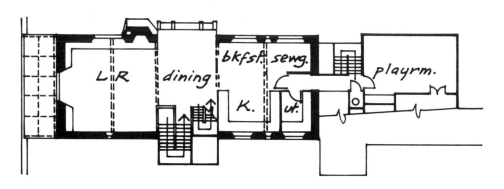

FIRST FLOOR PLAN

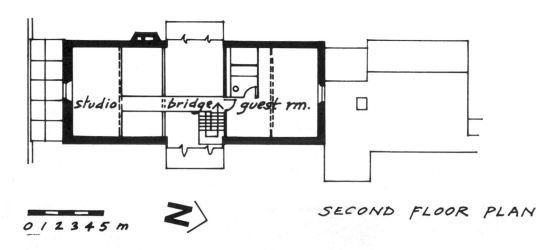

SECOND FLOOR PLAN

0 1 2 3 4 5 m

Fig 38

been applied to all new external and internal timberwork and is a conventional finish for the external woodwork of many local farm buildings.

The double-height entrance lobby leads to a ground-floor gallery which runs to the north end of the barn where it connects with the garages. Off this gallery all the principal bedrooms face west over an extensive private garden (Plate 5). From the gallery the main staircase leads up to a first-floor open-plan living/dining-room/kitchen area, the hefty roof timbers of the old barn being exposed overhead. A further dog-leg stair leads up from this level to second-floor guest accommodation located entirely in the roof space framed by the original trusses, and a narrow bridge leads across from the head of the stair to a complementary study balcony (Fig 38). A glasshouse was erected against the south gable to exploit the potential for solar heat gain to assist space heating of the dwelling. On sunny winter days, panels in the original south gable can be opened to allow air trapped in this conservatory and warmed by the sun to circulate in the body of the house. Also planned was a covered swimming-pool, linked to the main house through the former cow-houses, which would be converted into changing accommodation and general storage.

The reconstruction was undertaken by direct labour (ie, the building owner organised and executed much of the work), starting in the spring of 1979, the house and playroom link being occupied in October 1979. Because the bulk of the work was supervised by the owner, the overall cost is difficult to assess, but a figure of £50,000 at 1979 prices probably represents the right order of expense.

Place Barn, Wilmington, Polegate, East Sussex

Place Barn, Wilmington, is a flint-walled barn which was formerly attached to Priory Farm at the head of the hill that leads out of the village to the South Downs. It has a long, narrow plan, the northern end of which may have been used for stabling horses or housing the cattle. This combination of uses is suggested by the existence of a dormer-roofed pitching hole close to the roof eaves at the north end and the two high-level square ventilation openings which are closely associated with it (Plate 6). The waggon door was close to the south end of

Plate 6   Place Barn, Wilmington, East Sussex: the barn, seen from the north, before conversion

the barn, serving crop storage areas to either side. The only differences between its layout and that of the 'classic' threshing barn were the inclusion of a hay loft, carried on brick pillars, to give an upper level at the south end and an attached cart-shed adjoining the west elevation, also at the south end. When ·the new owners who proposed to convert the barn first saw it in 1978, the whole structure had been used for stabling horses, and accordingly, brick partitions had been erected to form stalls inside. This modified use meant that the original waggon door opening had been reduced in width (Plate 7). It was the new owners' intention to restore a more barn-like appearance. They had lived in Holland for twenty years and had been much impressed by Dutch conversions of barns into dwellings which tend to be more simple, 'scrubbed' and 'puritanical' than the often over-elaborate treatment that is applied to British projects.

Planning permission for its conversion into a dwelling existed when the barn was purchased, but the scheme was particularly disliked by one of the new owners who believed, partly for the reason cited above and partly because of her training as a sculptress, that a simpler treatment, more strongly evocative of the barn's original

Plate 7 Place Barn, Wilmington, East Sussex: the south end of the east elevation before conversion work began showing brickwork infilling the former waggon-door opening

function, might be adopted and still give comfortable and convenient living accommodation. Hence, in conjunction with a local architect who provided technical advice and who prepared drawings for statutory approvals, a new scheme was developed.

The strategy for the exterior was to reintroduce a 'barn-like' appearance. This was more possible on the east and south elevations which adjoin the head of the village street and a public car park access road respectively than it was on the west and south sides. This is because the former faces lack either a sunny aspect or a pleasant prospect and the preservation of privacy is an important consideration on elevations so close to the highway. Thus, changes to the east elevation included the necessary insertion of a small and unpretentious front entrance door in a pre-existing opening and the modification of the partly infilled former waggon-door opening to simulate the appearance of the original double doors. This was achieved without restoring the opening

Fig 39

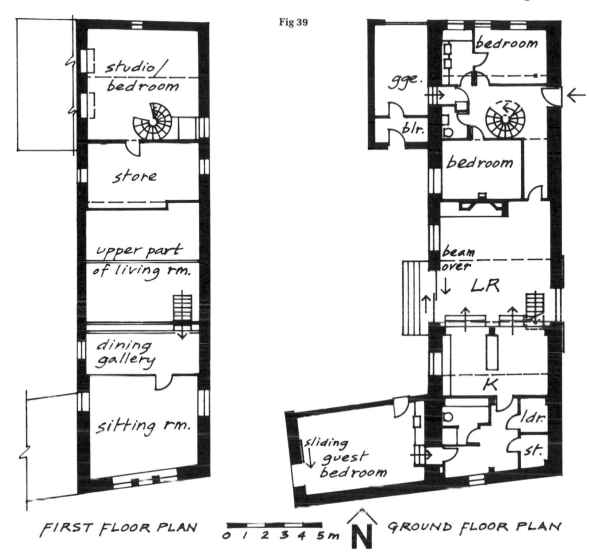

studio/bedroom

store

upper part of living rm.

dining gallery

sitting rm.

FIRST FLOOR PLAN

bedroom

gge.

blr.

bedroom

beam over

LR

K

ldr.

st.

sliding guest bedroom

0 1 2 3 4 5m   **N**   GROUND FLOOR PLAN

to its former width by applying a pair of new timber-boarded and dark-stained doors to the east elevation. The southern leaf of the double doors was fixed open against the wall and the opposite leaf was fixed closed over a new infilling cavity-wall construction of concrete blockwork (Fig 39 and Plate 8). Thus the appearance of a double door is created, although the actual opening is only of single-door width and is filled with one large panel of clear double-glazing. Ensuring that the glazing of such new openings is kept well back from the external face of the walls (at least 225mm (9in)) has meant that reflection has been minimised and the 'black hole' unglazed-opening appearance of apertures in traditional barns has been re-

Plate 8 Place Barn, Wilmington, East Sussex: the restored waggon-door opening at the completion of conversion work

Plate 9 Place Barn, Wilmington, East Sussex: the barn's south end, showing the three square windows which have been inserted at high level in the end elevation

Plate 10 Place Barn, Wilmington, East Sussex: the west elevation; the 'catslide' roof of the former garage outshot is seen on the extreme left

created. This treatment was also applied to the smaller door, reached via a short flight of external stone steps that previously served the upper-level hay-loft, so that the new infilling panel of clear double-glazing, set well back from the external face of the wall, helps to light a sitting room while a 'door', which can be swung like a shutter to seal this opening, is fixed back against the face of the adjoining flintwork.

It might be argued that this device, although an ingenious reference to the converted barn's former purpose, is not a practical feature in a dwelling because even double-glazing will not prevent the excessive heat loss and cold radiation caused by such large windows. There is some substance to this criticism, but developments in glass technology since the date of the completion of the Place Barn project have much improved the thermal performance of double glazing. It is now possible to obtain purpose-made double glazed units incorporating 'low E', or low emissivity, glass which includes a thin and imperceptible metallic coating on the inside surface of the outer leaf of each unit to reflect interior heat back into the room while allowing solar heat to enter the building. Hence, much larger areas of double-glazing than could formerly have been contemplated, consistent with maintaining comfort, may now be built into external walls.

To give additional light to the new upper-level sitting room, it was decided to insert a group of three fixed windows in the south elevation above an existing opening (Plate 9) and in the north elevation two similar openings were added. The west elevation was subject to most change. Four additional openings were made in this external wall and three existing openings were modified in order to admit adequate light to the altered interior. The three new windows – which were flanked by brickwork jambs matching the existing brick dressings to the flintwork – were spanned by brick segmental arches, a treatment also applied to the reprofiled opening opposite the former waggon door which accommodates a new sliding aluminium 'patio' door within a hardwood frame. The brick-built garage which adjoined this west elevation was demolished and rebuilt with its new

Plate 11 Place Barn, Wilmington, East Sussex: a bedroom (previously the studio) at the head of the iron spiral staircase; note that a roof tie-beam has had to be re-sited at a higher level in order that this 'room-in-the-roof' could be created

external walls showing a flint facing matching the remainder of the structure. This change also allowed a more harmonious treatment to be adopted for the roof of this outshot. By using salvaged slates, it was possible to revise the roof of the garage to a 'cat-slide' form projecting out and down from the eaves of the main rear roof-slope at a slightly shallower pitch than this surface (Plate 10). The addition of three roof windows close to the eaves of this upper roof-slope could then augment the daylighting of the upper-level studio that enters through the newly-glazed original eaves-level pitching hole of the east elevation. It was not necessary to re-roof the attached cart-shed on the west side, the pitched and hipped shape of which was retained, but the original timber-framed and boarded north elevation of this 'wing' was removed and replaced with a cavity wall, finished externally with salvaged facing bricks. This projection, with the addition of a sliding door at the rear of an existing door opening, could then accommodate a bedroom.

Internally, two further bedrooms were provided, both at ground-floor level. Between this pair of northern bedrooms adjoining the entrance door, a cloakroom with a WC and hand basin and a bathroom were installed (Fig. 39). This is also the point at which access to the upper-floor studio and store is obtained via an iron spiral staircase. In order to create sufficient headroom within the studio, it was necessary to remove an exist-

Plate 12 Place Barn, Wilmington, East Sussex: the painted and coarsely-plastered brick 'funnel' of the new living-room chimney; a heavy salvaged timber beam carries the chimney breast over the hearth

building prior to its conversion, but its insertion has been undertaken so carefully and with such sensitivity towards the simple, almost primitive shapes and textures of the original interior that it looks like a perfectly natural element. A huge 'inverted funnel' of painted, coarsely plastered brickwork lies on top of an oak beam which acts as a fascia spanning a very broad fireplace, also lined with white-painted brickwork (Plate 12). To give a suitably 'thick' appearance to the painted plaster surface applied over the new brickwork of the chimney, 'Sirapite' plaster was mixed with wallpaper paste and smeared over the over-precise profiles of the new work. On other

Plate 13 Place Barn, Wilmington, East Sussex: the mezzanine-level dining area and lower-level kitchen seen from the central living room

ing tie-beam which spanned between two timber posts that helped to support the roof structure and to adapt and re-site this member at a higher level, just below the soffit of the ceiling (Plate 11). Naturally, the greater part of the volume of this room is within the roof space and a consequence of this is that a small pre-existing ventilation opening, which was sited high up below the eaves of the barn and is now glazed to form a window, has its sill at floor level. This room-in-the-roof terminates to the rear of a massive brick-built chimney which dominates the main central living space of the barn. Plainly, there was no such feature in the

new internal surfaces some good 'rough plastering' was undertaken by very skilled tradesmen. The introduction of the equally direct and simple brick-built chimney above the rear roof-slope hardly detracts from the reposeful form of the old barn's roof.

The central living-room extends right up into the apex of the roof, the original heavy roof timbers – rafters, purlins and tie beams – being exposed to the interior (Plate 13). To emphasise fully the drama of this grand space, rather than remove the raised hay-loft occupying the south end of the building, it was decided to retain this area as a dining gallery overlooking the living-room, with a private sitting room at the same level lying behind a new partition. By excavating the existing ground-floor surface at this south end, it was possible to obtain a minimal, although legally acceptable, 2m (6½ft) headroom for non-habitable accommodation below the gallery. This comprises a shower room and WC, a dry-goods store, a larder, the passage leading to the third bedroom and the kitchen. The kitchen is thus three steps down from the living-room floor level and is paved with the same material – York stone slabs approximately 60mm (2½in) thick, below which a low-pressure piped hot water central-heating system is installed. The upper-level dining gallery and sitting-room are reached from the living-room via a short flight of open-riser timber stairs.

The owners who undertook the conversion of Place Barn were Mr and Mrs J de Geus – Mrs Ann de Geus being responsible for the concept and much of the detailed design of the conversion. They received invaluable technical advice from architect Colin Humphrey. The builder was H. Wilson Ltd. The conversion of Place Barn received the accolade of a Civic Trust Award in 1982.

Conversion Potential of Other Crop-Storage Buildings

Apart from the fairly standardised buildings housing the animals and the customary crops, some areas of the country also boast more specialised buildings for housing other crops, and these structures may be susceptible to conversion to valued and highly characterful accommodation. Prominent among these buildings is the hop-kiln, which was used for drying hops (the main use for which is in beer, although they are also incorporated in other delicacies) before they could be despatched to market. These structures are found in the hop-growing areas of Kent and East Sussex, where they are called oast-houses, and the westernmost part of Surrey, Herefordshire and West Worcestershire. The most obvious kilns that survive are the square or circular-plan nineteenth-century type which are high rooms with tall conical roofs terminating in cowls. They were invariably attached to a two-storey building of more conventional shape. Circular kilns first appeared in Kent around 1805 and soon became the normal pattern there. They are called 'roundels'. Roundels with tiled conical roofs require special tiles. These are known as Kent peg tapered tiles as they narrow in length, holes being incorporated at the narrow ends to accept wooden pegs which locate them on the roofing battens. Until recently, these tiles were made by hand, but now finding suitable second-hand replacement units is becoming difficult. Square-plan kilns were not used in the South until shortly before World War I. The kilns had brick walls; inside, at ground level, there was an open brick box to contain the fire, the draught being controlled by the entrance door. The drying floor was sited about 3m (10ft) above the furnace and was of slatted wooden construction, being made of laths or battens set fairly close together. The hot air from the fire passed up between the laths. The hops were spread on a horsehair cloth laid on the battens, access to this upper level being gained through a high-level door in the side of the kiln. Above was a steep-sided cone, usually timber-framed like a roof, with a plastered internal finish and clad with tiles or slates externally. In a few instances, the cone itself was of brick and this form of construction existed at Tibb's Oast, a mid-nineteenth century oast-house, the conversion of which is described later. Capping this cone was the cowl.

Repair of the cowl, the most distinctive part of the oast, requires a craftsman's knowledge and skill. Its purpose is to venti-

Plate 14 A derelict oast in East Sussex which displays the characteristic paired kilns and the central drying shed of timber construction; note the typical carved wooden vane which projects from the rotating cowl of the right-hand kiln

late the kiln, enabling the moisture-laden air to be drawn from the hops. This air is known as the 'reek'. The vane is the oast's rudder and ensures that the boarded surface always faces the wind, thus preserving the opportunity for moist air to escape (Plate 14). Considerable dexterity is required to lower and raise a cowl. It is quite normal for a cowl to weigh 200kg (31st) and extend to 4.5m (15ft) in height with a diameter of 1.8m (6ft) at its base, and four men are required to manoeuvre it. Where vaned cowls are to be replaced, it is not advisable for them to be fixed in place, not only for the sake of authenticity, but also to simplify maintenance. Damp must not be allowed to enter as rot can quickly result. Until recently, cowl bases (or 'curbs') were made from elm, but Dutch elm disease has made this material difficult to obtain. Today, it is more usual to replace the base with marine ply. Tradition

demands that the cowls should be painted white and it is common practice to spray their surfaces with glass-fibre to improve durability. Normally, cowls require considerable maintenance and possible replacement every ten years – a costly consequence of owning an oast. The vane is sometimes called the 'finger' or 'flyboard' and it gave farmers an opportunity to display their individuality. In Kent, many

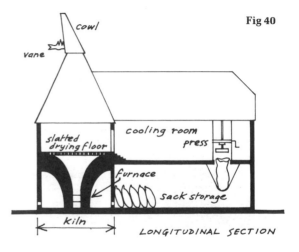

Fig 40

cowl

vane

slatted drying floor

cooling room

press

furnace

sack storage

kiln

LONGITUDINAL SECTION

vanes were completed with the Kentish horse motif and hunting scenes were popular. Other animals were also depicted. Additionally, most 'fingers' bear the personal mark of the executant craftsman.

Adjoining the kilns was a two-storey building, the upper floor of this structure being about 1m (3ft) below the drying floors of the kilns which were reached via short flights of timber stairs (Fig. 40). This area was used for receiving the hops and for spreading them out to cool after they were removed from the kilns. Once the redistribution of moisture had taken place, the hops were swept into 'pockets'. These were long sacks which were suspended through a circular hole in the floor, called the treading hole (until presses were introduced, the hops were compressed by a man treading them in). A later development introduced a press to compress the hops in each pocket which was held in a pocket sling. After pressing, the pockets were tied and then stored in the ground-floor storage area, which was only required as a space in which the pockets were hung and for stoking the fires in the kilns. Otherwise, it had no connection with hops and might be used for cidermaking, housing livestock, or as a cartshed. The pockets of hops were stored here until they were shipped off to market or to a brewery. It was common for the storage building to be accompanied by a pair of kilns and a complete range of such structures might be erected adjacent to a very long storage building on a site where the cultivation of hops was undertaken intensively (eg, at the hop farm of a brewery).

Tibb's Oast, Udimore, Rye, East Sussex

This oast-house conversion is rather unusual in that four kilns or 'roundels' are attached to the central storage shed, a pair being placed on both sides of this building, giving a symmetrical composition. The shed itself

Plate 15 Tibb's Oast, Udimore, East Sussex: the eastern kilns and central drying shed before conversion work commenced

Plate 16 Tibb's Oast, Udimore, East Sussex: the east elevation at the conclusion of conversion work

Plate 17 Tibb's Oast, Udimore, East Sussex: the central entrance hall, created from the old drying shed, showing the door to the mezzanine-level WC and the landings serving first-floor bedrooms which are located in the upper parts of the former kilns

Fig 41

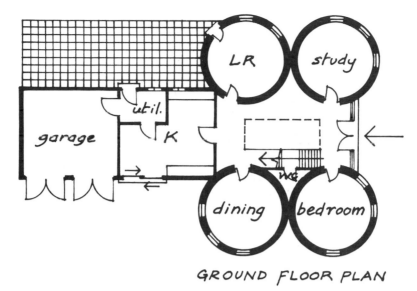

GROUND FLOOR PLAN

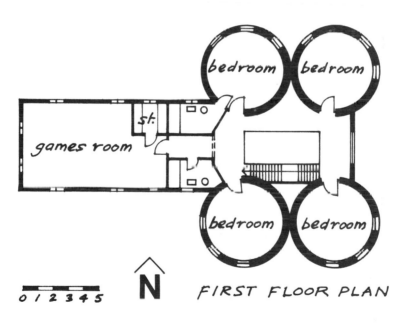

0 1 2 3 4 5   ⌃N   FIRST FLOOR PLAN

was largely of wooden construction, and as the photograph of its pre-conversion condition indicates (Plate 15), it was in a very ramshackle state. Hence the first job for the new owners in the autumn of 1983 was the demolition of the decaying boarded 'front' elevation of this structure which filled the gap between the eastern pair of roundels. This action enabled the new infilling east elevation clad in painted timber boards to be installed to the rear of the original wall-plane, better exposing to view the cylindrical forms of the kilns (Plate 16). The upper floors of the storage shed were also at inconvenient levels and the discovery of wholesale decay in this joisted construction supported a policy of removing these elements and replacing them with a new upper-floor set at a level which could be extended into the roundels to give adequate headroom in the new ground-storey rooms, while ensuring that the four upper-storey bedrooms located in these projections had a sufficiently deep vertical wall surface to accommodate conventional windows. With the drying floors removed, the brickwork of the roundels proved not to be very strong and it was necessary to span the circular spaces with timber beams before the new upper floor was installed. It was also necessary to fabricate and fit a new rotating cowl to replace the louvred terminal which was missing from the apex of the south-east roundel. Where the louvred cowls had survived, glazing had to be added internally in order to prevent wind-blown rain from entering the vents, and efforts were made to waterproof the sloping brick surfaces of the roundels' conical roofs by coating them with bitumen.

Because the junction of a pair of roundels produces a triangular interstitial space internally as well as externally, one of two such internal areas was used to accommodate a WC, which is reached from an intermediate landing of the staircase (Fig 41 and Plate 17). Apart from the four first-floor bedrooms, all of which are housed in the roundels and which are 5.1m (17ft) in diameter, the upper storey was used to house a large games room, an airing cupboard and a bathroom. The north-east roundel bedroom was provided with an en suite bathroom. The lower storey includes a very generous stair and entrance hall, extending to two storeys in height at its centre within a peripheral first-floor gallery, a double garage, utility room and a large kitchen being accommodated in the western half of the former storage shed. The dining room occupies the south-east roundel, the lounge the north-west roundel, a study the north-east roundel and the south-east roundel accommodates a fifth bedroom.

After several months' work, during which time they lived in a caravan parked on the site, the owners, Mr and Mrs Bates, were able to move into the future garage area of the building in August 1984 and to continue work on the upper-floor accommodation under the shelter of the reslated roof. The quickly erected boarded external finish of the former storage shed and the predominantly 'dry' construction of the internal wall linings made this a practical policy once reconstruction, during the spring and summer months, of the decayed lower-storey brickwork was complete and had produced a habitable shell. The complete interior of the house could not be occupied until the final months of 1985 and the owners stayed for only one further year before the challenge of converting a local barn tempted them away!

6 Churches and Chapels

Before considering the methods which various owners and developers have adopted to achieve the satisfactory conversion of church buildings to domestic use, it is important to be aware of the procedure through which the majority of churches become available for conversion. In the case of the Anglican Church, whose buildings make up the largest group of ecclesiastical structures, there exists a quite involved and considered procedure which is defined by the Pastoral Measure of 1983. Although there is no generally agreed forecast of the number of Anglican churches likely to be declared 'redundant', the Bridges Commission of 1960 suggested that 790 buildings could be involved. It is noteworthy that by 1976, eight years after the original Pastoral Measure came into effect, almost 500 churches had been declared redundant by the Church Commissioners. Of these, 37 per cent were destined for demolition. The remainder were to be preserved or put to other uses, but delays in reaching decisions often meant that the buildings had been severely vandalised by the time they were available for conversion.

The procedure is first for the Pastoral Committee of the Diocese to consult the Council for Places of Worship, receiving from it a report which sets out the architectural qualities and historic interest of the building. Reference is also made to other Anglican churches in the area as a choice may have to be made between one building and another. Having decided upon a recommendation that a particular church should be declared redundant, the Pastoral Committee sends the papers relating to the proposal to the bishop of that diocese. He has the opportunity to comment on these documents before forwarding them to the Church Commissioners. The Pastoral Measure defines the interested parties, including the local planning authority, who must be consulted before this stage is reached. If the Church Commissioners subsequently agree to seal a Declaration of Redundancy, advice is sought on the future of the building from the Advisory Board for Redundant Churches, a national body which was set up under the Pastoral Measure. If the building is of architectural or historical importance, or contains fine built-in furnishings, the Advisory Board may recommend vesting the church in the Redundant Churches Fund. This fund is another creation of the Pastoral Measure. It is provided with an income from central government and church sources and acts as a 'holding body' for churches which are of sufficient importance to be preserved, unmodified, 'in the interests of the Nation and the Church of England'.

For those churches not vested in the Redundant Churches Fund or retained by the Board of Finance of the diocese, two categories can be perceived:

a) those that will be demolished (although the Advisory Board may initially withhold a demolition certificate) and
b) those that can be adapted to a range of alternative uses.

Plainly, it is this latter category that is of most interest to readers of this book. Because the resources of the Redundant Churches Fund are fairly slight related to the large number of churches which are falling into disuse, it should be equally clear that conversion is often the only way in which a creditable building can be saved from complete destruction through neglect and vandalism. Of course, conversion can only be considered as an exercise in the conservation of a noteworthy building if the alterations are as sympathetic as possible to the fabric and general appearance of the original building.

The Church Commissioners have the right to declare a particular use as being unsuitable, and the Advisory Board is required to approve or withhold approval of the proposed adaptation. Every diocese that is actively pursuing the problem has appointed a Redundant Churches Uses Committee whose task it is to seek out suitable alternative uses.

Enquiries related to redundant churches, and especially their adaptation, should be addressed in the first place either to the secretary of the Redundant Churches Uses Committee of the Diocese (see diocesan handbook) or to the Secretary of the Advisory Board for Redundant Churches of the Church Commissioners. In relation to churches serving other denominations, it has been the case until recently that Roman Catholic churches have rarely fallen out of use, although the general decline in religious observance is beginning to affect some of these buildings too. In the circumstance of their redundancy, the usual prescription has been the demolition of the buildings and sale of their sites, but it is likely that where redundancy affects noteworthy buildings – and an increasing number of Roman Catholic churches, lacking the exemption from 'listing' currently enjoyed by the Anglican churches, are being listed as buildings of architectural or historic interest – the church hierarchy may have to consider offering them for conversion to alternative uses.

Information regarding the ownership of churches belonging to the various non-conformist sects can be obtained either from the General Secretary of the Free Church Federal Council or from the appropriate denominational headquarters. In general, the property of the non-conformist churches is administered either directly by the denominational headquarters as managing trustees, or else legally held by this body as custodian trustee and managed by honorary officials from the local church membership. Baptists and Congregationalists encourage the incorporation of property in the regional or County Union and the Wesleyan Methodist Church (now combined with the Congregationalists in the United Reformed Church) usually prefers the system of local personal trustees. Among the free churches there is

no set system of redundancy procedure as there is for the Anglican Church, so that it may be for officials from the local congregation to decide if and how to dispose of vacant church property.

Planning

A problem with the conversion to domestic use of a church planned in the conventional way arises from the cross-sectional shape of the building. Staple features of the church plan since early Christian times have been the cruciform shape and the division of the interior into a high central nave, flanked on either side by lower aisles. Although satisfactory for accommodating a large congregation in a uniformly lit space, such an arrangement does not offer the possibility of simple subdivision into a series of identical spaces suitable for use as dwellings.

One feature of this cross-sectional arrangement which is immediately apparent is the large area of roof surface which it generates, the roof surface of the central nave normally being sloped at a very steep pitch. Thus a large, lofty volume is enclosed by the roof and is useless except for the purpose of admitting daylight to the 'spinal' space of the building via high-level clerestory windows. The architects of the Gothic period exploited this device to the full, for they recognised that greater religious impact could be made by stressing the luminosity and verticality which result from its adoption. Many converters of churches which incorporate this arrangement have naturally regarded this space as a zone in which living-rooms might be accommodated, and the beneficial use of such roof space has largely been made possible by the widespread employment of standard reversible ventilating and double-glazed roof windows. However, the adoption of this policy alone does not solve the problem of making optimal use of the volume, because filling up the highest part of the nave with habitable accommodation arranged on one or several storeys deprives the lower-level spinal space of the church of natural light. The solution adopted in converting several two-aisled church interiors into dwellings has been to regard this low-level central strip as a spinal access corridor serving all, or most of the flats – a sort of internal 'street'. This policy is shown in the scheme for the conversion of All Saints and St Barnabas, Stockwell, London, which is described and illustrated in this chapter.

In the few cases where the church plan diverges from the conventional arrangement by including only a single side aisle rather than the normal two, this volume, rather than the nave space, can be used to accommodate the dwellings access corridor, although it is noteworthy that in the conversion of St James's Church, Farnham, Surrey, which is also described in this chapter, the optimum cross-sectional treatment of such an asymmetrical plan placed the longitudinal access corridor in the former nave space, the aisle projection being used to accommodate living-rooms. A complementary difficulty is the achievement of a physically and visually satisfactory interface between the large western window characteristic of neo-Gothic cruciform-plan churches and the floors which must be inserted in the formerly unitary volume of the high church interior in order to provide functional habitable rooms. These new levels invariably clash with such a feature and variations on one means of convincingly disguising what might be an unattractive junction of new and retained construction are illustrated in the following sections, which include accounts of the conversion of two conventional nineteenth-century Anglican churches.

Chapel of Nunc Dimittis and Saint Mark, Bilton, Rugby, Warwickshire

This building was erected by Richard Orme Assheton, Rector of Bilton and a local landowner, in 1893 in memory of his wife. Its chief importance to architectural history lies in the fact that it is a very early example of the work of J. Ninian (later Sir Ninian) Comper (1864-1960), a notable church architect of the early twentieth century. The commission to design the memorial chapel was first given to G.F. Bodley (1827-1907), an eminent church architect of the late-

Victorian period, but Bodley passed it on to Comper who had been his most highly talented pupil. Although the building was largely complete by 1893, the bell turret at the north-east corner was added in 1904 and is of a more conspicuously 'Arts and Crafts Movement' style than the body of the church (Plate 18). The Rev. Assheton was an avid collector of stained glass and the original grouped 'lancet' windows of the side walls contain stained glass from several periods (including the Middle Ages). The liturgical 'east' window – which is actually in the south wall – contains glowing Victorian stained glass designed by G. F. Bodley. Richard Assheton may have employed the best church architects of his day because he was himself an amateur architect (he designed a church at Flecknoe, near Daventry, south of Rugby) and hence may

Plate 18 Memorial Chapel, Bilton, Warwickshire: the new low-level three-light windows are seen clearly in this view of the chapel from the north.

Fig 42

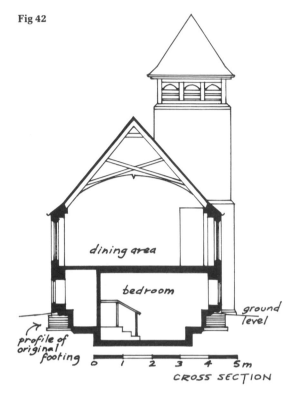

CROSS SECTION

thick brickwork external walls continued effectively to exclude wind and rain, although an attack of dry rot had affected the suspended timber ground floor. This problem did not extend to the roof timbers as this construction was very well ventilated. However, it was necessary to renew the roof covering of clay plain tiles with identical material. The policy adopted for the conversion involved exploiting to the full the high, undivided volume of the interior to create two storeys of living accommodation. This scheme was suggested by the need to remove the partially rotten wooden floor, thus deepening the space available for subdivision. A small amount of excavation down to a new lower-level concrete floor slab then provided sufficient height for two habitable storeys in the central zone of the building (Fig 42). This volume was confined to the central area because excavation was restricted to the 'core' of the plan in order to avoid undermining the existing external wall foundations (Fig 43). As most of the original windows were located quite high in the side elevations of the chapel, they could

have appreciated the difficulties of architectural design and the ability of talented practitioners to resolve them happily.

After many years of use by the local community, with regular services continuing into the early 1970s, the chapel was declared redundant in 1975. A chance inquiry into an old debt revealed that the building had never been fully consecrated and thus would revert to Assheton family ownership after a year and a day's disuse. Hence, around 1980, William Assheton, an architectural student whose forebears included the Rev. Richard Assheton, found he was the new owner of the building. As his course of study at the School of Architecture, University of Manchester, demanded a period of practical training in an architect's office, William Assheton decided to spend this time working in Coventry so that in his spare time he could design and supervise the conversion of the chapel into a dwelling for his own use.

The work was carried out during the period 1980-1 and the existing building construction was found to be generally in good condition. The well-built and massively

Fig 43

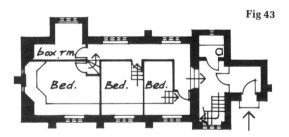

GROUND FLOOR PLAN

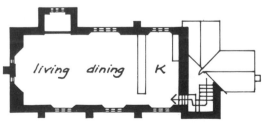

FIRST FLOOR PLAN

become low-level windows lighting the new upper storey, and space enough remained in the formerly imperforate lower-level panels of the side walls to introduce new 'tripartite' windows sited vertically below the original openings in order to light the rooms of the lower storey. This area – which, throughout, is somewhat lower than the original ground-floor level (necessarily retained in the entrance hall) – accommodates three bed-rooms. Because the achievement of a habitable room height in this lower storey necessitated deeper excavation of the central zone, the bedrooms too incorporate a change in floor level. A short flight of stairs adjoins each entrance door and leads down to the central sleeping area. This arrangement also produces a shallow perimeter 'ledge', parallel to at least one external wall, which can be used as a window seat.

This disposition of rooms made it possible to treat the residual high-level space as a single living/dining/cooking area, with the kitchen located at its northern end, divided from the generous living-dining-room only by a head-height folding screen. This arrangement allowed the elaborate wooden structure of the steeply pitched roof – now much closer at hand following the insertion of the upper floor – to remain unmodified, an impressive preserved construction 'over-sailing' the new living accommodation. The original windows of the 'east' gable and the side walls having become low-level lights closely related to the new upper floor, the fine stained glass they contain can now also be admired at close range.

William Assheton's attitude to the design of the conversion was based on the view that although the building might function as a house, it ought still to be recognisable as a church. This preference has produced at least two problems. First, the adoption of lightweight construction for new partition walls and the structure of the upper floor, although kind to the integrity of the original building fabric, has led to excessive sound transmission between rooms, a condition which is exacerbated by the inversion of the normal domestic arrangement – ie, the siting of the living-rooms over the bedrooms. The architect owner admits that it might have been better to regard the converted building primarily as a house and to order

priorities for the location and constructional 'envelopes' of rooms accordingly. This would have meant adopting dense and heavy new construction for partitions and the upper floor (ie, solid-brickwork dividing walls supporting a slab or concrete planks). Secondly, the new proximity of the original side windows to the floor of the living-room quickly revealed the propensity of the stained-glass panels to admit draughts and clearly it would be wise to install secondary glazing within these openings to seal leaks, even at the expense of losing an uninhibited view of the coloured glass. Also, following the removal of the suspended timber ground floor and the excavation of sub-floor earth so that adequate headroom could be obtained in the lower-storey bedrooms, it was necessary to install a continuous waterproof membrane below the new concrete floor slab in order to prevent penetration of the construction by rising damp. The product adopted for this task was a laminated bitumen and polyethylene sheet material which demands very careful attention to the formation of joints between sheets if groundwater penetration is to be entirely excluded. On reflection, the owner felt that it would have been better to adopt the traditional method of 'tanking' the semi-basement lower floor with in situ asphalt.

An aesthetically satisfactory answer to the need to insert additional windows to light the new lower-level accommodation was found by not only siting the new openings in the same vertical alignment as the original tripartite lights, but also by aiming to reproduce the general appearance of the existing windows. Absolute fidelity to the prototypes would have demanded the use of stone mullions, sills and lintels framing wrought-iron casements as well as the reproduction of the segmental-arched profile which caps each opening. However, insufficient height was available to install windows copying the attenuated shape of the original 'lancets' and the unquestioning reproduction of the arch form in the new windows would have produced a weaker visual result than the treatment which was adopted – the insertion of new tripartite lights capped by a simple square-headed profile (Plates 18 and 19). In this way the original window apertures 'read' satisfac-

Plate 19 Memorial Chapel, Bilton, Warwickshire: the south elevation showing the pair of small windows which have been inserted at low level

torily as the high level 'extension' of lower, squatter openings, rather in the manner that, in the internal view of a cathedral nave, the triforium openings of the nave arcade are vertically extended and handsomely terminated by the high-level clerestory windows. Also, expense was spared by the adoption of a simple square-headed shape in contrast to the original arched profile, and it was the cost consideration which similarly led to the new window sills, mullions and lintels being manufactured in reconstructed stone to match the existing dressings, rather than the natural material. Reproduction of the slender frames of the original wrought-iron casements was effected by having the new fixed and opening lights fabricated from standard steel sections, colour-coated to match the finish of the original metalwork.

St James Court, Farnham, Surrey

The conversion of St James's Church, East Street, Farnham, Surrey, which was completed in 1980, was probably the pioneering development of the current spate of residential conversions of churches for multiple occupation. The church was built in 1876 to the designs of Henry Woodyer (1816-96), an accomplished church architect who designed many ecclesiastical buildings, a large number of which are located in Surrey. The building's external walls are faced in ironstone setts with Bath stone dressings to corners and door and window openings. By virtue of its considerable size and its elevated site, the church makes a significant contribution to the townscape of Farnham's 'east end'. It is the sole building of good quality in this predominantly commercial and rather nondescript part of the town. As Farnham's second Anglican church, it was never very successful in attracting large congregations and was declared redundant in 1974. The Church Commissioners proposed its demolition because they were unable to identify any alternative use for the building.

As often applies in such cases, it became evident that the church was held in some affection by the local residents and, in response to public concern, the local planning authority, Waverley District Council, initiated a search for alternative uses. The council's Conservation Officer interested his colleagues in the Architect's Department in investigating possible residential use of the building. An architectural analysis of the structure showed that conversion of the church into council-owned dwellings, rented to young single people, was practicable. It was also the only alternative use for which finance was available. Thus the church and its site were purchased for £20,000 in 1979 by Waverley District Council, while the adjacent church hall was sold off separately by the local diocese for conversion into two small private dwellings.

The fact that the church was not of the highest architectural quality eased some of

Plate 20 St James Court, Farnham, Surrey: a bed-sitting room interior on the first floor.

the problems that could have been associated with its conversion into flats. The creation of several dwellings within a building previously devoted to one use necessitates the division of the original large single volume of the church interior and the loss of the special qualities of light, spaciousness and acoustics which that large volume possesses. Compartmentation of the interior means that the building is experienced in a new way – details which were once distant (and which may have been executed in the knowledge that they would not be viewed at close hand) are seen in 'close-up' for the first time and in relation to much smaller and more intimate spaces (Plate 20).

Despite the architect's awareness of the radical transformation that would be effected by conversion of the church into dwellings, it remained his objective to retain the essential character and best qualities of the original building and to keep the existing stonework as untouched as possible. This aim could have been frustrated by the need to keep costs to the minimum in order to maintain the economic viability of the project, but both requirements were satisfied by confining all new openings to the roofs of the aisle and the nave. Alterations to

these surfaces were less expensive than any modification of the walls and had less impact on the overall appearance of the church. Cost considerations also controlled the amount of restoration work which was undertaken. Such work had to be minimal if the project was to remain viable. Fortunately, the church was in very sound structural order – only one small area of dry rot was found in the course of the conversion – and restoration work was confined to the replacement of several crumbling gable coping stones and related 'kneelers', together with wire-brushing of some small areas of stonework where this was necessary. No attempt was made to return either the interior or exterior stonework to its original condition.

The accommodation provided by the conversion consists of 16 flats of which 6 are two-person units. The remaining 10 dwellings comprise 9 bed-sitters and one apartment with a separate bedroom. As it was difficult to convert the square-ended chancel into living accommodation and it

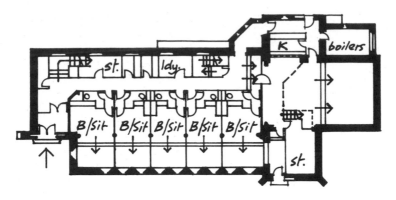

GROUND FLOOR PLAN

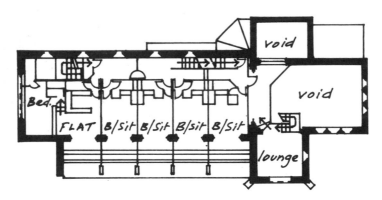

FIRST FLOOR PLAN

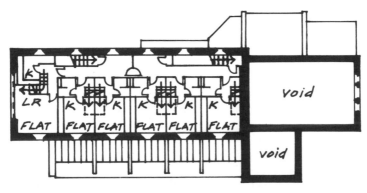

0 1 2 3 4 5 m

N

SECOND FLOOR PLAN
(third floor not shown)

Fig 44

was felt important to retain part of the church in its original state, this area was left almost untouched in order to operate as a multi-purpose 'community room'. An intermediate floor was inserted in the adjoining transept to form a small communal lounge linked to the first-floor corridor by a balcony crossing the chancel and by a small staircase to the ground floor (Fig 44). This space had previously accommodated the organ loft. Preservation of the chancel as a single space allowed the rich stained glass of the east window to be retained in its original form without interruption from new intermediate floors. Other communal accommodation includes a kitchen, laundry, two bathrooms (a shower is provided in each flat) and two store rooms.

The conversion of St James's did not result in the classic consequence of the conventional church conversion — namely, the creation of a central lightless dwellings access corridor between two lateral banks of living accommodation. This is because the church has an asymmetrical plan with a single southern aisle rather than the more usual arrangement of south and north aisles flanking a central nave. Thus the interior

Plate 21 St James Court, Farnham, Surrey: the interior of the church before conversion work commenced; note the single row of nave arcade columns

contained only a single row of nave arcade columns (Plate 21) and the comparative narrowness of the plan meant that there was space for only a range of shallow ancillary rooms — stores, bathrooms and laundry (Fig 44) — on the north side of the ground-floor flats access corridor once dwellings of suitable size, restricted to the spans of the nave arcade bays, had been accommodated. This arrangement has helped to reduce the potential oppressiveness of the resulting internal corridor because the northern 'strip' of service rooms also accommodates the two staircases that serve the two publicly accessible upper floors of the building and natural light spills into the ends of the corridor through the glazed enclosures of these features, reducing the room's apparent length. Only the second-floor dwellings are on two levels. Single-storey units occupy the ground and first floors (Fig 44 and Plate 22).

Constructional Details

With the exception of the stained-glass east window, all the original windows of diamond-shaped leaded lights set in wrought-iron frames were removed and replaced with purpose-made steel frames containing simple rectangular side-hung casements. The residual top section of glass within the arched section at the head of each window was replaced by a panel of glass directly bedded in the stonework. The tiled roof over the single south aisle was stripped

Plate 22   St James Court, Farnham, Surrey: a cross-section through the converted building showing the new living accommodation on four levels

off and partly replaced with bronze-coloured aluminium glazing bars framing bronze-tinted 'anti-sun' glass, the upper panels of which are laid to the same slope as the original roof, the lower panels producing a range of shallow vertical windows, the combination of which gives 'conservatory' lighting to the first floor flats (Plate 23). The remaining small areas of flat roof, extending from the vertical glazing almost to the eaves of the aisle roof, accommodate roof-lights admitting natural light to the ground-floor flats which would otherwise be only poorly lit by the original lancet windows of the aisle wall.

The end wall of the aisle, adjoining the main entrance, is the only place where alteration of the existing stonework was undertaken. The original tiled roof over-sailed this wall with a conventional tiled verge. In order to 'contain' the higher profile of the new, glazed aisle roof, the wall was raised slightly with new ironstone masonry, producing a parapet wall under a new sloping stone coping. The architect, Roy Toms, of the Waverley District Council, was worried about what could have been an un-sympathetic alteration to a venerable build-ing, but a visit to St Martin's, Dorking, another Woodyer church, confirmed that its architect had adopted raking parapets to terminate the aisle roofs there, and the dis-covery of this period precedent vindicated the use of this treatment at St James Court.

The original suspended wooden ground floor was entirely removed after penetra-tion of this structure for the installation of the new cross-walls and their foundations showed that some residual sections were badly affected by woodworm. The new ground floor is of in situ concrete and con-tains horizontal drainage ducts. Few addi-tional loads were placed on the original structure. The two main additional floors are largely carried on new masonry cross-walls which are, in turn, carried on their own new strip-footing foundations. The structure of these intermediate floors com-prises closely spaced pre-cast concrete beams, the intermediate voids being infilled with 'hollow pot' units. On top, a sand/cement screed gives a solid, level floor finish. This heavy construction, which has good sound-insulating properties, provided an economic solution to the problem posed by the need to insert new floors in spite of the fact that all the beams had to be man-handled into position because there was no access for mechanical handling. The new third floor, which is the upper floor of the two-storey dwellings, is of conventional

Plate 23 St James Court, Farnham, Surrey: the south end of a first-floor 'bed-sit' interior showing the new 'conservatory' windows which replaced the original aisle roof

joisted timber construction. As applies almost invariably in the conversion of columnated church interiors, compartment-ation of the interior of St James's adheres strictly to the original division of the nave into bays which, in this case, placed the columns at approximately 3.5m (11½ft) centres.

Contract Details

When detailed drawings of the scheme had been prepared, they were put out to com-petitive tender and the resulting offers were assessed by the Department of the Environ-ment against a 'cost yardstick' related to similar newly built accommodation. Conse-quently, the ministry concluded that the conversion represented 'good value for money' and the contract was awarded to

Plate 24 St James Court, Farnham, Surrey: the exterior of the church before conversion

Plate 25 St James Court, Farnham, Surrey: the exterior of St James Court after the completion of the conversion work; the radical alterations to the aisle roof are clearly visible

builders John Worman Ltd on a fixed price basis. The eventual cost of the conversion was £238,000 and the reconstruction period extended to fifteen months, the work being completed in the last quarter of 1980. In late November of that year, the first tenants moved into the building and the development almost immediately became the only award-winning refurbishment scheme in the Department of the Environment Housing Awards for 1981, despite tough competition from more than four hundred entries.

It is important to recognise that an identical project promoted at the present time would not offer good value for money in comparison with a new-build scheme. This is because St James's Church was not listed as a building of architectural or historic interest after it was declared redundant and thus the cost of the building work would attract Value Added Tax at the standard rate. A new-build scheme providing equivalent accommodation would be exempt from this tax. Only if a building is listed can this significant premium on construction costs be avoided, although the majority of disused churches which are offered for conversion are of 'listed' status.

The only note of criticism which can be sounded in relation to the admirable job of careful conversion which created much needed and characterful dwellings within the shell of a disused church at St James Court emerges from the preservation-conscious atmosphere of the present day. This mood might question the suitability of making the radical alterations to the aisle roof and the almost equally severe remodelling of the south slope of the nave roof which were implemented here (Plates 24 and 25). Although it is clear that these changes were made in order to admit light to the new, deep-plan living accommodation, it is conceivable that the judicious use of ranges of standard reversible and ventilating roof windows might have provided an answer to this requirement which would have been less erosive of the original external appearance.

Church of All Saints and St Barnabas, Stockwell, London SW8

This church was erected in the mid-nineteenth century in an area of South London which was being developed, to an overall plan, as a residential estate. In a pattern of development which took the form of a circus containing a garden at the centre, with roads radiating towards the cardinal points, the land was divided into small plots which were developed by various builders between 1843 and 1850. While the estate was being developed, a site was conveyed to the Church Building Commissioners for the erection of the church of St Barnabas. The foundation stone was laid on 27 July 1848 by the Duke of Cambridge. The building was erected by builder George Myers at a cost of £4,800 to a design by architects Isaac Clarke and James Humphrys. Accommodation was provided for a congregation of about 1,500 people and the church was consecrated on 24 June 1850 by the Bishop of Winchester. It is noteworthy that Ralph Vaughan Williams was at one time the organist here.

The axis of the nave of the church is also the centre-line of the road which leads east from the central circus of Lansdowne Gardens. Before conversion, the building had a simple plan with a nave and aisles of six bays terminated by a shallow semi-octagonal apse at the east end. In conformity with the principles of the Ecclesiological Society, whose views on church design were increasingly influential in the 1840s and '50s, no internal gallery was provided. Also in deference to their preferences, the building was carried out in the Early English Gothic style, its structural brickwork being faced externally with Kentish ragstone dressed with Bath stone at corners and door and window openings. The central nave of the church was clerestoried and a slender bell-turret of octagonal plan was subsequently installed against the south-west corner of the nave, projecting slightly beyond the south aisle. The interior was plain with two-light windows lighting the apse. The nave arcading was borne on alternate octagonal and circular stone columns with foliated capitals and supported a timber roof carried on 'hammer beam' trusses. Originally, the east window contained rich stained glass portraying St Barnabas and St Paul. The church was restored in 1948 and was refurnished with the organ from All Saints Church nearby. All Saints Church had been erected in 1876-8, but after being damaged during World War II, it was demolished and most of its parish was combined with that of St Barnabas so that the latter church was renamed All Saints and St Barnabas.

In the post-war years and partly in consequence of much local redevelopment, congregations declined and the church was eventually declared redundant in the early 1980s. The building and its site were purchased from the Church Commissioners by the Society for Co-operative Dwellings, a secondary housing co-operative, in mid-1983. The society's proposal to convert the church into dwellings followed on from the same sponsor's conversion of a similar local and redundant Anglican church, St James's, Knatchbull Road, Stockwell Park. SCD acted on behalf of a primary housing co-operative, Ekarro Housing Co-operative, who were active in the area, housing single people referred to them by various caring agencies. They had already purchased and converted the adjacent vicarage into twelve dwellings and seized the chance to convert the church to provide more units to house the majority of the co-operative on one site. In the early 1980s, such churches were not yet recognised as vehicles for providing housing and this ignorance of the potential of All Saints and St Barnabas generated a low purchase price which was a vital element in making the financing of this publicly funded scheme work within accepted limits. The support of the client co-operative, the local planning authority and the earlier experience at St James's, Knatchbull Road, helped to persuade the Housing Corporation to fund the scheme.

Quite independent of the social merits of re-using a redundant building to provide comfortable dwellings for local people at modest rents, a main factor encouraging the retention of All Saints Church was the value accorded by the local authority planners to the building for its contribution to the townscape. In this respect the Planning Department preferred the 'permanent' use offered by conversion to rented housing to a transitory use, such as might result from re-use of the building as, say, a carpet sales warehouse. In fact, the alternative course open to the Church Commissioners of demolition of the building and sale of the site might not have been easily pursued, had they chosen to adopt that route. Although All Saints is not a listed building, it lies within a conservation area so that any proposal to demolish it would have been subject to the same scrutiny as plans for the demolition of a listed building. It is far from clear that the necessary Listed Building Consent for demolition would have been forthcoming from the local authority. By the same token, in contrast to the conversion of St James's, Knatchbull Road, where 50 per cent of the cost of external repairs to this listed building was met by English Heritage, only 25 per cent of the cost of this work at All Saints was covered by a central government grant. Funds were also provided by Lambeth Council as the local Inner City Partnership Authority, for the execution of landscaping and external works. Fortunately, the church did not have the problems or liabilities which result from the existence of an associated graveyard. Although an adjoining area of ground had been purchased for this purpose, it was never developed as a burial ground and its virgin state allowed the Ekarro Housing Co-operative to complement the conversion of All Saints and St Barnabas with a new building, in the style of the surrounding villas, accommodating further flats for co-operative members (Plate 26). The total contract cost of the church conversion and the adjacent new building was of the order of £1.25 million and the work extended over twenty-one months.

The accommodation provided through the conversion of All Saints and St Barnabas comprises 25 flats, consisting of 4 bed-sitters, 2 single-bedroom units, 8 double-bedroom units, 5 two-study-bedroom units, 2 three-study-bedroom units, 2 two-double-bedroom units, 1 three-bedroom unit and 1 single-bedroom unit, the last two dwellings being sited at ground-floor level for the use of disabled people. The planning principles adopted included keeping the common circulation areas and services central – all-

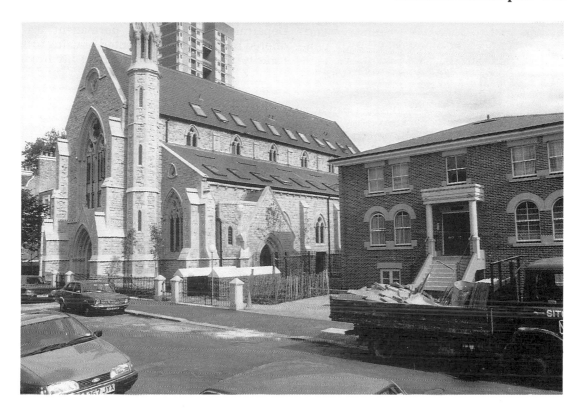

Plate 26 All Saints and St Barnabas, London SW8: the south side of the converted church faces the flank wall of a new 'villa-style' block which is the other part of this development of dwellings for a housing co-operative

internal kitchens and bathrooms back on to the spinal corridor which occupies the central strip of the former nave space (Fig 45). To obtain additional internal volume and a satisfactory relationship between new floor levels and existing or modified window openings, the original ground floor, which consisted of two panels of suspended timber construction under the areas formerly accommodating pews, separated and flanked by strips of tiled floor on a solid base where the gangways ran, was removed to give a further 400mm (16in) of height. The resulting cavity below the central ground floor corridor has been used to house horizontal drain-runs and other services. Naturally, the new dwellings had to be so arranged as to satisfy the requirements of building regulations and a significant stipulation of the old Constructional By-laws for Inner London under which this design was produced, relates to the amount of daylight which must be admitted to habitable rooms. The requirement of the old London Building Acts was that an area of window equal to at least 10 per cent of its floor area should be provided to light a habitable room. This requirement is continued by the current Building Regulations (1985).

Thus it can be seen that there is a clear relationship between the depth of each habitable room which is confined to the width of a church's nave arcade bay and the usable area of the related existing window in the side wall. It is common for these perforations in the broad surfaces of church external walls to be small. At All Saints and St Barnabas the difficulty of a comparatively small total area of existing windows failing to light adequately a much increased area of floor-space has been overcome in two ways. First, the reduction of the ground-floor level so that five storeys could be accommodated satisfactorily in the building height meant that the new first floor would cut across the aisle windows if they were left unmodified. As the existing windows were more than large enough to light the second-storey

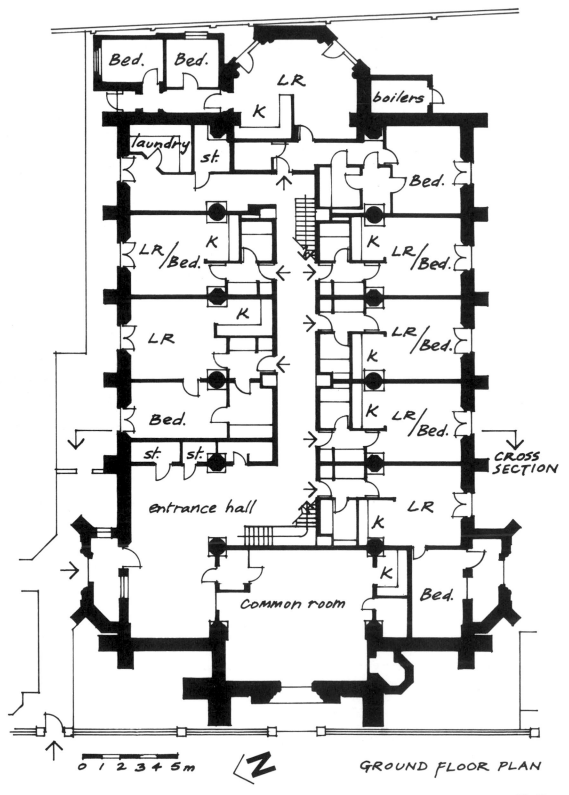

Bed.   Bed.

LR

K

boilers

laundry

st.

Bed.

LR/Bed.

K

K

LR/Bed.

LR

K

LR/Bed.

K

Bed.

K

LR/Bed.

st.   st.

entrance hall

K

CROSS SECTION

LR

K

Common room

K

Bed.

0 1 2 3 4 5m

GROUND FLOOR PLAN

Fig 45

accommodation to building regulations standards, it was decided to shorten these openings. The enlarged opaque panel thus formed below each of these 'paired lancet' windows was then perforated with a new opening containing a steel-framed French window to admit light to each living-room of the outer ranges of ground floor rooms (Plate 27). Secondly, the third-floor accommodation, lit only by the small clerestory windows of the nave (composed of shallower paired lancets), managed to obtain the necessary amount of daylight from the glazing being placed at the rear of the original traceried stonework where the splayed internal window-reveals generate an area exposed to daylight which is larger than the window area seen from outside (Fig 46).

Plate 27 All Saints and St Barnabas, London SW8: the south elevation of the converted church seen from the rear garden displays the new openings for French windows serving the ground-floor flats which are located below the original 'paired lancets' of the aisle

Plate 28 All Saints and St Barnabas, London SW8: much of the high level stonework of the west gable had decayed because the original coping had trapped rainwater; here the detail is being upgraded by the insertion of a lead 'secret gutter' between the gable and the slating

Services and Construction

Individual gas supplies were not provided in the services included in the rebuilding, partly because of the difficulties in projecting the resultant chimneys and flues through the external surfaces – the appearance of which was closely watched by officials of English Heritage. The dwellings are heated by communal gas boilers, the fuel used being heat-metered into each flat – occupants have the option of reducing or suspending the flow of the low-pressure hot water central heating – while a 'landlord's meter' records the amount of heat used in common areas.

The structure of the 'infilling' construction relies on support provided by new load-bearing masonry cross-walls which were installed in this lateral alignment on the

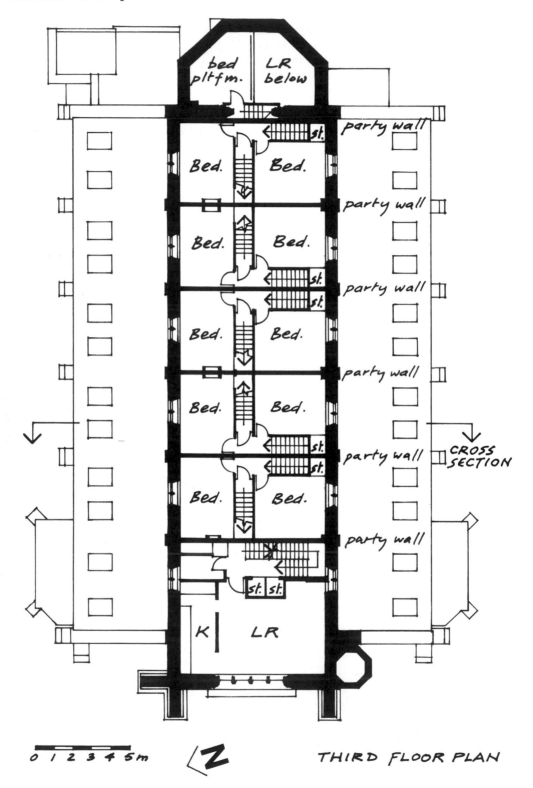

bed
pltfm.

LR
below

party wall

st.

Bed.

Bed.

party wall

Bed.

Bed.

party wall

st.

st.

party wall

Bed.

Bed.

party wall

Bed.

Bed.

st.

party wall

st.

st.

CROSS
SECTION

Bed.

Bed.

party wall

st. st.

K

LR

0 1 2 3 4 5m

THIRD FLOOR PLAN

Fig 46

centre-lines of the nave piers. 'Separating' floors – ie, those which separate one 'layer' of dwellings from the flats located above or below – are of concrete construction and most of the new concrete floors were executed by laying down pre-cast concrete planks which then received a steel-reinforced concrete screed as a structural topping. As the existing and new foundations are founded on a common 'ballast' subsoil, it was not found necessary to install movement joints between the new and the old constructions, although this policy was adopted in the reconstruction of St James's, Knatchbull Road. Where individual dwellings have intermediate floors, these were carried out in traditional timber joisted

Plate 30 All Saints and St Barnabas, London SW8: the location of living rooms at high level in the former nave of the church was facilitated by the use of many roof windows

Plate 29 All Saints and St Barnabas, London SW8: the new artificial stone coping is added to cap the gable stonework and overhang the secret gutter before the slates are fixed

construction, the joists being hung from the new masonry cross-walls on joist-hangers.

In addition to the residential accommodation, the converted church includes an entrance and main stair lobby which extends to the full height of the north aisle, incorporates two arches of the original nave arcade and gives an impressive indication of the powerful verticality of the original church interior. An adjoining one-and-a-half-storey-high common-room and a laundry associated with the rear entrance are also provided for the use of residents.

Constructional problems which were encountered during the contract included the discovery of the serious decay of a considerable area of the Kentish ragstone facing. Where this problem was found at high level on the aisle gable walls, it was

Fig 47

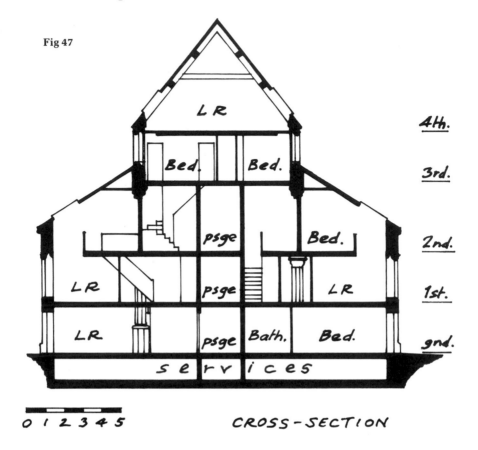

CROSS-SECTION

0 1 2 3 4 5

owed to a poor constructional detail. The original stones of the sloping gable coping had simply been bedded on the slate-roof covering of the aisles at their verges so that rain entering the joints between the coping stones had saturated the top courses of the stone facing and caused premature decay. This condition has been corrected by replacing the defective detail with a conventional sloping stone coping oversailing a 'secret gutter' of in situ lead which terminates the new roof slating, the new coping being bedded on an impervious damp-proof course (Plates 28 and 29).

Replacement of the eroded ragstone facing could have provided a problem were it not for the fact that the builder who was employed to undertake the conversion was dismantling an identically constructed church at Canterbury at the same time and thus it was possible to import salvaged ragstone from the demolition for re-use at All Saints and St Barnabas. As this description of the reason for the decay of the stonework

suggests, the original roof surfaces also presented increasing problems and complete replacement of the roof slating was necessary. In contrast to the policy adopted at St James's, Knatchbull Road, it was decided to re-roof All Saints and St Barnabas with natural slates rather than the cheaper synthetic slates that had been used on the earlier project. In this way, slates salvaged in the process of stripping the roof could be re-used, and, in fact, one complete nave roof-slope was reslated with salvaged material. Because the salvaged slates were of a size which is not readily obtainable today, the other roof-slope was reclad with new Welsh slates of conventional 'Countess' dimensions; 500 x 250mm (20 x 10in). The different sizes of slate used on each main roof-slope is of little consequence because the two surfaces cannot be seen together.

Because All Saints and St Barnabas has a broadly symmetrical plan and it is therefore logical to dispose dwellings to either side of a spinal corridor, the church has been converted in accordance with this principle at the lowest levels where the cross-section is widest (Fig 47). In conformity with the conventional treatment, where the cross-section narrows from a church with a central nave and side aisles at the lower levels to a narrow, lofty nave only at upper levels, optimum use is made of this space by filling it with a single range of dwellings. Because it is a high volume, it is usually necessary to install two-storey units in this space (compare St James Court, Farnham). In the case of the very high void at All Saints and St Barnabas, three-storey units take up most of the volume. This arrangement denies natural light to the body of the spinal corridors which serve the ground-, first- and second-floor dwellings, giving them an institutional quality that is only slightly reduced by the relief from the cellular treatment of space offered by the lofty entrance lobby and main staircase space at the west end. Nevertheless, the insertion of twenty-five comfortable and characterful dwellings into the complicated interior of this church is a tour-de-force of three-dimensional geometry. The 'collegiate' quality of the three-level dwellings which are sited in the topmost section of the nave and which are reached via integral winding staircases is particularly delightful.

The project architect was Angela Clemo of Southbank Architects who continued the work following the reconstitution of the Society for Co-operative Dwellings into a secondary housing co-operative which does not offer in-house architectural services. The builder was R. Durtnell Ltd.

7 Schools

Specialised buildings for the education of children have a relatively short history in Britain. Throughout the greater part of the nineteenth century, most people were averse to official intervention in social and family affairs and the Victorian age can be seen as an era in which individualism was the leading social ethic. The two main political parties – Tories and Liberals – agreed on a minimal role for the state in the nation's affairs. It was widely believed that if the individual was allowed to follow his own interests, within the law of the land, then general good would result. Yet many people in Victorian Britain were not indifferent to the widening divisions between rich and poor that seemed to be a consequence of this ideology. Most saw it as an evil, although the ways suggested to combat the condition varied greatly. Eventually, it was recognised that some of the results of the laissez-faire mentality could pose a threat to social stability and the health of rich and poor alike. Hence there was an extension of the powers of local government and the state intervened after 1870 to provide universal elementary education. The establishment of a system of elementary education available to all the country's children was one of the great achievements of late Victorian Britain. Before W. E. Forster's Elementary Education Act of 1870, educational provision was haphazard. Secondary education was available for the more fortunate and higher education was reserved for the privileged few.

In early Victorian times illiteracy was widespread. The churches played a significant part in dealing with this condition and the parish schools were the most important providers of elementary education. They were usually built with donations from private individuals, many prompted by charitable feelings, others by the belief that education was an antidote to revolution. Government grants became available later in the period to assist all denominations to establish schools.

The parish school was usually small and relied on one teacher, whose small house was often part of the school buildings. The schoolmaster might be assisted by an unqualified 'pupil-teacher'. There was a shortage of trained teachers and the planning of schools reflected this circumstance; most of the instruction was done in a large school-room, off which there might be one or two classrooms which were used for teaching smaller groups. A larger school might have separate school-rooms for boys and girls. An entrance porch, cloakrooms and lavatories made up the rest of the accommodation. The simplest arrangement is apparent in the original building of the village school at Shawell, Leicestershire, the conversion of which is described and illustrated later in this chapter.

The original fabric of Shawell school also displays another quality that is characteristic of mid-Victorian church schools – the neo-Gothic style of architecture. An urban example of this type of school, St Peter's at Vauxhall, South London, is also described in this chapter. Probably the adoption of the Gothic style for church schools is not so surprising when it is considered that the design of schools was a subject in which the influential Ecclesiological Society – the significant impact of whose views on church design has already been referred to – was prepared to interest itself. In an article of 1847 in its journal, The Ecclesiologist, the society advocated a separate roof for the school-room and the headmaster's house with the classroom set at right-angles to it and a lean-to cloakroom. Separation of the sexes was also considered desirable where this could be achieved. The school should be 'the prettiest building in the village next to the church'. Of course, in conformity with ecclesiological principles, schools were expected to be in the Gothic style.

High Anglican architects such as William Butterfield (1814-1900) and George Edmund Street (1824-81) took up these ideas and produced a series of parish schools which combine simple planning and construction with details they had developed for church architecture. The elevations, as well as the planning, are frequently extremely plain. In St Peter's school at Vauxhall which is described later, we see the work of another very talented church architect, John Loughborough Pearson (1817-97).

The design of Victorian village schools often manifests a concern for the use of local building materials and the desire to create a picturesque silhouette. In the vast majority of these buildings, the entire accommodation was single storey, the central school-room being lit by very high, arched windows located in the gables. The problem of designing parish schools in towns was greater. Often they are not unlike village schools, but where space was limited on a cramped city-centre site, multi-storeyed buildings were erected. In an extreme case, it might be necessary to put the playground on the roof. J. L. Pearson avoided this arrangement at St Peter's by confining the two-storey teaching accommodation to the perimeter of the wedge-shaped site at the rear of his church, the central 'spine' of the plan linking the blocks on the east and west site boundaries to create two largely internal courtyards which operated as children's playgrounds (Fig 53).

Like Shawell school, St Peter's was built in the 1860s and so preceded the Elementary Education Act of 1870 that called for large numbers of schools, mainly in crowded urban areas, to be built with public rather than private money. London, for example, had over four hundred such Board schools by 1895. Many of them were designed by E. R. Robson (1835-1917) who was the first architect to the London School Board. Robson's work was influential, partly because in 1874 he published *School Architecture*, a book in which he illustrated a number of London Board schools.

As they often occupy cramped sites, London Board schools are usually multi-storey buildings. In their planning they retain the large central school-room, but the provision of classrooms is greater than the norm established by the church schools. The members of the School Boards were more secular in their thinking than the builders of the earlier parish schools, and although some designers used the Gothic style, it was argued that '. . . a continuation of the semi-ecclesiastical style . . . would appear to be inappropriate and lacking in anything to mark the great change which is coming over the education of the country'. The new 'Queen Anne' manner of the time seemed to be a style that would permit greater freedom of planning and lacked the associations with religion evoked by neo-Gothic forms. The London Board schools were usually built of yellow London stock brick with red brick dressings, although the later buildings, and the majority of contemporary schools erected in provincial cities, were carried out entirely in red brick. Tall, white-painted window frames, subdivided by many glazing bars, were placed under segmental arches of red brickwork and the most prominent features were the high gables which gave the buildings a varied and lively skyline. This craggy silhouette invariably was further enhanced with tall chimney stacks and, often, a crowning bell-cote, cupola, or turreted staircase towers.

Most of the early London Board schools have been replaced or altered and most of those which survive remain in use as schools. However, the inner city depopulation of recent years has led to falling rolls in city schools and the consequent rationalisation of local education has caused certain Board schools to become redundant, releasing them for alternative uses. In Bethnal Green, in East London, two such schools, at Olga Street and Bow Brook, have been converted into dwellings. The planning principle of converting the barrack-like main blocks of these buildings into flats has been the exploitation of the 4.2m (14ft) standard height of each classroom by siting a mezzanine 'sleeping gallery' on the internally located kitchenette/bathroom areas, overlooking a 'double-height' living-room which is lit by the large and lofty classroom windows. An identical approach has been adopted in the conversion into flats of the former Ducie High School, Greenheys, Manchester. The conversion to a house of the former village school at Airton, in the Yorkshire Dales, which is one of the following case studies, shows how a similarly 'standard' type of local authority school – in this case in a rural location – can be transformed into a convenient and characterful dwelling without adversely affecting its external appearance.

The Old School, Shawell, Leicestershire

Shawell is a small village close to the boundary of Leicestershire with both Warwickshire and Northamptonshire. As an old-established settlement, it had boasted its own school since 1604 and the schoolmaster's house of this date, although much altered, survives on an adjoining site. The school was founded as the result of a bequest made by a local landowner, John Elkington Esq, and a copy of his will, dated 2 April 1604, is in the possession of the present owners of the school, Mr and Mrs Goddard. Although the surviving school building is of much later date, it has a fairly complicated history.

A school-room of brick construction was erected on the site of the ancient building in 1862. A simple, single school-room with an entrance porch on the east side, it catered for the children of Shawell and the surrounding villages until after World War I. It is significant that even such a simple building as this was not immune from the stylistic preferences of contemporary architects and the steeply pitched roof-slopes of the school-room are 'stratified' with bands of alternating plain and fish-scale pattern tiles in true 'High Victorian' fashion. This treatment is shown clearly in the photograph of the east elevation, taken in Edwardian times, with the schoolchildren crowding the entrance steps (Plate 31). Similarly, the three-light windows sit below pointed arches and the brickwork of the otherwise plain gables is

Plate 31 The Old School, Shawell, Leicestershire: an Edwardian view of the school and its pupils showing the decorative banding of roof tiles and 'diapered' brickwork of the 1862 building

relieved by a diaper pattern formed in 'header' bricks of contrasting colour.

By 1922 the single school-room was no longer adequate to meet the needs of the local school population, so the full width of the building was extended eastwards under a pair of pitched roofs to create a second classroom, head-teacher's room and internal side entrance lobby replacing the demolished attached porch (Plate 32). The final alteration came in 1959 when, at long last, internal WCs serving the staff and pupils were added in a single-storey flat-roofed extension to the south.

It will be appreciated that even after these enlargements, Shawell school was not a large building. When a new junior school was built in a nearby village in the late 1970s, the building became redundant. The present owners knew the village through visits to a local pub and became aware that the old school was standing empty. Their offer to buy the building was accepted by the Leicestershire County Council and they moved into the building in 1981. Since then they have been effecting a gradual programme of repair, restoration and alteration.

Plate 32 The Old School, Shawell, Leicestershire: the 1862 block is still visible behind the twin-gabled 1922 extension in this modern view; the water-pump seen in the Edwardian photograph remains in the playground

It was plain that the existing accommodation – two classrooms separated by a half-glazed folding partition, a head teacher's office and WC block – did not provide an arrangement that could be easily adapted to give convenient living space. An essential first step was to create a bedroom and this was formed from the larger part of the former WC block. By retaining the other elements of the plan of this block, the main entrance that had been created in 1959 could be maintained as the 'front door' with the bathroom/WC being reached from the adjacent entrance hall (Fig 48). It was similarly easy to convert the head-teacher's office into a kitchen adjoining the side-entrance lobby. This left a suitable strategy for conversion of the former classrooms to be decided. Because twin gables flanking a central valley gutter had been adopted to cap the elevation of the 1922 extension, it

Fig 48

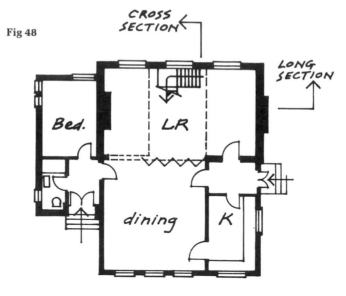

GROUND FLOOR PLAN

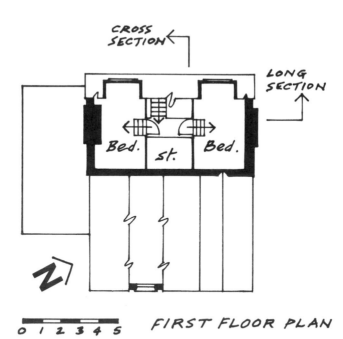

FIRST FLOOR PLAN

0 1 2 3 4 5

was not possible to form an upper storey in this section. Fortunately, the classroom located below this block was the smaller of the two, and because it adjoined the kitchen, it made a logical dining-room.

To the rear of the glazed, folding partition lay the larger, higher volume of the original school-room. It was believed that this area offered more opportunities for conversion into convenient living space. However, the most significant obstacles to this plan were the deep trusses of heavy timbers which spanned the roof space at two locations to brace purlins supporting the rafters of each roof-slope (Fig 49). Instead of giving a clear internal height of 6.9m (22½ft) (extending up into the apex of the roof space), headroom beneath these two trusses was reduced

Plate 33 The Old School, Shawell, Leicestershire: the dormers added to the rear roofslope and the flat-roofed WCs extension of 1959 feature clearly in this view from the field behind the school

to 4.4m (14ft) at the junction of their curved braces with the tie-beams, thus denying the opportunity to install two storeys of habitable accommodation at these points. To make optimum use of the volume, an ingenious device was employed. It seemed sensible to reserve each end bay of the roof space for a bedroom, lit by a new window installed either in an adjacent roof-slope or in the flanking gable. Each bedroom would be reached via a staircase sited in the central bay, but headroom for a lower-storey living-room could not be achieved below this stair and still give an adequate height for a door opening beneath the truss tie-beams, allowing unobstructed access from the main landing into the bedrooms. Thus the stair was installed with a mezzanine-level landing, giving a headroom below of only 2.05m (6½ft) – ie, the height of a conventional internal door – and allowing an equivalent headroom below the tie-beams of the roof trusses above. A short flight of three steps

beyond the line of each truss and to the rear of each bedroom door then ascends to the floor level of each end-bay bedroom (Fig 50). In this way, the new upper floor is prevented from crossing the original three-light arched windows which serve the end bays of the lower storey, and the stair is prevented from

Fig 49

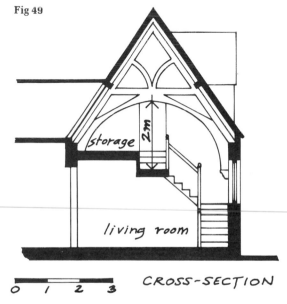

CROSS-SECTION

0   1   2   3

Fig 50

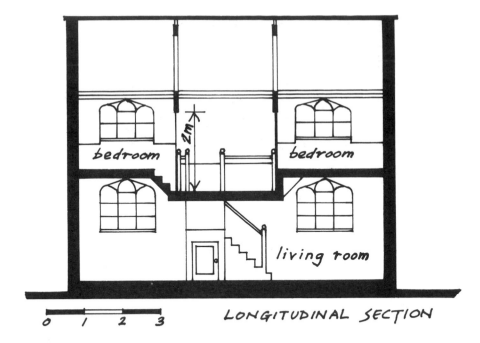

bedroom

bedroom

2m

living room

LONGITUDINAL SECTION

0 1 2 3

conflicting with the central window of this range by the introduction of a further quarter-landing at an intermediate level that turns its lowest flight parallel to the side elevation at a level just below the window-sill (Fig. 49). The area below the stair then becomes part of the lounge, extending back from the glazed folding doors that separate it from the dining-room (Fig 48).

To introduce daylight into each of the new upper-storey bedrooms, instead of puncturing the patterned brickwork of the gables, it was decided to construct large dormer windows matching the style of the existing windows of the lower storey. These have been installed under new steeply pitched roofs which harmonise with the form of the main roof (Plate 33). The cost of installing these features and retiling the remainder of the roof was assisted by a Repairs Grant provided by the local authority. The need for remedial work on the roof covering became apparent when the worn-out lead valley gutters began to leak, although discomfort from this source had to be endured for almost two years until the Repairs Grant was awarded.

Perhaps the one regrettable feature of the conversion of Shawell school – which is being carried out with great care and sensitivity – is the retention of the 1950s flat-roofed WCs extension which, almost gratuitously, fails to relate in any way to the form of the original building. It is unfortunate that the space enclosed by the 1862 building, together with its 1922 extension, was too small or too lacking in services provision to offer a convenient corner for installation of the new bathroom and WC. The logical re-use of existing services has led to the retention of the overly utilitarian post-war outshot when it would have been better to demolish it and to restore the four-square appearance of the pre-war building.

Village School, Airton, North Yorkshire

This village junior school, built to a standard county council plan in the inter-war period, like Shawell school, was converted into a dwelling by the efforts of the occupants. The building was purchased by a local clothing manufacturer to provide a family dwelling and a small office for the administration of his company. Like Shawell school, it is a high-roofed structure, but it is slightly more complicated in having a T-shaped plan (Fig 51). Separate entrances for boys and girls were located in the small north wing which forms the leg of the 'T'

Fig 51

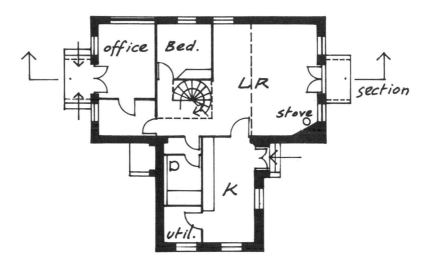

GROUND FLOOR PLAN

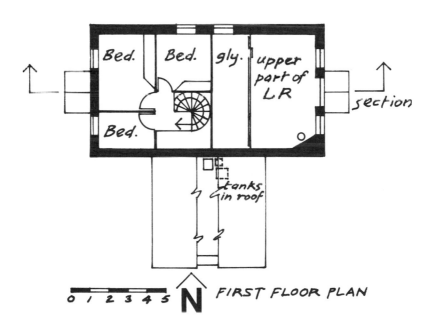

FIRST FLOOR PLAN

(Plate 34). In 1980, the owner approached a local architect, John Wharton, to provide him with a design that could be easily executed by direct labour and it was immediately apparent that exploitation of the high volume of the main east-west wing of the building would be the best way of obtaining the maximum accommodation.

Although the apex of the pitched roof of this wing was 6.5m (21ft) above floor level, unlike the arrangement that applies at Shawell school, the internal space did not extend up to the roof ridge-board. A broad central strip of flat ceiling existed above the classrooms to give a maximum headroom of only 4.3m (14ft) which could not be divided horizontally to give two storeys of habitable room-height. Hence it was decided to remove this ceiling and its supporting joists and to resite it at a higher level. This was

Plate 34 Village School, Airton, North Yorkshire: a view of the school from the north showing the lower entrance wing and the simple, standard design

achieved by installing new ceiling joists, at 400mm (16in) centres, bearing on the top surfaces of the large purlins that support the rafters at the centre of their span. Following the installation of a suspended ceiling of plasterboard and plaster skim coat below these joists, a headroom of 2.6m (8½ft) could be achieved in the new upper storey, the floor of which was formed from boards nailed to 50 x 150mm (2 x 6in) joists at 400mm (16in) centres. Below this floor, a headroom of more than 2.4m (8ft) resulted in the residual lower-storey space.

The main east-west wing of the school originally accommodated two classrooms – as at Shawell, divided by a glazed, sliding-folding partition. Above this central partition lay a heavy timber roof-truss, supporting the purlins and extending down to suspended ceiling level. As it was impractical to remove this essential structural element, the new first-floor construction had to terminate on this line, so the added floor was restricted to the east side of the central truss. The western half of this wing could then be dedicated to a 'double-height' living-room with French windows opening out, through a deepened former window opening, on to the garden. Hence, over this section, it was not necessary to remove the

existing ceiling, but a desire to emphasise the still lofty volume of this room caused the client to request the insertion of a 'minstrel's gallery' upper level over part of this area. By the introduction of a 75 x 75mm (3 x 3in) square-section hollow steel post sited close to the centre of the room for the support of heavy timber trimmers, it was possible to construct a gallery which extends between the flank walls on modestly-sized 38 x 150mm (1½ x 6in) joists, carrying boards which give a platform 2m (6½ft) wide over-looking the larger part of the living-room.

Fig 52

LONGITUDINAL SECTION

Headroom equivalent to door head-height could just be achieved both below and above this gallery and under the retained ceiling. Access to the gallery is obtained via a removable ladder.

The remainder of the upper-storey accommodation, which was created at a slightly higher level in the eastern half of the main east-west wing, is reached from the ground floor via a spiral stair. It comprises two single bedrooms and a double bedroom. At ground-floor level, the stair devolves into a central hall, from which access is gained to the single lower-storey bedroom, a waiting lobby associated with the office, and the bathroom/WC as well as the living-room which is reached by passing below the gallery. Also reached through a door located below the gallery is the kitchen, which re-uses the former 'Boys' Entrance' to the school as the new main entrance to the dwelling. Apart from housing the bathroom/WC and the kitchen, there is sufficient space in the small northern wing of the school for a small utility room to be provided en suite with the kitchen.

Apart from the deepening and modification of the existing central window openings of each main gable to create garden access doors, the only other alterations to

Plate 35 Village School, Airton, North Yorkshire: the school's south elevation showing the boarded infill panels between new windows serving the original ground-floor rooms and the new upper storey

the external appearance were modifications to the existing very high classroom windows of the east and south elevations to reconcile them with the newly inserted upper floor and gallery. Because these two constructions are at different levels, the existing fixed and 'hopper-vent' windows of eight lights were removed and replaced with sash-pattern frames incorporating top-hung, open-out casements, boarded panels infilling the gap between the head of the lower-storey vent and the sill of the upper-storey window (Plate 35).

As there is a trio of high and narrow lights in each main gable, the problem of reconciling this glazing with the added upper floor was less critical than in a case where large windows, surmounted by pointed arches, occupy the gables – this is almost a standard feature of Victorian village schools. As applies with the treatment of such windows in the western gables of churches, it is probably kinder to the existing architecture to avoid a 'collision' between the new floor and the broad and high-arched opening. In most cases of the conversion of schools that incorporate this feature, the owners have wisely left space between the edge of the added floor and the window to give a mezzanine platform overlooking a 'double-height' living-room, as in the arrangement adopted at the west end of the main wing of Airton school.

Because the stone-built, partly render-clad building proved to be extremely sound, little alteration to the exterior or renewal of materials was necessary. Indeed, it was even found possible to reuse the characteristic roof-top ventilator of the school-room as the vented enclosure in which to terminate internally located pipes that provide fresh air to the new bedrooms.

St Peter's School, Vauxhall, London SE11

The church of St Peter, Vauxhall, was built between 1863 and 1865 on part of the area formerly occupied by the Vauxhall Pleasure Gardens; its altar is on the site of the Neptune Fountain, and the late-eighteenth-century house which adjoins the church and is now the vicarage was originally the home of the manager of the gardens. Its architect was J.L. Pearson, a highly accomplished church designer, most of whose work was for the 'High Church' wing of Anglicanism. Because the established church played a major role in the provision of education before the passing of the Elementary Education Act of 1870, it is not surprising that the lofty, brick-built church of St Peter shares its site with a school.

The site is shaped like a truncated wedge and Pearson placed the majority of the school buildings along its east and north sides. However, this did not provide sufficient accommodation, so a high two-storey wing was erected on the west boundary and was linked across to the eastern range by a short 'spinal' block, creating two courtyards following completion of the church, for the erection of the school preceded construction of the church by two years. The northern courtyard, with a fairly open aspect to the west, was the boys' playground, while the south court provided a play area for the girls. The building not only accommodated schools for boys and girls, but also an art school and a soup kitchen (later converted into a school-room). Alterations to Pearson's design were made by the architect J. T. Knowles in 1873.

Over the years, the buildings were subject to many more changes and extensions as facilities were added or improved. The aspect of the north playground to the west was largely lost with the construction of an independent WC block, and part of the eastern range fronting St Oswald's Place, which originally accommodated the art school, was rebuilt as a flat-roofed block after bomb damage during World War II (Plate 36). In terms of consistency of architectural style, this was a regrettable change, because Pearson's carefully crafted High Victorian Gothic treatment of tall sash-windows spanned by pointed arches of 'polychromatic' brickwork was replaced by a much more utilitarian brick 'box', fenestrated with standard steel-framed casements arranged horizontally and contrasting strongly with the pre-existing forms.

The development of more modern schools in the locality, combined with falling numbers of pupils from this depopulating 'inner city' area, caused the closure of the school in 1977. The north wing of the otherwise redundant building was leased to a gymnasium/health club. In 1982, the school was put on the market by the agents to the Church Commissioners and the Inner London Education Authority. At that time, Russell Mills, an artist who was looking for a dwelling that would be large enough also to provide studio space, realised that the building might subdivide suitably to meet, at low cost, the similar needs of fellow artists and designers. With the help of an architect, Tony Fretton, he deduced that even if the north wing continued as a gymnasium, the remainder of the accommodation would divide satisfactorily into six residential/studio units. Despite the fact that only three weeks were available between his first viewing of the premises and the date for submission of offers, Russell Mills managed to find five collaborators, and their tender succeeded in competition against bids from office developers, engineering firms and an art college. The would-be occupants and

their architect had successfully demonstrated to the vendors that the character of the Grade II listed building would remain undisturbed by its conversion into dwellings. The six participants also took a risk in buying the building without planning permission, but some months later they obtained consent for change of use from school premises to residential/studio units and the architect was able to instruct a builder to commence Stage 1 – the conversion of the building into six basic, serviced 'shells'. This stage of the work took nine months. The north wing of the school would have made three extra units, but as it was rented out to the health club, the new owners decided to maintain this arrangement.

Because it is not possible for more than four people to share a freehold, the owners of each of the six units formed themselves into a management company in order to buy the building; each became a director of the company and was given a 999-year lease of his or her dwelling. The purchase price of each unit was chiefly related to its area, although other factors entered in, such as the amenity offered by the single private garden. It was also clear that some of the

Plate 36 St Peter's School, London SW11: St Oswald's Place; the apse of the church is on the left, the former schoolmaster's house arches over the entrance to the south courtyard, centre, and the flat-roofed block which replaced the original Art School after wartime bombing is on the right

new occupants needed studios with specific qualities. For instance, two potters who share a unit required ground-floor premises to accommodate their heavy kiln and to allow easy access from the street for the delivery of materials. Similarly, a photographer who also occupies a ground-floor unit needed a huge room that could operate as a photographic studio. A designer chose the only flat with a garden and a fashion consultant, Juliet Mann, who is similarly keen on horticulture, chose the only unit with a flat roof so that she could establish a roof-top conservatory above her flat.

From the start, the participants decided that firm agreements should be made in advance in writing. Thus, their solicitor drew up a document detailing joint responsibility for communal maintenance of roofs, courtyards and external paintwork. Money from the rent of the gymnasium is put back

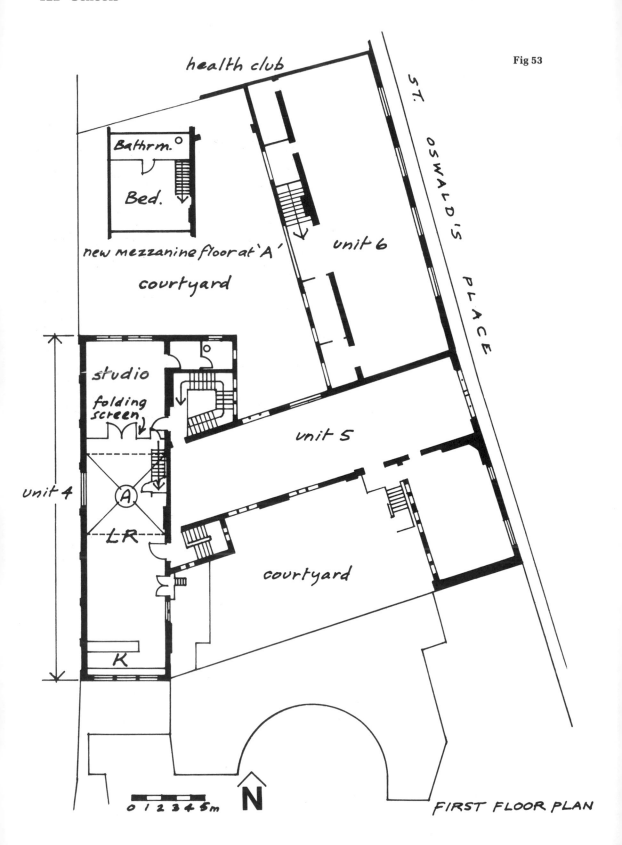

Fig 53

health club

Bathrm.

Bed.

new mezzanine floor at 'A'

courtyard

unit 6

ST. OSWALD'S PLACE

studio

folding screen

A

LR

unit 4

K

unit 5

courtyard

0 1 2 3 4 5m

N

FIRST FLOOR PLAN

into the company to pay for repairs, contract window-cleaning and other matters of mutual concern. If any of the present owners wish to sell their share of the converted building, the remaining directors must approve the new purchaser, but otherwise the dwellings can be sold in the normal way.

It is clear that a main attraction of the project for its participants was the opportunity it offered to obtain a large amount of space in a Central London location for a modest outlay. In fact, the average size of unit is 110sq m (1,200sq ft) and since the school was purchased in 1982 for £162,000, an average-size unit cost £27,000. However, all the new occupants were faced with considerable expense in converting their areas of the building into habitable accommodation because each newly formed unit lacked even basic services provision, and by 1986 most people had spent an additional £55-60,000 on their conversion. Tony Fretton, the architect who had devised the original division of areas to form six units and who had advised on the allocation of flats, was retained by both Russell Mills and Juliet Mann to design the interiors of their dwellings.

Russell and Ann Mills' flat is particularly impressive as it is located on the upper floor of the school's west wing (Plate 37 and Fig 53) and so extends up into the apex of the steeply-pitched roof. The vast room of 21.3 x 5.4m (70 x 18ft) had been divided into three classrooms separated by half-glazed partitions. One of these was removed to form the large general living area, at the end of which is the dining table, with the kitchen hidden behind panelling formed from painted tongue-and-groove boarding. The partitioned end of the room is north-facing and makes an ideal studio, lit, as it is, by the original tall neo-Gothic windows. The architect has cleverly preserved the integrity of the lofty space by restricting an inserted upper level to the central section of the room. This zone accommodates a double bedroom with en suite bathroom and, being mainly in the roof space, is lit by a large new roof-light. The necessary insulation of the thin roof construction against heat loss was achieved by draping a glass-fibre quilt, laminated with aluminium foil, beneath the rafters. The silvery underside of this

Plate 37 St Peter's School, London SW11: neo-Gothic windows in the south gable of the west wing (formerly an infants' school) light the first-floor flat of an artist

material is exposed to the interiors of the studio and living/dining areas, but these are such lofty spaces that this inexpensive treatment does not detract from their grandeur. The colour scheme is monochromatic throughout in accordance with Russell Mills' preference to keep the space '. . . clear and simple, everything visually quiet'.

Selective demolition of some post-Victorian accretions (like the independent WC block on the western boundary) helped to make the building more suitable for its new use, but otherwise external alterations were very modest. This follows the ethic pursued in the conversion of similarly old city-centre premises in New York of leaving exteriors more or less alone so as not to attract attention. Other than some water-washing of the exuberant polychromatic brick arch that surmounts the entrance to

Plate 38 Two views of a 1970 building of 'rationalised traditional' construction make the point that even very modern buildings may offer opportunities for conversion into characterful dwellings; this shot of the redundant Tilehouse Primary School at Denham, Bucks, which was taken in 1983 could suggest that the scope for its re-use was limited

Plate 39 The same view of the school taken in 1987 following its conversion into sheltered housing for elderly people shows how the smaller scale associated with domesticity has been achieved by the quite simple means of replacing the 'ribbon' glazing and low infill-panels of the original building with dark-stained chevron-boarded full-height infill-panels and French windows

the former south playground (now the communal car park), no cleaning of external brickwork has been undertaken. In the same way, only modest repairs were needed to the steeply pitched slated roofs – wholesale reroofing was not necessary. The northern playground is in the process of being transformed into a communal garden as earth and foliage replace characterless tarmac.

The scheme is an impressive realisation of the idea of combining uses within units contained in a single building – in this case, living space and craft/design studios. However, it must be emphasised that the flexibility shown by the local authority in approving this combination of residential and occupational functions within individual units is very unusual and was probably encouraged by the planners' recognition that this approach could act to conserve a listed building with the least possible alteration of its character. The combination of different uses in separate parts of one building, rather than within individual units, is dealt with in the final chapter.

8 Mills, Factories and Warehouses

Probably the most common type of conversion project at the present time is the adaptation of a mill or warehouse into a block of dwellings. The riverside warehouses of the London docklands have become favourite subjects for this treatment during the last decade and an outstanding conversion of one such building – Thames Tunnel Mills – is described in this chapter, while the final chapter of the book contains an analysis of a similar building that has been converted to house a range of new uses, including sixty apartments. However, conversion of more modest manufacturing and storage buildings into individual dwellings has occurred over many years – possibly even centuries. It will be appreciated that before widespread industrialisation, the erection of highly specialised buildings was something of a rarity. It used to be the normal practice to adapt buildings for different purposes over their lives. Evidence of the logical development of this practice can also be found in one or two early industrial buildings. At least one small nineteenth-century factory in Denton, Greater Manchester, an area noted for the manufacture of hats, was built with certain architectural features included so that it might easily be converted into a terrace of houses, should there be a downturn in trade. Only since the general adoption of the policy of specialisation engendered by the Industrial Revolution has it become common to demolish and rebuild rather than to adapt and extend. So natural had this practice become that only in the past fifteen or twenty years has there grown up in Britain the idea of conserving redundant industrial and commercial buildings and putting them to new uses.

Early candidates for this treatment among industrial buildings, and prior to the enthusiasms of the last twenty years, were traditional watermills and windmills which had become redundant with the introduction of steam, and later electrical power. Before describing the opportunities and shortcomings of such structures for conversion to domestic use, it is necessary to say something about the process of grinding grain to produce flour, because the anatomy of these buildings was dictated by this process.

Corn-milling is one of the oldest and most necessary human occupations. The main food grains on which we depend for an essential part of our daily diet come from plants belonging to the family of grasses and cannot be readily digested until the tough outer shells are broken up and, sometimes, removed. A grain of wheat, for example, consists essentially of three parts: the bran, made up of several outer coverings, the germ (the embryo of the new plant) and the endosperm, the starchy centre which is made into flour. Various methods have been developed to break open such cereal grains and to extract flour. During the Iron Age, the first rotary mill appeared in Britain. It consisted of a stationary lower bed stone and an upper stone that was turned above it while grain was fed through a central hole or 'eye' in the top stone. The grain was ground between the faces of the stones which came to be grooved to give a better cutting action, and the ground meal was distributed to the outside edge of the stones for collection.

This method of grinding grain had to await the human skill to fabricate tools from two materials because three wooden parts were essential to the rotary mill: the *rynd* which bridged the eye of the runner stone and enabled it to be hung on top of the wooden *spindle*, and the *handle*, used for turning the runner stone. The spindle, projecting upwards from the centre of the bed stone, was at first fixed to carry the runner stone a little above the bed stone, but later the elevation of the spindle could be altered to allow regulation of the gap between the stones and so control the fineness of the meal. The rynd and the spindle soon came to be made from iron to be more durable, and the handle was developed to become a lever for turning the runner stone by animal power. Eventually, the handle was superseded by a power drive applied to the spindle, and its successor is the central shaft of all windmills and watermills.

Water power was first used to turn millstones about two thousand years ago, the earliest waterwheels being horizontal, fixed to the projecting lower end of the spindle. From the first century AD, the principles of gearing were understood and used by the Romans, so that a horizontal millstone could be turned by a vertical waterwheel. The Romans probably introduced the geared mill to Britain. Windmills seem to be a medieval invention derived from the geared watermill and are first recorded in England during the last quarter of the twelfth century. By the end of the thirteenth century, they were common landmarks in the English countryside.

During the eighteenth century, corn-milling had to keep pace with the growth of population and industry. The form of mills had developed only slowly since the Middle Ages, but by the middle of the eighteenth century the technology of wind and water power was being investigated scientifically and there was competition for mill sites because of enlarging industrial needs. Established corn mills often had first claim to the use of watercourses, but their machinery needed modernising to improve efficiency. Steam power was first used to drive corn mills in the 1780s following its adoption in textile mills and the building of Albion Mill, beside the Thames at Blackfriars, London, in 1784, greatly influenced the development of milling. It was the first purpose-built flour factory and had twenty sets of millstones driven by two steam-engines. The success of Albion Mill marked the beginning of the move from the trade's dependence on small country watermills and windmills, often with only two or three sets of stones, to larger merchant mills built close to centres of corn trading and importing. In the late nineteenth century, when vast quantities of grain were shipped into British ports from overseas, the milling industry became concentrated at ports and in towns with good canal, rail or road links.

The method of milling grain between two stones probably reached its peak in Britain in the watermills and windmills of the early nineteenth century. The rival method of using metal rollers for milling corn had been tried as early as the sixteenth century but was generally only adopted for malt-milling until, in 1834, a Swiss engineer substituted rollers for the original stones in the reconstruction of an existing mill. In consequence of his success, mills using both stones and rollers were built in Britain from the 1860s. The first successful flour-manufacturing plant using only rollers was the Manchester mill established by Henry Simon in 1878. By 1881 he had built the first fully automatic milling plant at Chester and from that time, mechanically powered roller-milling rapidly supplanted stone-milling in the mass production of flour.

In medieval times, bringing corn to the mill was the responsibility of the customer. It was brought by the customers when required for use rather than all at once so that large-scale storage was not needed at the mills. Horse-drawn and water-borne transport became important with the expansion of trade during the eighteenth century. To simplify the handling of sacks of corn, facilities such as loading ramps, waggon bays and internal or external hoists that could lift sacks to the top of the mill for storage were installed. Both windmills and watermills were built taller or larger to accommodate additional machinery and grain storage space, and an extra floor was often provided above the rest of the accommodation so that grain could be emptied into bulk storage bins and led through spouts to millstones as required. In modern mills, grain is stored in silos which are often separate from the mill and near to a bulk intake point. The business of manhandling sacks has been replaced by automation, the grain being conveyed mechanically or pneumatically direct to the mill.

Types of Mills

Windmills

Various types of windmill emerged, and it is possible to distinguish the characteristics of these among the survivors.

Post mills were first built in the twelfth century and there is little difference in design between the early examples and those constructed in the nineteenth century. Built mainly of wood, the rectangular boarded body of this type of mill turns on a central post to face the wind. At the foot of the post are horizontal beams and diagonal beams to carry the weight of the uprights. It is plain that such essentially lightweight structures, the form of which is determined almost entirely by operational considerations, may offer few opportunities for conversion into comfortable living accommodation.

Smock or **frock mills** are so called because their shape is said to resemble a man dressed in a smock. Constructed from wood on a circular base, this type of mill was usually eight-sided, although six-, ten- and twelve-sided mills were also built. In this type, only the cap of the mill and sails rotate to work the grinding stones, so the wooden walls are either sloped or battered to allow free movement of these elements. These mills, which sometimes have a tarred brickwork plinth with the wooden structure painted white, are more frequently converted into houses than the less enduring post mills.

Tower mills are similar to smock mills in shape and working machinery, but brick or stone is used for the structure instead of wood. Porous brickwork tower mills were often tarred against the weather and in Sussex they were frequently tile-hung. Tower mills can be seen all over Britain, but south-east England houses more wooden smock mills. In East Anglia, the Midlands and the North, stone and brick-built mills

Plate 40   A kitchen/dining area on the first floor of a converted windmill; it is clear that standard built-in fittings must be adapted if the cubical forms of conventional furniture are to be reconciled with the circular plan of a typical tower-mill interior

Plate 41 The ruin of a brick-built tower mill at Ramsey, Cambridgeshire, before its conversion into a house; surviving windmills which have not yet been reused as dwellings have commonly descended to this level of dereliction

become more common. Many mills in low-lying country were built to power drainage pumps.

Although many windmills have been converted to domestic use, it is plain that there are distinct limitations on the opportunities for winning convenient living accommodation from these structures. A major constraint upon the straightforward re-use of a windmill as a dwelling is imposed by its circular or polygonal plan which tends to conflict with conventional cubical furniture and may only be reconciled satisfactorily with purpose-made, built-in fittings (Plate 40). The cylindrical rooms which are logically formed within the tower at several levels are usually of quite small diameter – indeed, decreasing diameter the nearer they are to the top of the tower. Windmills share these limitations with other cylindrical structures such as lighthouses and martello towers and these qualities have tended to cause most owners of these types of buildings to regard the tower form as only one element of a new house created from the salvaged structure, the remainder of the accommodation being a newly built extension which more suitably houses a spacious entrance hall, additional bedrooms and,

possibly, an attached garage. An example of such a conversion, in which the former windmill is only partly recognisable, has recently been completed at Ramsey, Cambridgeshire (Fig 54). However, it is only fair to add that, in this case, the surviving windmill structure was little more than a ruinous stone stump before conversion work began (Plate 41). Most owners of 're-cycled' windmills are also naturally disinclined to reinstate the wooden sail structures of their mills because of the considerable maintenance liability which is imposed by restoration of these complex and highly exposed features.

Watermills

Following the Romans' introduction of the geared watermill into England, many such mills were established – the Domesday Book lists 5,624 mills, although a good proportion of these would have been worked by horses or oxen rather than water. In the Middle Ages these mills were the property

Fig 54

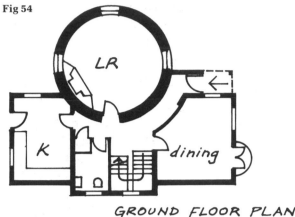

GROUND FLOOR PLAN

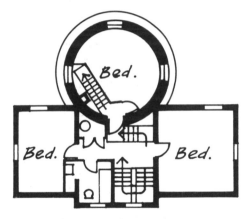

FIRST FLOOR PLAN

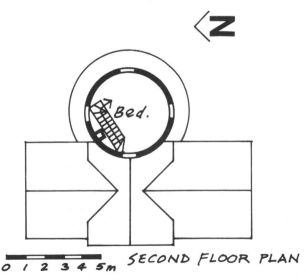

SECOND FLOOR PLAN

0 1 2 3 4 5m

of the lord of the manor who possessed 'soke rights', which meant that anyone growing corn on his manor was obliged to have it ground at the lord's mill because hand mills were outlawed. The miller would then deduct a proportion of the grain in payment for his services. As a result of the soke system, the medieval miller was often the subject of suspicion and distrust. The amount of toll-in-kind payable for the service of milling the grain varied according to region and period, but the average charge was one-sixteenth part of the grain by volume. No miller was allowed to buy or sell grain or flour except surplus toll corn until after the reign of Elizabeth I and although the influence of the soke began to wane during the seventeenth century, toll-in-kind was not replaced by a monetary charge until an act of 1796. Even then, old habits died hard, and at Wakefield, Yorkshire, one of the most important grain markets outside London, the milling soke was not finally abolished until 1853.

Arguments and local strife were often caused by the building of a new watermill because the necessary raising of weirs and cutting of races would affect the flow of water to other mills on the same stream. The number of mills that could work effectively on the same stream was limited, which led to smaller streams being used by means of building dams to create mill-ponds. In these smaller waters, the miller could work by day and his mill-pond would be replenished at night. Seasonal and tidal changes posed problems for mills situated on larger rivers. Waterwheels could not function at low water, so adjustable wheels were made. Installation of these devices proved costly and very few were used. The floating mill, moored to a bridge or pier in the cities, solved this problem, but in the country the miller had to moor in open stream and the grain had to be conveyed to him by boat. Use was also made of the power of the sea by constructing tidal mills along the coast. As these buildings were constantly threatened by storms and high tides, it was important to choose a sheltered position protected from gales. Several such mills have survived along the south coast of England on shores where the Isle of Wight gives protection from the prevailing south-westerly winds. Mills were often built on an estuary where

Plate 42 Lockyer's Mill, near Crewkerne, Somerset: an example of a working watermill; note the boarded lucarne, enclosing the sack hoist, which projects from the front roofslope and, to the left, the modern cylindrical metal silo for bulk storage of grain

the water could be trapped upstream at high tide by sluice gates. In other parts, a sea wall would be built at a suitable inlet to enclose a mill-pond. The miller's day was dictated by the movements of the tides because his source of power would only be available for short periods of two or three hours at a time.

Early waterwheels were made of wood, but as cast iron developed the miller made use of this new material for his machinery. Wooden wheels decay quickly with the cycle of immersion in and emergence from the water. Thus it is rare to find a wholly wooden wheel intact today. Cast-iron wheels were too expensive for the miller to install, so a hybrid construction emerged. The hub, bearings and rims of otherwise wooden wheels might be made of iron. Wheels made completely of iron began to be used during the eighteenth century. Each wheel was made in sections and assembled at the mill, paddles made of wood being retained. Iron fittings could replace wooden components gradually, allowing major alterations to take place over a long period. This atmosphere of making changes only slowly and of preferring a tried and tested 'free' source of power to more efficient engine-driven plant can be savoured at Lockyer's Mill, Clapton, near Crewkerne, Somerset, a mill of 1864 in which grain is still milled commercially by water power provided by the River Axe (Plate 42).

As well as milling corn, water-powered mills have been used for weaving and spinning. In Sheffield, until the 1930s, power from a waterwheel was even used to grind cutlery.

Textile Mills

When the mills of the North of England are referred to, we think immediately of the nineteenth-century factories which were built for the purpose of manufacturing yarn and textiles, rather than buildings containing corn-grinding machinery. The earliest textile mills were similar to the traditional water-powered flour mills because they consisted of load-bearing masonry external walls and wooden floors held up by timber posts or cast-iron columns and often occupied equally remote rural locations in order to exploit fully the power provided by the rushing streams of narrow Pennine valleys. With the introduction of steam power from the later eighteenth century, the necessity for a streamside location disappeared and, particularly in regard to cotton spinning, a climate of high humidity became a more important requirement. Hence the enormous success of Oldham, a hilly settlement in East Lancashire with considerable reserves of coal, situated only 11km (7 miles) from Manchester, the greatest yarn market in the world in the nineteenth and early twentieth centuries. By 1871, Oldham had more cotton-spinning spindles than any country in the world outside the USA and it maintained that position of superiority until 1937. At the peak of production, around three hundred cotton mills were concentrated on Oldham. A writer in an edition of the *Manchester City News* of 1908 recorded that such a vast hive of industry could overpower even a worldly-wise observer:

> the smoke of the innumerable tall chimneys lies over all like a poultice . . . houses and shops go on for ever, and at the back of them, blotting out all the rest of the world, rise great precipitous mills like frowning cliffs, at whose base are the small houses where the folks live like coneys at a mountain foot.

The cotton mill was essentially a container for machinery, simple in design and unfussy in appearance. Many multi-storey mills impressed – and continue to impress – by their sheer size. The basic dimension of a mill was its width which determined both the length and the height, and which was itself determined by the length of the cotton-spinning 'mule'. The increase in maximum width of these buildings from 30m (99ft) in 1868 to 48m (158ft) in 1905 was necessary in order to accommodate the longer mules which were enlarged to their technical optimum, consistent with rigidity, of 1,392 (116 dozen) spindles. These wider mills were thus squarer than their predecessors which had tended to be long and narrow. Consequently, it was necessary to introduce more daylight into the broader interiors and this became possible in the 1890s with the use of reinforced-concrete floors and steel girders. The arched window was allied to the brick jack-arch system often employed to achieve an incombustible floor construction and tended to produce an opening which was disproportionately high related to its width. In contrast, the square-headed window spanned by the steel beam of the new technology could have a width disproportionate to its height. Taken together with the replacement of the solid, load-bearing external walls by rows of brick piers flanking narrower infill panels, this development allowed the area of window relative to wall to increase to a maximum in the 1900s when the facades of mills became more glass than brick. Elevations were ultimately reduced to a matrix of concrete-encased steel beams and columns, the voids between which were filled with large, gridded, steel-framed windows surmounting low infill panels of brickwork.

Mills of the Oldham type were usually

five storeys high with a warehouse and conditioning room in the cellar. The most impressive interior space of the mill was the engine room, from which power was transmitted to each floor by means of a rope-race that used cotton ropes of local manufacture. This arrangement was adopted from the 1870s. Because raw cotton is an inflammable material, mills had to be made fireproof either in whole or part. The adoption of iron instead of wood for floor beams helped to achieve this aim. The sprinkler, invented in the USA in 1881, was a further safeguard against the dire effects of fire and its introduction into cotton mills produced the water towers which crown the main external staircases of many of the later mills. Internally, a hardwood floor surface helped to maintain an equable temperature, permitted work to be done in bare feet and simplified the recovery of waste cotton. In Oldham, and other towns of East Lancashire (but not in West Yorkshire where stone was plentiful), the chief constructional material was brick because it was cheaper than stone. At first bricks were made on site from abundant local clay. Later they were supplied by specialist brickmakers whose numbers increased greatly during the last quarter of the nineteenth century. Each mill was likely to require around 4 million bricks, 2 acres of glass and 2,200 tons of iron and steel. Mill-designing architects and mill builders avoided any superfluous decoration, dispensing with the external rendering and cornices between the storeys that would have been demanded by classical precedent. Often the sole ornament applied to mills was projecting angle piers and a small cornice near the top of the facade, surmounted by a 'blocking course' of bricks, although some very large mills built during the Edwardian period, when labour and materials were cheapest, display elaborate decorative brickwork.

It is apparent that the conversion to domestic use of a textile mill up to 48m (158ft) wide is likely to pose problems. Partly for this reason and partly because of slight local demand for living accommodation so markedly individualistic as apartments created in former textile factories (which may not be entirely free from unpleasant associations), only one or two of the smaller, older and picturesquely situated textile mills have, to date, been converted into dwellings.

Warehouses and Factories

The large urban or dockside warehouse is a building type strongly related to the grander grain and textile mills, not only because it often stored the raw materials or products processed by these latter buildings, but also in its constructional composition. The storage of grain or many bolts of cloth imposed loads upon the structures of these buildings almost as heavy as the machinery contained in the textile mills and therefore their construction had to be equally robust and similarly fireproof. Many cotton warehouses displaying gridded elevations reminiscent of those of the mills themselves were erected in central Manchester, 'Cottonopolis' in the period leading up to the start of World War I, and the later the building, the more elaborate and showy was the architecture. For the largest and most prominent buildings, located in that city's Whitworth Street area, colourful cladding of their steel skeletons with elaborately moulded glazed terracotta blocks was de rigueur. The conversion of one building of this confident era, Granby House of 1900, is the final project described in this chapter.

Following a series of projects in which it has been shown that mills and large warehouses may satisfactorily be converted into dwellings, some interest has been shown in the possibility of treating redundant factories similarly. A four-storey former clothing factory at Ipswich, Suffolk, has been converted into 103 flats, 24 of which are roof-top penthouses which were sold to leaseholders, the remaining 79 dwellings being 'fair rent' flats for council and housing association nominees. The cost of this project, which was completed in 1983, was almost £2 million. In Glasgow, the former Wylie and Lochhead Cabinet Works on Kent Road has been converted into a block of 196 flats for sale and its sumptuous Grade A listed stone-clad main elevation has been carefully restored. In the other main cities of Scotland, where most city-centre residents are flat-dwellers, tenements being the predomi-

nant residential building type, several other large commercial or industrial buildings have recently been converted into dwelling complexes. In Dundee, a former jute mill has been converted into 72 flats, while in Edinburgh a scheme at High Street/Bell Street is creating 172 flats in former bonded warehouses. A Glasgow 'suburb' is to witness a very large scheme involving the restoration of the five warehouses at Spiers Wharf, the terminus of the Glasgow branch

Plate 43 Watermill, East Sussex: the waterwheel and entrance elevations of the mill; the launder which accepts water from the mill-pond and ducts it on to the wheel below can be seen against the side elevation

of the Forth and Clyde Canal at Port Dundas, to create almost two hundred dwellings for sale.

However, apart from the pioneering Ipswich project and Glasgow's Kent Road Cabinet Works scheme, elsewhere in Britain little has yet been done to promote, or to try to demonstrate, the advantages of re-using redundant factories as dwellings. This may be because the 'classic' factories of the twentieth century tend to be low-rise, usually single-storey structures, built to very broad plans from cheap and impermanent materials. Consequently, they require radical alteration and major upgrading of their constructional envelopes, local environment and services to make them suitable for subdivision into saleable dwellings. To date, it appears that no developer has been prepared to challenge the accepted policy by retaining and adapting a low-rise factory structure for housing rather than choosing demolition and redevelopment.

Watermill, East Sussex

This building was erected in the nineteenth century and was the first mill on the site. A stream, which is a tributary of the River Ouse, was dammed to create a large mill-pond which feeds the waterwheel. The structure of the wheel remains alongside the north-west elevation of the mill, although the wooden paddles have entirely rotted away and it cannot be made to turn (Plate 43). A broad wheel of small diameter, it is of the overshot, pitch-back type and sits below a *launder*, or large iron tank, which accepts water from the *flume*, connected with the mill-pond, so that water is ducted on to the top of the wheel, causing it to rotate backwards. The benefit of this arrangement is that the wheel does not lose efficiency in the manner of the traditional overshot wheel which is continuously fighting backflow turbulence at its junction with the tailstream.

As in many early industrial buildings, the original layout of this mill was very simple. A large block of rectangular plan, containing all the mill machinery — axles, gearing, etc — adjoined the waterwheel. The construction of this block comprised a ground-storey brickwork plinth, perforated with a handful of windows where these were necessary to light the interior, surmounted by a timber-framed and boarded upper-storey structure, a third 'attic' storey being accommodated largely in the void formed

by the steep-sided pitched roof. From the gable of the south-west elevation projects a boarded *lucarne*, or sack hoist enclosure, a feature which is characteristic of many older flour mills. Because this main block is quite wide at more than 8m (26ft), and the considerable weight of stored grain and flour sacks had to be supported safely, the span of the floors between the flank walls was halved by introducing a central row of cylindrical cast-iron columns sited at approximately 2m (6½ft) intervals from front to rear. These columns support stout timber beams, on to which bear the joists, running parallel to the flank walls, that carry the boarded floors. This is the classic structural/constructional arrangement of the small watermill of lowland England. However, this mill differs from the simple prototype in having a brick-built outshot against its south-east elevation which was constructed to house an auxiliary steam-engine that would be brought into use during periods of drought. A prominent detached brick-built chimney served the engine and adjoins the north-east corner of the extension (Plate 44).

The present owners purchased the mill in 1976 after part of it had been used to house chickens and the mill-pond had been used for fish-farming. It had ceased to operate as a flour mill as early as 1938 and in the immediate post-war period it was used as a seed store. Thus it will be appreciated that the building was in a rather unkempt and neglected state when the present owners began to restore the structure in 1983. Prior to their purchase of the building, the owner of the adjoining mill house had made two attempts to obtain permission from the local authority to change the use of the mill from industrial premises into a dwelling, but it was only with the current owners' application of 1977 that planning permission for this change was granted.

The mill-pond was drained for a three-year period in order to allow some necessary excavation. Derelict pig-pens were demolished and a vast amount of chicken droppings had to be dug out and carted away. A goose paddock was transformed into the garden. Following the demolition of a wooden fuel-store lean-to that had adjoined the south-east elevation of the engine house, most of the restoration work

Plate 44 Watermill, East Sussex: the rear elevation seen reflected in the mill-pond and showing the brick-built outshot with its tall chimney that originally served the auxiliary steam engine; the chimney has been re-used to vent a domestic hearth

consisted of the replacement of decayed material. The pitched roof of the main block was re-tiled and large areas of the painted external weatherboarding (including the whole of the rear gable) were taken down and replaced with new material backed with a lining of bituminous felt to better exclude the wind.

The plan for converting the large volumes of the mill interior into living accommodation involved retaining the entrance into the lean-to engine house and using it as the main entrance to the building. The brick shell of this element could then accommo-

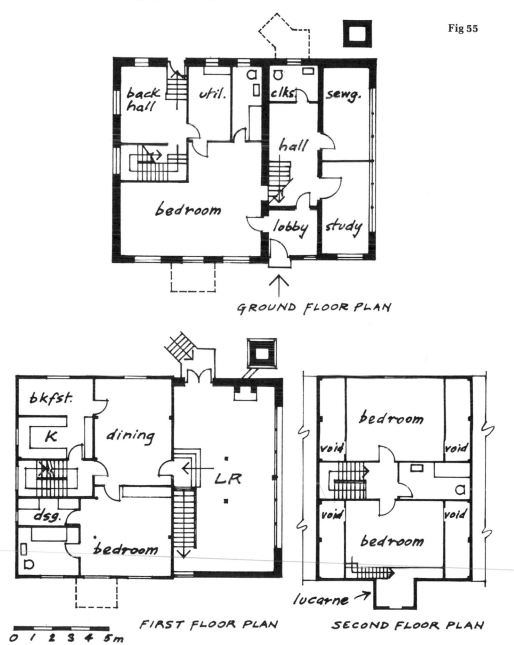

Fig 55

GROUND FLOOR PLAN

FIRST FLOOR PLAN

SECOND FLOOR PLAN

0 1 2 3 4 5m

date an entrance lobby, study, cloakroom, sewing-room and stair hall, giving access to the main first-floor living room, also entirely located in the engine-house outshot (Fig 55). To light this room it was necessary to introduce a range of large windows into the flank wall of the engine house, just below eaves level. More importantly, the existing upper floor of this outshot proved to be too close to the lean-to roof to give a habitable room-height, so rather than raise up the roof level of the entire extension, it was decided to reduce the level of the upper floor to create adequate headroom. Access to the dining room in the north-east corner of the main block was then made via a short flight of stairs. Beyond the dining-room, in the north-west corner of the main block, a breakfast/dining-room was located, separated from the bathroom and dressing room associated with the main bedroom, by a dog-leg staircase located at the centre of the north-west elevation (Fig 55). The lowest level of the main block accommodates the foot of the main stair with its related rear hall, a large L-plan bedroom with en suite bathroom and a utility room, while the top storey has been reserved for two more bedrooms and a further bathroom. Conversion of this space has yet to take place and the unlined timber skeleton of the boarded external-wall construction of the upper storeys remains on view to the interior, awaiting its insulation and internal finishes.

In consequence of its importance as a relic of local industrial archaeology, the mill has been listed as a building of architectural or historic interest (Grade II), a status which has not been jeopardised by the very careful treatment of the building by its present owners in their continuing programme of conversion and conservation.

Castle Mill, Dorking, Surrey

The existence of a mill on the site of Castle Mill, Dorking, is noted in the Domesday Book. It takes its name from Betchworth Castle, a medieval mansion that was altered in the seventeenth and eighteenth centuries, but is now a ruin. The original building (which can still be discerned today) was a simple block of rectangular plan adjoining a 'breast-shot' waterwheel, powered by a mill-stream fed from the River Mole. With the construction of the South Eastern Railway Company's nearby Reading–Tonbridge line in the mid-nineteenth century, an increase in trade for the mill was anticipated, and an extension, equal in height to the main block, was built on its south side. Naturally enough, the new, faster, mode of transport acted to reduce trade rather than to increase it and the mill suffered declining fortunes until it ceased to operate as a flour mill shortly after World War II. It became derelict rapidly, a picturesque feature of the local landscape, until the late 1960s (Plate 45). During this period it was recognised by the local planning authority as a building of considerable local importance, and, accordingly, was listed Grade II. The family who had owned and operated the mill continued to live in the imposing nearby mill house, but were unable to fund a restoration of the redundant mill, so that when a Repairs Notice was served on them by the local authority, they were obliged to sell the building. It was purchased by an architect, Michael Manser, in 1969, for what would now be regarded as a nominal sum.

At that time, Michael Manser lived and practised in South Kensington. He was anxious to obtain a weekend retreat close to London and the derelict mill promised conveniently located, characterful accommodation. His decision to purchase the mill heralded the start of a thorough and extensive process of restoration. The construction of Castle Mill consists of a brickwork plinth, surmounted by timber-framed and weather-boarded upper storeys, and an attractive mansard roof capped its blocky form. It is easy to see that this was a practical means of enclosing a large volume which then could be used for the storage of grain, and the profile is reminiscent of the gambrel-roofed hay barns of the USA. This treatment contributes to the quality of verticality and stateliness which characterises the building, soaring above the tail-race of the mill-stream (Plate 46).

The essential structure of the mill – both masonry and timberwork – was found to be very sound. Even the boarded cladding was in need of only piecemeal repair rather than wholesale renewal. The slate roof was treated

Plate 45 Castle Mill, Dorking, Surrey: the derelict mill before conversion work began at the end of the 1960s

similarly, although the need to install central heating meant that the roof ridge at the junction of the main block with the nineteenth-century extension had to be punctuated by a new chimney. Internally, the existing building incorporated floors on seven levels because the floor levels of the Victorian extension did not ally with those of the original block. As the majority of the mill machinery remained – waterwheel, axle, pit wheel, 'wallower', power shaft and millstones – and these components were chiefly situated in the lowest storey, Michael Manser decided to retain most of these items in a 'set piece' display, reminding visitors of the mill's former function, and visible from the generous entrance hall of the house through a glass door (Fig 56). An existing external door was re-used as the main entrance and the new straight-flight stair, giving access to the first-floor living-rooms, was located on the site of the former upper storeys' access ladder. The rest of the ground floor, occupying the Victorian extension of the main block, converted satisfactorily into a garage, boiler room and tankroom for oil storage once the existing timber floor of this section had been replaced by a concrete slab. Below this new slab it was practical to install a sewage

collection chamber of 1,818 litres (400 gal) capacity, associated with a macerator and pump, allowing waste to be reduced and then pumped through a small-diameter pipe to a private sewer manhole 150m (492ft) away. All new soil stacks installed in the building discharged into this sealed sub-floor collection chamber.

At first-floor level, the volume of the main block allowed the inclusion of a large stair hall, kitchen/breakfast-room and dining-room en suite with a 'gazebo' formed from the original outshot that projected over the waterwheel. An attempt was made to preserve a sense of the large, formerly unitary space of the mill's second storey which had had to be subdivided to create the dining- and food preparation rooms, by 'unifying' the stair hall and dining-room through very large sliding doors which formed the end panels of the dining-room rear wall. In normal circumstances, these full-height panels would be slid back to ensure a 'flow' of space up the straight-flight stair from the entrance hall, through the first-floor stair hall and into the dining-room. To satisfy the

Plate 46 Castle Mill, Dorking, Surrey: the mill following its conversion into a dwelling and the restoration of the waterwheel

demands of the local authority's building inspector, who was not happy with this lack of fire compartmentation in a single-staircase building incorporating many levels, these sliding doors were tensioned against counterweights so that in the event of a fire, fusible links in the cables restraining the counterweights would melt, causing the weights to drop and drawing the doors closed. This area of the first floor had housed four millstones as well as the upper section of the power shaft. The architect-owner decided to retain one of these stones as well as the timber shaft and these features make a prominent contribution to the character of the dining-room.

From the first-floor accommodation of the main block, and to the front of a brick-built hearth serving the new chimney flue, the slightly raised floor of the Victorian extension, reached via a pair of steps and through double doors, provided the site for the drawing-room. The loading door formerly incorporated in the east elevation of the extension was replaced by a large fixed window of plate glass. The second floor could then become the bedrooms level. A further single-flight stair, in this instance incorporating winding treads at its base, discharges on to the large second-floor landing, off which radiate all four bedrooms (Fig 56). Because, at this level, the floor of the extension is considerably higher than the floor of the main block, the master bedroom is reached from this landing via a flight of five stairs. Extension of this elevated level into the south-west corner of the main block allowed an en suite bathroom to be attached to the master bedroom. The subdivision of the remaining, very large volume of the third storey of the main block into three further bedrooms and a bathroom was accomplished by installing new timber-framed partitions, cranked on plan, which thus provided built-in wardrobes for all the secondary bedrooms. From the second-floor landing, a ladder-like stair, more steeply raked than those serving the lower floors, leads up to a large loft, wholly accommo-

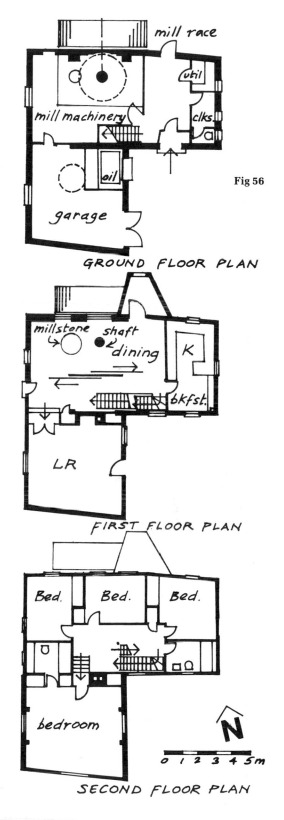

Fig 56

GROUND FLOOR PLAN

FIRST FLOOR PLAN

SECOND FLOOR PLAN

0 1 2 3 4 5m

dated in the roof space of the main block, which was not exploited as living accommodation in the original conversion scheme.

Michael Manser sold Castle Mill soon after its conversion was complete and since that time it has had two further owners, the first of whom installed a lift linking the ground-floor entrance hall with the first-floor dining-room, the generous volume of which has been somewhat reduced by the intrusion of the lift shaft into its south-east corner. The flow of space between dining-room and first-floor stair hall so valued by the Mansers was shunned by the succeeding owner who replaced the large sliding doors and fixed centre panel with a conventional solid partition incorporating a hinged access door. Some further windows were added, puncturing the weatherboarded exterior and tending to reduce the opacity of the walls which is so characteristic of simple and strong early industrial buildings.

The third set of owners since the mill's 'reincarnation' extended the living accommodation into the former storage loft contained by the roof. They were also watermill enthusiasts and continued the work of restoration that was begun by Michael Manser by restoring the waterwheel to working condition. The elm paddles of the iron wheel were renewed and the mechanism was modified to operate on the 'undershot' principle because a lowering of water levels brought about by a local flood alleviation scheme made impracticable the restoration of the original 'breast-shot' arrangement. The great care taken by Michael Manser to conserve the majority of the existing building in his scheme for its conversion was recognised in European Architectural Heritage Year 1975 when he received a Civic Trust Heritage Year Award for the restoration and adaptation of Castle Mill.

Thames Tunnel Mills, Rotherhithe, London SE16

The story of the conversion of Thames Tunnel Mills at Rotherhithe on the south bank of the River Thames in central London provides a clear contrast to the foregoing accounts of the renovation of traditional water-powered, corn-grinding mills in Surrey and Sussex. Thames Tunnel Mills is, in fact, two buildings, which together formed a warehouse and flour mill. The western half of the block was a six-storey flour mill of around 1850. Internally, a grid of cast-iron cruciform-plan columns supported massive timber beams bearing joisted and boarded floors. The eastern half was a warehouse, a storey higher than the mill and built later, around 1890. Steel beams and columns supported its intermediate floors. The building was in use for its original purpose until the early 1960s, but by the time it was acquired for conversion into dwellings in 1977, it had lain empty for more than ten years and was decaying rapidly because the upper floors and roof covering of the mill had been destroyed in a fire.

At that time, the building could have been said to typify the dereliction of the whole London docks area. In the post-war period, these districts had undergone precipitous decline from their pre-war position as thriving communities servicing the world's largest port. Consequently, much demolition of 'life-expired' riverside wharves and warehouses was occurring. Many acres of land were cleared to await future development and there were few places either north or south of the river where a group of traditional waterside commercial buildings remained. Fortunately, Thames Tunnel Mills adjoins the handsome early-eighteenth century church of St Mary, Rotherhithe, so that when the Department of the Environment designated the church and the surrounding buildings as an outstanding conservation area, the building became eligible for grant aid from the Historic Buildings Council and their help was crucial to the funding of the development.

The scheme of conversion was designed to provide fair rent accommodation for 118 mainly young, single, local people, either in bedsitters or flats which two or four people would share. Seventy-one flats were created. Such provision was thought to be important in a borough where the majority of housing is in local authority estates with little provision for single people. The scheme was innovatory in providing housing at controlled rents in a converted building on a spectacular riverside site, something which previously had been regarded as the preserve of affluent owner occupiers. Although the flats are very compact, generally following the standards laid down for this type of housing in DoE Design Bulletin 29, they share the facilities of a jetty on to the river, and a roof-top conservatory and roof garden, all of which were made possible by a £200,000 grant from the Historic Buildings Council. These are features additional to the normal provision in this type of housing.

The brief for the architects, Hunt Thompson Associates, from their housing association client, was to explore the suitability of the building for conversion into flats, subject to the standards and cost limits laid down by the Housing Corporation and the Department of the Environment. It was immediately apparent that the main challenge to the ingenuity of the designers was the considerable width of the building, which, at 20m (66ft), was more than double the dimension usually found in residential buildings. It followed that it would be sensible to locate elements not needing daylight – stairs, lifts and corridors – in the interior of the building. Kitchens, bathrooms and entrance lobbies to flats could also be placed internally. As every flat needs to have these service spaces, and such spaces occupy a fixed minimum area in a flat of any size, it made sense to maximise this internal accommodation in order to utilise fully the broad interior, and this was achieved by making the majority of flats one-bedroom or bedsitter units. The advantages of adopting this planning policy informed the decision that the development should be primarily for single people.

Although it was beneficial both to optimal planning and the creation of much-needed accommodation to maximise the number of rooms that could be sited internally, the aggregation of these spaces was still inadequate to 'fill up' the middle of the broad interior, and in the flour-mill section of the building the residual central space was devoted to a full-height internal courtyard or 'atrium' which rises through seven storeys to terminate in a glass-roofed conservatory (Plate 47).

In the centre of the plan of the eastern half of the building, the original grain-storage

Plate 47 Thames Tunnel Mills, London SE1: the central 'atrium' showing the flats' access galleries faced with salvaged timber beams

silo structure of the warehouse was retained for use as a lift, staircase and refuse chute (Fig 58). Corridors giving access to the flats in this half wrap around three sides of the silo and are extended as galleries, supported by timber beams and cast-iron columns, salvaged from the original internal structure, to enclose the atrium, which allows daylight to penetrate down to every floor of the building. Grouped around the bottom of the atrium are a common room giving access to a riverside terrace, a laundry and the caretaker's office and flat (Fig 57). At the top of the

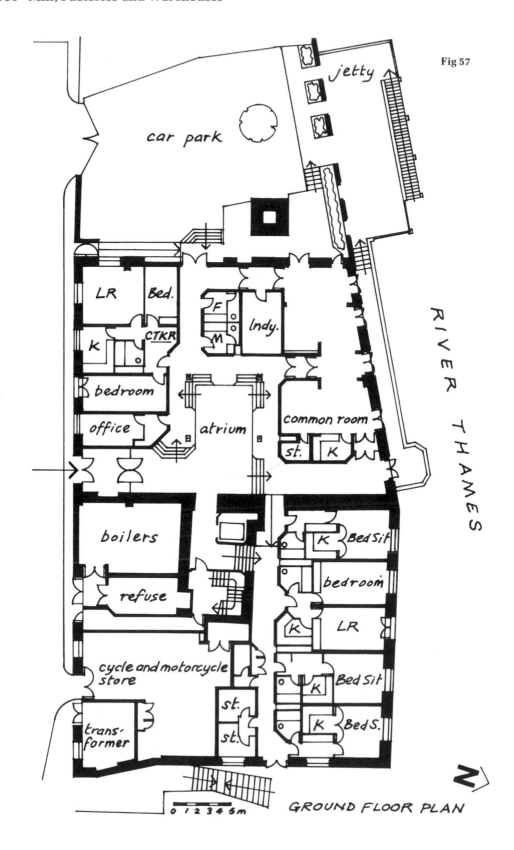

Fig 57

GROUND FLOOR PLAN

0 1 2 3 4 5m

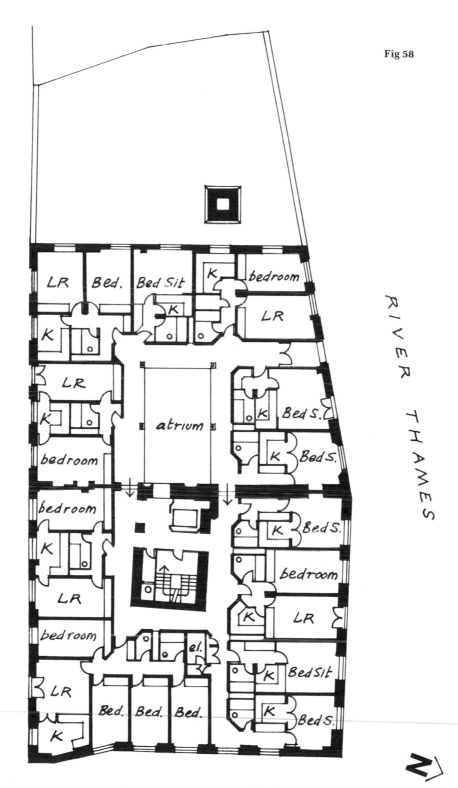

Fig 58

FIRST FLOOR PLAN

0 1 2 3 4 5m

Plate 48 Thames Tunnel Mills, London SE1: the rooftop conservatory at the head of the atrium

atrium, the pitched-roof-profile roof-light was made larger than was strictly necessary in order to provide a conservatory complete with tropical plants (Plate 48) which leads out on to a landscaped roof garden capping the western half of the building.

It is clear that some provision of communal rooms is important in the conversion of old buildings to multiple occupation, and consistent with other comparable projects analysed in this book, the common room of Thames Tunnel Mills is logically located at ground-floor level. However, the architects' view is that this communal aspect of the building is most clearly expressed architecturally by the central atrium, a space overlooked by the lift lobbies and the galleries of each upper floor that give access to the flats.

The difficulties encountered in negotiat-

ing all the necessary approvals, particularly the funding, for a scheme which departed from the norm of fair rent housing explain the exceptionally long period of four years that preceded commencement of the building contract. A major problem that arose at an early stage was the reconciliation of the local authority's requirements for one car-parking space per flat with the DoE's refusal to fund a scheme in which the entire ground floor would be used for parking. A compromise was eventually negotiated in which the space to the west of the building, originally planned as a garden, was devoted instead to a car park and to compensate for this loss of amenity, the Historic Buildings Council then agreed to pay for the provision of the jetty and roof garden. When the Housing Corporation refused to contribute to the cost of these features, the HBC relaxed its general policy of contributing only 50 per cent of the cost of eligible items and met the full cost.

The condition of the original internal structures of the existing buildings was so bad that cost studies showed that, as well as offering higher standards of fire and sound insulation, the provision of an entirely new structure within the retained shell of the building would be cheaper than a process of repairing and upgrading the surviving framing. This policy of renewal was effected by installing a replacement internal structure of load-bearing brick walls and in situ concrete floors. A consequence of this decision could have been the creation of evidence that the project was merely an exercise in 'façadism' – the policy of retaining only the external skin of a building as a 'screen wall' to new accommodation, which often creates a disagreeable distinction between the 'stage set' of the preserved shell and the entirely rebuilt interior. In order to avoid this 'skin deep' quality, in the central atrium the brickwork of the original party wall between the buildings has been preserved at the eastern end of this space to the full height and width of the block. Similarly, by re-using salvaged beams and columns to 'frame' the atrium, a character has been given to this space which is evocative of the interior of the original building, yet does not mock its new use.

All circulation spaces within the building

— corridors, galleries, staircases and lift lobbies – have been designed so as to exploit the brick-built elements of the original structure. Elsewhere, new brickwork flanking circulation spaces and certain living-rooms has been painted and in every flat at least one wall-panel of the original brickwork is left exposed.

Efforts to retain the character of the original building externally extended to a decision not to clean the brickwork. Repair and repointing work was kept to a minimum and new pointing was carefully matched to the colour of the original joints. Features such as cranes, loading bays and the 25m (83ft) high free-standing chimney were retained and the original windows were replaced with steel casements of similar pattern (Plate 49). The importance of maintaining the relationship between the building and the river was expressed not only in the provision of the boat jetty, which is linked to the common room, but also in the balconies, connected to the main circulation galleries of every floor, which overlook the water. Clearly, all flats located in the northern part

Plate 49   Thames Tunnel Mills, London SE1: the two blocks of the building, the rooftop conservatory and the freestanding former boiler-house chimney, seen from the north bank of the Thames; the church of St Mary, Rotherhithe, is seen on the right

of the building enjoy views both up and down the river, because the building is located in a concave curve of the Thames. Several flats have living rooms in which the loading-bay doors of the original warehouse have been converted into fully glazed French windows sited behind simple steel railings.

The contract for the construction of a residential development wholly or partly funded by the Housing Corporation may be awarded to a builder only if he submits the most favourable tender in competition. Thus, when Hunt Thompson Associates had completed the technical information, six contractors were invited to submit tenders for the reconstruction of Thames Tunnel Mills on a fluctuating price basis. When these offers were received, it was apparent that the lowest tender considerably exceeded the cost acceptable to the Housing Corporation, who insisted that savings of £170,000 should be made before this lowest price could be accepted. The architects duly made economies, although they were dismayed that these had to include the reduction to a dwarf wall of the high wall intended for the street side of the car park because they felt that the omission of a high wall at this point would detract from the character of Rotherhithe Street. However, the Housing Corporation refused to fund this item. The Historic Buildings Council was unable to increase its grant to pay for this work and it was only because of the intervention of the chairman of the planning committee that an exceptional grant to cover the extra cost was obtained from Southwark Council. At an earlier stage the council had accepted the architects' proposal to replace the chain-link fencing around the adjacent churchyard with cast-iron railings of period appearance. These were installed under a separate contract and Hunt Thompson Associates' supervision, and they have considerably improved the appearance of the conservation area.

The tender submitted by J. L. Eve Construction Ltd, was reduced to £2,024,681 after making economies, and this figure was accepted in November 1980. Work commenced on site in January 1981 with an anticipated contract period of 104 weeks. Practical completion of the project was ultimately achieved in March 1984. The resultant cost per square metre of gross floor area was £401.62.

The common areas of the building are maintained to an immaculate standard by the resident caretaker and a small team of cleaners – there is no evidence of abuse of staircases, lifts or corridors as is apparent in many local authority or other housing association schemes. Reflecting the great care taken by the architects to conserve and enhance the qualities of this former industrial building as a significant element in the metropolitan riverside scene, the project has received several awards, including a DoE Housing Design Award and a Civic Trust Award, both of which were presented in 1985.

'The Old Wharf', Arun Navigation Terminus Warehouse, Billingshurst, West Sussex

The River Arun, from Littlehampton on the English Channel to Pulborough in West Sussex, has been navigable since the seventeenth century. The upper reaches of the river remained unnavigable until, in the late eighteenth century, it was decided to construct a parallel canal, drawing water from the river, from Newbridge near Billingshurst to Pallingham Quay, above Pulborough, where the canal would join the river. This project was promoted by Lord Egremont who wished to improve the condition of local agriculture by upgrading transport facilities. A terminus wharf was established at Newbridge.

In 1816, the logical extension of this waterway to join the waters of the Wey Navigation, about 26km (16 miles) to the north, and hence to establish an inland navigation between London and the English Channel, was completed with the opening of the Wey and Arun Junction Canal, whose main sponsor was again the second Lord Egremont. Traffic carried by the new trunk waterway thus increased beyond the volume of goods which had been conveyed along the old cul-de-sac Arun Navigation and it was necessary to extend the waterside storage buildings that had been established at Newbridge. Hence, in 1839, the Arun Navigation Company erected a substantial brick-built warehouse on the Newbridge site and this wharf quickly became a busy centre for the collection and conveyance of agricultural produce from the Billingshurst area until competition from the newly constructed railway robbed the canal of most of its traffic in the late 1860s. Thereafter the canal went rapidly into decline. The Wey and Arun Junction Canal was formally closed in 1871, leaving Newbridge Wharf as the terminus it had been before construction of this waterway, until the closure of the Arun Navigation in 1888.

Following the demise of the canal, the old wharf buildings found a new use as hay barns for the adjoining farm. The buildings

Plate 50 The Old Wharf, Billingshurst, West Sussex: the terminus warehouse before the work of restoration and conversion began

continued to be used for this purpose until the mid-1980s when an enterprising manager of a local farm realised that something could be done to salvage the structures for a more profitable use.

Not until recently did the West Sussex County Council wish to encourage the development of tourist-related activities in parts of the county other than the Channel coast, but a change in policy, provoked by the recognition of the potential of the rural hinterland for attracting tourists, allowed the new owner of the wharf warehouse to contemplate its conversion into a guest house and family dwelling because the project became eligible for grant aid from the English Tourist Board. The warehouse had suffered considerably from the neglect associated with its low-grade use as a hay barn and was little more than a 'masonry shell devoid of weather-tight windows and doors when the work of conversion commenced. Large trees had rooted in the canal bank below its east wall, obscuring its impressive waterside location (Plate 50). Internally, some evidence of the building's commercial use remained – notably the shaft and pulleys of a large wooden rope-hauled hoist, sited close to the apex of the roof space, which the present owner has carefully restored and integrated into the building as a relic of its former use. This was possible because the topmost floor of the two-and-a-half storey building is entirely in the roof space, obtains all its daylight from a new roof-light and therefore cannot be used easily for habitable accommodation. It is reserved for use as a children's play area.

The first floor accommodates the bedrooms for the guests – each bedroom being paired with an en suite bathroom – together with sleeping accommodation for the proprietor and his family, while the ground floor includes a large guests' lounge, TV room and breakfast room to the east of the main entrance/staircase hall. To the west of this space lies the guests' dining-room, a large kitchen incorporating a dining area for the family, a pantry, living-room, utility room and small office adjoining the secondary entrance (Fig 59). Also included in this

Fig 59

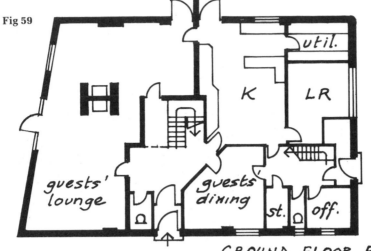

GROUND FLOOR PLAN

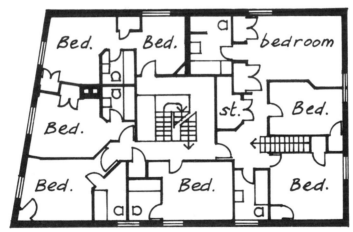

FIRST FLOOR PLAN

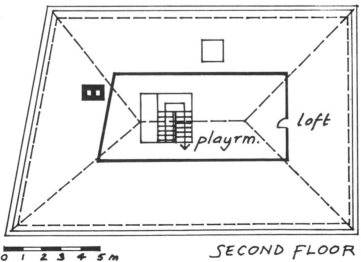

SECOND FLOOR PLAN

0 1 2 3 4 5m

'private' section of the building is a straight-flight staircase which leads up from the small hall containing the secondary entrance to serve the family's first-floor sleeping accommodation.

Plate 51 The Old Wharf, Billingshurst, West Sussex: the south elevation of the warehouse during the conversion work showing the natural finish of the new windows and doors, the roof-light straddling the roof ridge and the new chimney stack

The architects, Derek Irvine Associates, were obliged to locate the main 'public' staircase at the centre of the plan with light flooding in through the roof-light which straddles the roof ridge above, because the considerable width of the building – 11.4m (37ft) – necessitated some means of introducing light into the middle if gloomy internal corridors were to be avoided.

Considerable care has been taken to retain a 'period' appearance in the building. The existing roof covering was completely stripped and the rafters were brush-cleaned. Glass-fibre quilt insulation was laid between them and, following the application of roofing felt, new timber roofing battens were fixed to accept the sound slates which had been salvaged from the original construction. Only small quantities of imported second-hand slates were needed to supplement the re-used material. A brick-built chimney had to be integrated into the reconstituted roof and new lead flashings were provided to reconcile this feature, as well as the added roof window, soil vent pipes and roof-light, with the roof surfaces. Repairs to the existing masonry were carried out in matching brickwork and the purpose-made joinery of new windows and external doors has been retained in its natural colour under a clear sealant, rather than being painted, which might have detracted from the mellow textures of the renovated building (Plate 51). To furnish the interior authentically, the owner sought out period items – panelled doors, chimney pieces, etc – from local buildings that were to be demolished and installed them in appropriate positions. Various panels of brickwork have been left exposed rather than plastered over, and the original heavy timber floor beams generally continue to project down below ceilings.

Outside, equal care has been taken to ensure a picturesque setting for the restored building by removing most of the jungly vegetation which formerly swathed the canal banks, dredging the canal and regrading the banks so that guests are greeted with a pleasant prospect from the ground-floor

Plate 52 The Old Wharf, Billinghurst, West Sussex: the canalside elevation of the warehouse at the conclusion of the rebuilding work

lounge and the 'wharfside' location of the building is appreciated (Plate 52). The owner wished to reconstruct the wharf structure which had disappeared since the active days of the waterway, but no drawings or photographs of this feature could be found.

The restoration of the warehouse and the adjoining 457m (500yd) length of canal is viewed with enthusiasm by the Wey and Arun Canal Trust, a society which has worked since the early 1970s for the complete restoration of the Arun Navigation and the Wey and Arun Junction Canal between Pallingham and the River Wey, and which has restored the opportunity for navigation to several stretches of these waterways.

Granby House, Granby Row, Manchester

Granby House is a seven-storey building of 1908 which was built as a cotton warehouse. Its outside walls are largely of pressed red brick, although there is a plinth and decorative band courses at various levels, carried out in Portland stone (Plate 53). It is in the heart of Manchester, but for many years industry and commerce have been moving away from the city centre, increasing the risk that only a lifeless core will be left. The city council recognises the need to re-inject life into the potentially deserted central area, particularly after business hours, and it is considered that there is no surer means of achieving this aim than by encouraging young people to live in the city centre again. Before the conversion of Granby House, it was not clear how this could be done without incurring enormous expense.

A local housing association believed that the conversion of an existing building into an attractive block of flats would assist the process of regenerating the city centre, provided a sound building could be obtained cheaply. After several previous attempts, the Northern Counties Housing Association found and converted Granby House into

flats with the help of an Urban Development Grant. Northern Counties is a large housing association, with its headquarters in Manchester, which has specialised in fair rent and shared ownership housing schemes. In recent years, when there have been reductions in public funding for housing associations, it has been developing an increasing proportion of properties for sale in order to maintain and expand its activities. The association wished to be involved in a major city-centre conversion but needed to be sure that the selected project would succeed.

The essence of the association's idea was to develop flats for sale and this would make it possible to bring in private institutional finance – eg from a building society which might then become involved in providing mortgages for the individual purchasers. It is noteworthy that this type of conversion scheme was becoming fashionable in London, but the great difference was that flat prices in the capital were, and remain, very much higher than those applying in Manchester. However, in the latter city, building costs were almost as high as those of London, so some form of subsidy was necessary. It was believed that an Urban Development Grant might meet this need and Manchester City Council agreed to support the association's application for this form of government assistance. On the private sector side, the Nationwide Building Society were interested in participating. This left one further matter to be resolved. The development of housing for sale with the use of private funding cannot be carried out by a registered housing association, so a non-registered housing association – Northern Counties Provident Housing Association – had to be set up. While these arrangements were being formulated, the developer was looking for a suitable building.

Granby House is listed Grade II and stands within the Whitworth Street Conservation Area. Following its use as a cotton warehouse, the building had been the headquarters of a mail-order company and ended its commercial career accommodating the offices of a number of small businesses. It was the fourth building in the area that the association considered for conversion and had studied in detail. Selecting the optimum building and obtaining it on satisfactory

terms are matters of great importance where institutional finance is involved. In each case, the association had commissioned structural surveys, followed by feasibility and market studies. Indications of the purchase price of each building were obtained and full funding proposals were prepared. Although conversion of each of the first three buildings considered was potentially viable, all three failed one or more tests of the practicality/viability analysis. When Granby House came on to the market early in 1983, it looked more promising. It was in good condition, its shape and window arrangement made the formation of a central light-well unnecessary, and the city council were keen to prevent it from falling into long-term disuse. However, the Regional Development Officer of the housing association insisted on carrying out the same thorough appraisal of its potential that had been applied to the previous buildings. Consequently, an architect and builder were invited to prepare and cost a conversion scheme. The association's own quantity surveyor and marketing department made detailed investigations. On the basis of a building purchase price of £200,000, the total cost of the project would be £1 million, or about £16,000 per flat. The average selling price for a one-bedroom flat in Manchester was reckoned to be around £11,000 at that time (in contrast to at least £25,000 in London).

The prices being asked for vacant buildings in Manchester were quite high, being based on 'hope value' rather than use value. After much negotiation, the association was obliged to pay a purchase price of £210,000 for Granby House at the end of 1983. The Nationwide Building Society agreed to put up £703,000 at 2 per cent above their normal rates because of the experimental nature of the scheme. Manchester City Council supported an application for an Urban Development Grant of £300,000.

At this point, the builder on whose estimate the scheme was based went into

liquidation, so a new contractor had to be found. It was decided to enter into a fixed price 'design and build' contract with a major firm and to appoint an external project manager to oversee the building work. It was felt that these arrangements would lessen the risk of the association being drawn into difficulties if anything else went wrong. Following a tender competition, the offer from Fairclough Building Ltd was chosen, but the cost had now risen to almost £1.3 million, partly because of the imposition of VAT on building operations in the 1984 budget. Because Granby House was a listed building, the contractor eventually became exempt from this tax, but as he could not reclaim any VAT he had already paid to suppliers, he had to pass most of it on to the developer.

The increase in cost also necessitated a fresh application for Urban Development Grant. The Nationwide Building Society felt that they could not increase their investment because it was linked to unchanged valuations and therefore the new ratio of public to private funds had to be higher than before, even though the housing association was prepared to invest some of its own resources. £601,000 was applied for, including a contingency sum of £50,000. In the event, only £575,000 of this grant was taken up. It took several months to obtain approval and construction work started only in August 1984.

The fact that the building is listed limited the opportunities for external alterations, and internal layouts had to respect existing window locations (Fig 60). It was possible to leave untouched the greater part of the existing structure. The general construction is of brick external walls with a central masonry spine wall running from front to back. The building is covered by a reinforced concrete roof of mansard profile, which houses the seventh storey. The structure of the open warehouse floors consisted of cast-iron columns supporting steel, iron or heavy timber beams. On these members 75mm (3in) thick pine floorboards are fixed, performing a structural function as well as providing a floor surface sufficiently substantial to resist the heavy loads imposed by stored textiles. The structural alterations consisted of the removal of the

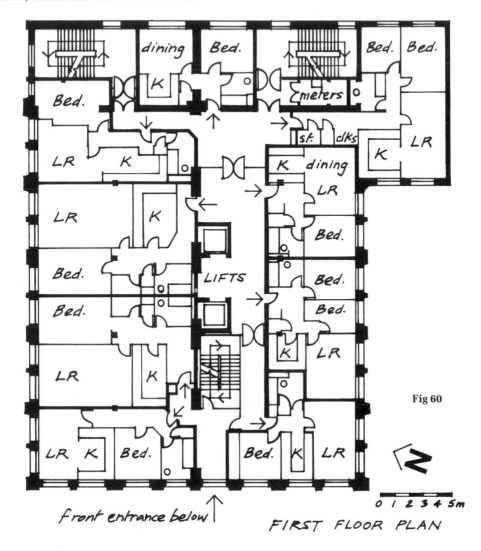

Fig 60

front entrance below↑

FIRST FLOOR PLAN

0 1 2 3 4 5m

existing goods lifts, the addition of two passenger lifts and the formation of various internal doorways in existing internal masonry.

The architects, John Cottam Partnership, found space for 61 flats, comprising 50 one-bedroom and 11 two-bedroom dwellings. The enclosure of individual flats within the large open floor spaces was achieved with the use of metal-stud and plasterboard partitions. Metal-framed suspended ceilings were installed throughout, two layers of 'fireline' board being incorporated at ceiling level in order to provide a one-hour period of fire resistance between storeys. The partitions contain sound insulation and thermal insulation to the level required for inclusion

of projects in the Electricity Board's Civic Shield Award Scheme. All dwellings and the hot water system are heated using off-peak electricity.

The flats were sold on 125-year leases and priority was given to first-time buyers. Owing to the delays that had occurred since the marketing studies were made in 1983 and because of the attractiveness of the finished scheme, it was found that considerably higher prices could be obtained for the flats than had been originally foreseen. Most of the apartments were sold quite quickly, raising a total of £1.1 million. Even so, this did not cover the full cost of the project, confirming that some form of subsidy was essential.

9 Transport and Service Buildings

Buildings for the public utilities – gas, electricity, telecommunications and water supply – are logically considered together with transport buildings because they all support services to the general public. The most familiar buildings of the statutory undertakers – power stations and gasworks – are perhaps generally too large or too highly specialised to be considered for conversion into dwellings, although the continuous monitoring of the performance of electricity-generating stations ensures the regular relegation of the oldest stations from the efficiency 'league table' as each new plant is commissioned, and this process is constantly producing redundant sites and buildings for sale and redevelopment. The only building which has been excepted from this apparently inexorable progression from redundancy to demolition is Battersea Power Station in central London, where its status as a listed building has ensured that it can be considered as suitable accommodation for an urban 'theme park'.

The gas industry's permanent buildings have usually been more related to the storage of its products than to the accommodation of staff or raw materials and it is clear that the traditional gas-holder functions as well in storing natural gas as it did in housing the locally manufactured town gas of yester-year. It is equally plain that these structures are not 'malleable' buildings, susceptible to easy conversion, and it is hard to see how any future redundancy of this plant can offer opportunities for its conversion into dwellings. In the same way, existing tele-communications buildings are proving to be readily adaptable to new technology and unless miniaturisation of equipment causes space demands to be much reduced, it is unlikely that large numbers of former tele-phone service buildings will be offered to private buyers. A more promising possi-bility for the release of former public utilities buildings for conversion lies in the 1990 privatisation of the regional water boards. Many of the industry's more marginal sites have already been disposed of and it is likely that further waterworks buildings will be sold, posing a new challenge because the ease with which they may be converted to domestic use will be constrained by demands for the careful conservation of structures which were once significant cultural symbols. Some build-ings which naturally form part of the estate of the water supply industry – namely, water storage towers – have already been restored for re-use as dwellings and one such project is described in this chapter.

A natural element of as much significance as the water contained in storage towers is fire and this phenomenon has produced its own service buildings in the form of fire stations. The smaller 'parish' buildings which were erected to house the horse-drawn steam-powered mobile pumps often became redundant through changes in the organisation of the county fire brigades or their inability to house modern motorised appliances. The conversion of such a 'village' station in North London is described later in order to illustrate the possibilities that buildings of this type may offer for con-version into a clutch of small dwellings.

This chapter concentrates on such build-ings of modest size which have been 're-cycled' as individual houses or pairs of dwellings. Among transport buildings, a prime candidate for such treatment in the years since World War II and, more par-ticularly, since the 'Beeching Report' of 1963, has been the country railway station.

Railway Buildings

Railway buildings, be they termini, inter-mediate stations, goods sheds or locomotive depots, provide some of the first examples of primarily functional industrial buildings, tailor-made for a specific purpose. Therefore it is particularly remarkable that, in recent years, they have been shown to be readily adaptable to a wide range of uses. As well as houses, conversions of railway buildings accommodate offices, restaurants, pubs, clubs, factories, workshops, art galleries, shops, field centres and indoor sports facilities. A full survey of railway conversions in Britain has not yet been carried out. However, in 1976 it was stated in parliament that since the 1963 report 'The Reshaping of British Rail', 3,539 railway stations had been closed to traffic, of which 1,570 had been sold. Responses to an earlier questionnaire sent to county planning officers in order to elicit the nature of planning permissions granted for change of use of railway buildings showed that conversion to dwellings emerged as the most common category (38 per cent of successful applications in the sample).

One of the obstacles encountered by potential purchasers when attempting to pursue such proposals has been the attitude of the vendor, British Rail. In many cases, an abnormally high price demand emerged in response to enquiries, resulting in buildings remaining unsold, inviting vandalism and structural deterioration to the extent that, ultimately, no one was prepared to buy them. Artificially protracted negotiations or simple procrastination on the part of the vendor turn assets into liabilities and frighten off potential purchasers.

Despite such significant obstacles, many owners have persevered and numerous stations have been converted into houses – this applies to stations on lines that are still in use as well as to those that have closed. Many small stations were designed in such a way that they resemble cottages, so conversion has involved virtually no external alterations. However, other former stations are hardly recognisable as such, platforms having disappeared and track-beds having been filled in. In at least one instance, the owner of a former railway station has even created a swimming pool in the track-bed, using the platform edges as retaining walls. Consistent with the general philosophy of this book, it is not proposed to deal with projects where a complete metamorphosis

of the building has been brought about; fanciful transformations of stations and other railway buildings have been omitted in favour of those which retain, in a coherent way, a sense of the character and purpose of the former working premises.

Characteristics of Small Railway Stations

The vast majority of station buildings were constructed during the nineteenth century. They were the product of numerous independent companies, each of which erected stations reflecting its financial state, its ambitions and the taste of the architects it employed. The station-building era has extended over a 150-year period which has seen the introduction of new building materials and many changes in architectural fashions, so it is not surprising to find evidence of these developments in the enormous diversity of railway station architecture.

Soon after the inception of passenger services on the new 'iron road', it became apparent to the railway companies that there would be benefits in introducing resident staff at stations and the earliest station houses were erected in the mid-1830s. For the issuing of tickets and the handling of parcels, offices were built either within the station-house structure or as an appendage. Similarly, passenger shelters were provided either as buildings in their own right or within the structure of the station house. Consequently, a feature of some station buildings is a covered area, recessed into the structure of the station house on the track side, where passengers could shelter. More commonly, an awning or canopy extended beyond the building towards the track. In a good number of stations, the station-master's house stands at some distance from the platform and other buildings. However, even in a 'combined' structure, the station house is normally the largest part. The buildings at a suburban station might omit the station house, including only offices, workshops, lavatories, waiting-rooms and shelters, yet the overall bulk of the structures could be considerable. 'Halts' were not built until early in the twentieth century. They were usually tiny, unstaffed stations with simple buildings, often formed from 'temporary' materials such as timber and corrugated iron and, as such, are unlikely to provide a satisfactory basis for conversion to domestic use.

In the majority of medium-sized stations, the buildings were strung out along the rear platform edge: ticket office, waiting-rooms, lavatories, bookstalls, porters' room and stores. Platforms were very long and mostly covered by awnings. Such an arrangement is expensive to staff and very costly to maintain. Roof canopies of cast iron, wood and glass need cleaning, painting and repair on a regular basis. Nowadays, it is preferred to group the passenger facilities around a single, square space, the station entrance, which abuts a 'travel centre', buffet, bookstall, lavatories and left-luggage office. Here, too, is access to the platform at one central point which, it is claimed, necessitates only a short canopy because most trains now have corridors. Clearly, this policy has acted to denude most intermediate stations that are still operational – let alone the redundant examples – of the elaborate platform canopies which were often their chief glory.

However, the traditional small station arrangement provides problems for would-be converters of these buildings as well as for British Rail managers, because the almost invariably elongated plan of the platform structures tends to demand the inclusion of long and space-consuming corridors to link the individual rooms and there is the danger that these passages will dominate the planning unattractively. This quality is present, although carefully minimised, in the conversion of a South Worcestershire station described later. It is avoided in the conversion of a former narrow-gauge railway terminus station in North Devon, which is also analysed, because two adjacent dwellings have been formed from the foregoing unitary accommodation. In the case of the conversion of a light railway terminus station, which is described first in the following examples, the original building was effectively little more than a 'halt' and so had to be enlarged by the addition of a domestic extension which greatly exceeded it in size. Thus the existing building did not place the conventional constraints upon the achievement of a compact, efficient and attractive arrangement of living accommodation.

Much of the most flamboyant architecture was reserved for major town stations where rival railway companies were anxious to outclass each others' buildings and the admiration of architectural masterpieces was assured by intensive use of the buildings by large numbers of passengers. Nevertheless, there are numerous minor stations of considerable architectural merit. One cause of the elaborate treatment of a small station building was the need to meet the strict requirements of a landowner who had consented to the railway crossing his land not only in exchange for generous cash compensation, but also on the understanding that a correspondingly expensive appearance would be achieved in the new railway structures. It is also clear that particular architectural styles were favoured by each railway company and generally there is some similarity between different stations on the same line. Where the site and anticipated traffic provided no reason to vary the arrangement of a rural station from a 'standard' design, neighbouring stations on the same line might be virtually identical.

In the early days of railway development, when a host of small companies built short local lines, a great variety of architectural styles might emerge in the buildings of one region. In due course, the larger companies absorbed most of the smaller companies so that later station buildings show greater uniformity over larger areas of the country. Without doubt the most dainty, diminutive and intentionally pretty small stations are of the cottage orné, or 'picturesque cottage', style which had developed in England during the Regency period as the conversion of influential people to the philosophy of the Picturesque raised the social status of the 'cottage' from an agricultural labourer's hovel to a middle-class habitation, or even a holiday retreat for the upper classes. Early railway stations adopting this style tend to exhibit an extravagant composition of sham half-timbering (ie, applied over a load-bearing masonry core rather than being self-supporting) which is arranged in fanciful lattice or polygonal patterns, lace-like pierced and carved bargeboards at roof verges and tiny bay, oriel and dormer windows. Such buildings may be found at stations in the south-east Midlands, the uplands of central Wales and the Yorkshire Dales.

Another architectural style popular with the railway companies was neo-Tudor. Owing to their pleasant aesthetic qualities and sound structures which make them easily adaptable into houses, many buildings in this style have survived the closure of the related lines more readily than the fragile cottage orné buildings. They may be found in north-east England, in north-west Cheshire and north Staffordshire.

The neo-Jacobean style, with curving gable ends, which was equally suitably executed in the mass-produced pressed red bricks of Leicestershire, the nationwide distribution of which was facilitated by the development of the railway system, was also used for station buildings, particularly in north Staffordshire, the East Midlands and East Anglia. In southern and eastern England in particular, sober Italianate buildings of symmetrical appearance incorporating semi-circular-arched openings stand at many stations. Sir William Tite (1798-1873) developed the original design for these fairly simple hipped-roof structures which were first erected on the London and Southampton Railway and later adopted throughout the network operated by the succeeding London and South Western Railway. Other Italianate station buildings are scattered throughout England and along the line that follows the North Wales coast to Anglesey.

Among railway companies, the Midland Railway enjoys a good reputation for its architecture. Its best-known country station style is the single-storey twin-pavilion platform building with a tall pitched roof and elaborate bargeboards such as is found on the main line running north from Settle in North Yorkshire to Carlisle, Cumbria. In this arrangement, the station-master's house stands away from the platforms. The buildings were constructed of whatever material was thought to be most suitable to the locality – generally Cumbrian red sandstone. In its south Midlands territory, the company combined a two-storey house with single-storey offices at its stations. Again, great care was taken to blend the stations with existing local architecture. This might

mean complementing the delicately detailed bargeboards so characteristic of many 'Midland' stations, with walls constructed in the local limestone. The station building in south-west Worcestershire described in this chapter, although built by the Tewkesbury and Malvern Railway, passed into Midland Railway ownership in 1877. By an apparent coincidence, it is of a style which generally matches the standard, vaguely neo-Gothic product of that company's architectural output (one of the best examples of the Midland's neo-Gothic style survives on the former Manchester–Derby main line at Darley Dale, Derbyshire).

In contrast to the policies of the Midland and Great Eastern railways, other companies had rather poor reputations for the architectural quality of the buildings they erected at minor stations. The delinquents included the Great Northern Railway, the Great Central Railway and the North Eastern Railway, although the latter two companies did inherit some excellent buildings from smaller lines which they absorbed (notably the many twin-pavilion stations of the Manchester, Sheffield and Lincolnshire Railway which became part of the GCR).

The Great Western Railway has been the object of more enthusiastic study than any other British railway company, but the architecture of its small stations could not be said to justify its pre-eminence. Buildings erected at the GWR's rural stations were usually small and of impermanent materials. Station-masters' houses were rarely included, although the company did produce a brace of delightful cottage orné style stations in east Somerset. It is also east Somerset (or, more properly, Avon, as part of that county was renamed with the restructuring of local government in 1974) which provides this chapter's first example of the policies that may be adopted to convert the smallest type of rural railway station into a residence.

'Little Halt', Blagdon, Avon

By the 1860s, the legal requirements for the promotion, construction and operation of railways had become so onerous that it was clear that the construction of new lines in

Plate 54 Little Halt, Blagdon, Avon: the original platform building of the former Blagdon station is seen in the centre of this view with the newer, stone-built extension to the right and the ex-GWR goods van tool-shed to the left

rural areas was virtually impracticable. This condition was not fully corrected until the passing of the Light Railway Act of 1896 which provided for the avoidance of parliamentary expenses, the reduction of operating costs and the availability of financial assistance. The new legislation attracted a spate of applications, the peak being reached as early as 1898 with thirty nine applications for a total of 896km (557 miles) of light railway. However, the age of motor transport was imminent and after thirty years of declining interest in this legal mechanism, by 1932 applications had completely dried up.

The Wrington Vale Light Railway was a child of the 1896 Act. It was opened on 4 December 1901 and Blagdon was its southern terminus. Farmers in the area west of Congresbury (the first station after Yatton on the Wells branch of the Great Western Railway) had found it difficult to market their dairy produce. With the help of some local landowners, they promoted the construction of a 10km (6½ mile) single-track railway from Congresbury to Blagdon. The scheme was supported by Bristol Corporation who were contemplating the construction of the large Yeo reservoir of their waterworks at the latter place. The Great Western Rail-

way agreed to work the line. Apart from carrying equipment for the reservoir works in its early days and coal to fuel the steam engines that worked the waterworks pumps until they were converted to electric power in the 1920s, the line led a quiet rural existence for many years. Bus competition reduced the number of passenger trains in the early 1920s and this service was withdrawn on 14 September 1931. Goods traffic continued to decline and on 1 November 1950 the line beyond Wrington was closed completely, isolating Langford, Burrington and Blagdon from any rail service. The remainder of the line, between Congresbury and Wrington, closed on 10 June 1963.

The present owner of 'Little Halt' became interested in purchasing the site of the former Blagdon station and its derelict buildings in the late 1950s and persisted in his attempts to persuade British Railways to sell the land until they relented and sold most of the area to him for £100 at the start of the 1960s. The original station building

Fig 61

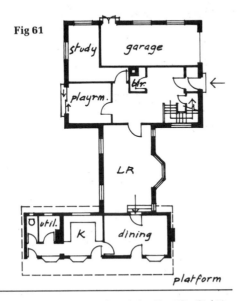

GROUND FLOOR PLAN

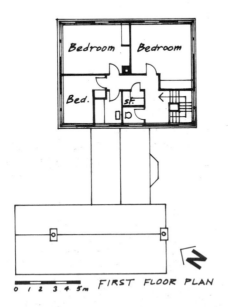

FIRST FLOOR PLAN

0 1 2 3 4 5m

was little more than a shack of largely timber construction which occupied the centre section of the single long platform overlooking the vacant trackbed and facing a grassy embankment (Plate 54).

Clearly, this structure was not adequate to accommodate the rooms required in a family dwelling and so, if he was to try to retain some of the qualities of the working station, the new owner was obliged to consider how the existing building might be added to or extended without too severely injuring these qualities. To his credit, he employed an architect, Peter Ware, to produce a design and the result of his deliberations was the suggestion that the most satisfactory way of preserving the 'station character' was to provide only a minimal connection between the old platform building and the new accommodation rather than to attempt to add to it in a matching style. In this way the retained and preserved platform building could continue to be looked at 'in the round'. This policy was also justified by the existing structure's comparatively elevated location on the platform surface (Fig 61). For economy's sake, the extension would have to sit on adjoining and lower ground which would have the visual advantage that the platform building, despite its small size, could continue to assert itself as a structure of significance. It was equally plain that the new living accommodation would be most economically contained within a single, larger structure, ideally clearly separated from the former station building. Quite apart from the aesthetic shortcomings of the policy, the constructional drawbacks of 'colliding' this larger structure with the old platform building were avoided by connecting this accommodation to the latter structure through the single-storey 'link block' containing a sitting-room. The affinity of this structure with traditional railway architecture was strengthened by incorporating a splayed bay-window, built above a brick plinth, on its south-east elevation. The overall height of this element could have posed a problem for its connection with the platform building, because its roof was required either to connect with, or pass below, the wide, overhanging eaves of the latter structure. This condition was

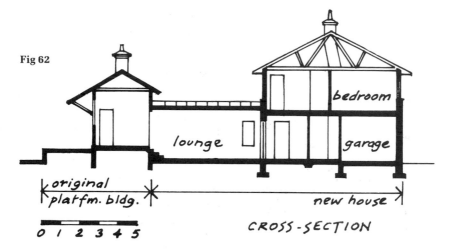

Fig 62

bedroom

lounge

garage

original platfm. bldg.

new house

0 1 2 3 4 5

CROSS-SECTION

resolved by adopting a very low-pitched roof, clad in a sheet aluminium roof-covering, which could then meet the rear elevation of the platform building some way below its overhanging eaves (Fig 62, Plate 55).

It was felt that the newly built larger part of the domestic quarters might also harmonise better with the retained station building if it in some way exploited associations with railway architecture. Thus the new 'house' was erected to an almost-square plan, and the stratified appearance which

characterises many station buildings and which was adopted in the single-storey link was also reproduced in this element – this time with fenestration and boarded infill panels sitting above a lower-storey plinth of natural stone. In this way, it was felt that associations with a conventional hipped-

Plate 55 Little Halt, Blagdon, Avon: the entrance elevation of the house; the 'signal-cabin' extension of the 1960s is on the right and the original platform building is on the left

roof railway signal cabin might be evoked. The formula is partly successful.

Traditional signal boxes often included a lower-storey masonry plinth to hide the mechanical linkage between the control levers and the points and signals. At the upper level, the signalman enjoyed a commanding view of approaching trains through extensive glazing, but any windows in the brick, stone or timber plinth were invariably small, square and regularly spaced. Plainly, living-rooms sited behind such a construction impose different demands for window space, so the necessarily larger windows inserted in the stone-faced lower storey of the main block of 'Little Halt' tend to detract from the 'signal cabin' associations. Similarly, it was not possible to reproduce the continuous matrix of small-paned windows that make up the 'observation' level of the standard signal box because some areas of the upper storey, which accommodates mainly bedrooms, require privacy. For this reason, weather-boarded infill panels alternate with windows. However, windows have been carried around all four corners of the block, which tends to stress the 'floating' quality of the low-pitched pyramidal roof, a quality that the building does share with some signal boxes. It is, perhaps, regrettable that horizontal boarding was used for the infill panels. While it harmonises with the horizontal bias of the paired aluminium-framed sash-windows, and is a traditional cladding material for the upper storeys of signal cabins, the combination of textures and shapes used here fails to reflect the vertical stress of the high-level fenestration of old signal boxes. It would have been better to include a larger number of narrower sash or casement windows to give an equivalent glazed area and, perhaps, to clad the infill panels in painted vertical boarding. It is also interesting that the owner observes that the aluminium windows have not proved to be as serviceable as conventional painted timber-framed lights.

A further association with railway architecture exists in the building, although it is not readily apparent. The 'coursed and snecked' rubble stonework of the main block came from dismantled railway buildings at Worle Junction, near Weston-super-Mare.

Construction of 'Little Halt' was completed in 1965 and the role of the site as evidence of the railway heritage has been reinforced since then by the addition of an ex-Great Western Railway guard's van, which acts as a shed for garden tools. All external woodwork on the buildings is finished in the familiar chocolate-and-cream colour scheme of the GWR and a resident pony now helps to keep down the considerable quantity of grass that grows on the former track-bed.

Station House, Lynton, North Devon

Like Blagdon station, the station at Lynton was also a terminus, but of a rather different concern. The Lynton and Barnstaple Railway, of which Lynton was the northern terminus, was opened in 1898, primarily as a means of conveying tourist traffic from the London and South Western Railway main line at Barnstaple to the coastal holiday villages of Lynton and Lynmouth. As the terrain between these two locations was difficult, to save expense it was decided to construct the line as a narrow-gauge railway on the 2ft gauge, terminating at an interchange station with the standard-gauge line at Barnstaple. The adoption of this policy allowed curves in the track to be of smaller radius, and locomotives and rolling stock could be lighter and of smaller loading-gauge than the standard-gauge vehicles, thus permitting the required civil engineering works to be more modest than would have been necessary to carry a conventional branch line.

The consequently diminutive look of the railway – many of its features had the aspect of a 'toy railway' – were reflected in the treatment of the station buildings (Fig 63), three of which, including Lynton and Lynmouth (as the station was originally named), were erected by a local builder, Mr R. Jones. They have been described as being of the 'Nuremburg' style, which is presumably meant to refer to their visually-dominant pitched, hipped and half-hipped roofs with broad eaves. Possibly a closer resemblance is to be found in contemporary American small rural and suburban stations in which a

Plate 56 Station House, Lynton, Devon: a wartime view of the station after the track had been lifted; the goods shed can be seen in the background

Plate 57 Station House, Lynton, Devon: the road elevation of Station House; the former booking-office door is in the foreground

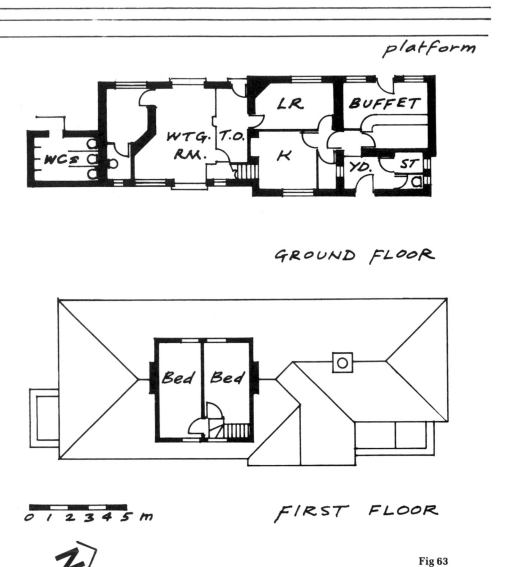

GROUND FLOOR

FIRST FLOOR

0 1 2 3 4 5 m

Fig 63

similarly heavy-roofed treatment was sometimes adopted. This affinity was reinforced in the design of the original locomotives which, in true American fashion, had 'cow-catchers' fitted at front and rear. On a more practical note, it is clear that the inclusion of broad, wide-spreading eaves on the platform side of the pitched and hipped main roof of the station building removed the need for a separate canopy for sheltering passengers, and the builder may have copied this feature from some small station buildings erected by the Great Western Railway, if he did not arrive at the arrange-

ment independently. Brunel himself had exploited the capability of a pitched and hipped roof which is too large for its building to project a deep eaves which could act as a platform canopy when he designed the small, simple station building at Mortimer, Hampshire, in the mid-nineteenth century, and similar buildings were erected at other stations in the GWR network which embraced North Devon.

An economy resulting from the adoption of narrow-gauge standards was the omission of high platforms – only a nominal 'single-step' improvement of the station platform

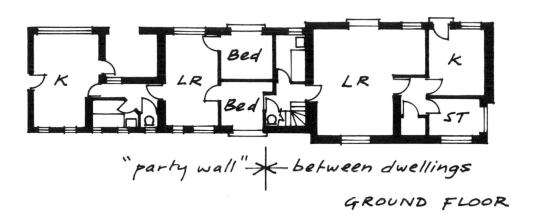

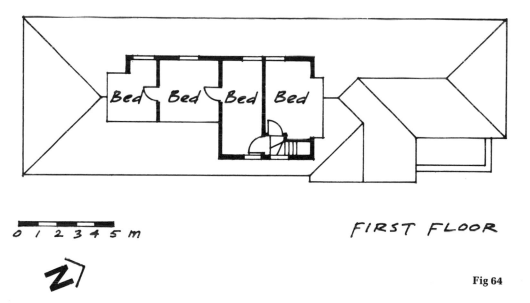

GROUND FLOOR

FIRST FLOOR

Fig 64

level above the track was employed (Plate 56) and the carriages were built with a continuous low step-board along each side to assist passengers in mounting and dismounting.

The railway was taken into the ownership of the Southern Railway in July 1923 following the 'grouping' of the multitude of railway companies that took place in the wake of World War I. This development spelt change for Lynton station. The Southern Railway decided that money had to be spent on the line if it was to have a chance of survival. A new bungalow home for the station-master was built on the bank opposite Lynton station and the station buildings were enlarged and altered internally – partly by extending the station offices into the former station-master's accommodation, although the lavatories at the south end were relocated and a new flat-roofed ticket office entrance replaced the yard, WC and fuel store on the north-east corner (Plate 57). The alterations to the south end necessitated the extension of the main hipped-roof structure and the supporting walls of rubble stonework, as can be deduced from a photograph of the platform side of the derelict station building, taken during World War II (Plate 56). The Southern Railway also demolished the original high chimney stacks, thus removing the considerable maintenance liability posed by such features in this exposed and elevated hillside location.

The building had become derelict by the time of World War II because the railway had failed to survive new motor-bus competition. The 'writing was on the wall' for the line by 1931 as passenger traffic continued to decline and the strength of road competition was acknowledged by the inclusion of times of local bus services in the railway timetable. The line remained a favourite with holidaymakers but the tourist season was all too short and takings from these few weeks of the year were insufficient to subsidise the poorly patronised service operated during the winter months. Consequently, it was decided to close the line at the end of the 1935 summer season and the last passenger train ran on Sunday, 29 September 1935. The track at Lynton station had been lifted by November 1935 and the dismantling of the entire line was complete by the end of 1936. When Lynton station was later sold as a derelict shell, it realised £475. As evidence that platform buildings may not be the only type of railway structures suitable for conversion into dwellings, it is interesting to note that Lynton station goods shed was sold off separately and subsequently converted into a pair of cottages.

The present owner of Lynton station has aimed to re-create something of the atmosphere of a working station by relaying about 30m (100ft) of narrow-gauge track alongside the still-recognisable shoulder of the former passenger platform. On certain occasions, he operates a small industrial diesel locomotive on this short stretch of line. The site's history as a railway terminus is also alluded to in the leaflet he has produced to publicise the availability of part of the building as holiday accommodation. During the summer months, the owner's family restrict themselves to the northern half of the building and the upper-storey rooms while the southern section is let to holidaymakers (Fig 64). It would be difficult to summarise the peculiar charm of this self-catering flat, part of a building which surely occupies one of the most obscure locations of any former British railway terminus, in better words than those adopted by the owner in his own publicity leaflet in which he states that it

has the novelty of being housed in the delightfully picturesque old Lynton and Lynmouth Railway Station, the terminus of the Lynton and Barnstaple Railway; closed as a station in 1935, and converted to a residence long since, it has the added attraction of a 2ft gauge Ruston locomotive alongside the platform.

Station House, South Worcestershire

If the conversion of Lynton station has avoided the problems posed by the conventional 'lineally extended' plan of the small railway station by effectively creating a pair of semi-detached dwellings, these difficulties could not be avoided in the conversion, to single family use, of this former Midland Railway station in south-west Worcestershire. The station was built by the Tewkesbury and Malvern Railway Company which opened a single-track line from a new station at Tewkesbury, Gloucestershire, to the Great Western Railway's existing line at Great Malvern, Worcestershire, on 16 May 1864. The Tewkesbury and Malvern Railway was absorbed by the Midland Railway in 1877. Weekday passenger services on the line were reduced from Great Malvern to Upton-on-Severn in 1952, and this stretch of almost 11km (7 miles) was closed. The Tewkesbury–Upton line, on which this station was located, retained passenger trains until 1961 following local protests that Tewkesbury's tourist trade would suffer without them, and this section did not close completely until July 1963.

One of the present owners of the station works in Cheltenham and preferred to live in the Severn valley area to the west of that spa town rather than in the Cotswold hills. While searching for suitable accommodation in this district in 1979, he discovered the near-derelict station building, part of which was occupied by an aged tenant who was related to the former station-master (Plate

58). The building was for sale and he succeeded in purchasing the platform buildings and the surrounding land which included the former coal-yard of 1½ acres. Unlike the two station conversion projects described earlier, in which the existing accommodation was either very small, requiring a large, purpose-built residential extension, or it was essentially 'livable' before its change of use, purchase of this station signalled the start of a very long, extensive, expensive and time-consuming alteration, renovation and restoration programme. In the opinion of the owners, only by 1986 had the building attained a 'suitable' state.

The existing accommodation incorporated two bedrooms on the upper floor of the two-storey southern pavilion of the platform building, sited above a kitchen, scullery and larder at ground-floor level. To the north of this 'cross-pavilion', the rest of the building was effectively single-storey, housing the station-master's living-room, ticket office, booking hall (reaching upwards two storeys in height, almost to the apex of the roof) and ladies' waiting-room with adjoining WC. To the south of the residential cross-pavilion, a

Plate 58 Station House, South Worcestershire: the platform elevation of the station before conversion work began

walled yard led to a wash-house and outside WC. Beyond this area lay a porters' room and gents' lavatories accessible only from the platform (Fig 65).

The policy of the new owners in planning and executing the conversion was to add to and modify the southernmost rooms, primarily to create additional bedrooms. The former gents' WC enclosure was retained as a garden store and the adjoining porters' room became a study. The external WC and wash-house enclosures were demolished, thus enlarging the foregoing walled yard so that when the combined space was roofed over it could be subdivided to provide a downstairs bathroom/cloakroom, a short passage giving access to the study and new downstairs bedroom formed within the new construction at the south-east corner, and a utility room en suite with the kitchen, which was retained in its original position. Demolition of the front wall of the enclosed yard meant that the replacement wall, of cavity construction for improved weather-

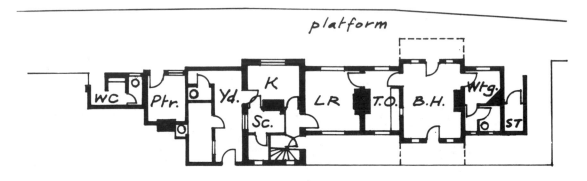

GROUND FLOOR PLAN

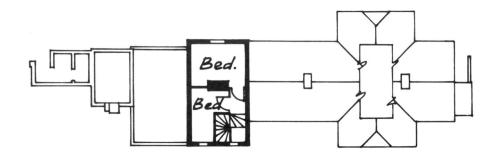

FIRST FLOOR PLAN

Fig 65

resistance, could be indented to form a porch incorporating an external door from the utility room. The whole of this reshaped and enlarged single-storey accommodation was covered with a pitched and half-hipped slated roof, matching the covering of all other original roof slopes of the building. The roof space thus formed, lit by new roof windows, provides a useful children's playroom and potential additional bedroom (Plate 59).

To the north of the cross-pavilion, the station-master's living room has become a dining-room and the former booking hall has been combined with the ladies' waiting-room and WC to form a lofty and rather grand living-room, direct access to the exterior having been retained by way of the original glazed platform-access door of the booking hall. To avoid disruptive diagonal circulation across rooms, two internal door openings were bricked up and two substitute openings were formed in formerly 'blind' panels on the opposite side of adjacent chimney breasts, thus creating a straight route alongside the eastern flank wall from the central entrance hall to the living-room at the north end. All chimney breasts were left in place and most fireplaces were restored, although the aperture for the range in the original kitchen was modified to accept the cooker in the new arrangement.

Plate 59 Station House, South Worcestershire: the platform elevation at the conclusion of conversion work; the new wing in the foreground has been roofed with salvaged slates whilst the body of the building has been re-roofed with synthetic slates

Plate 60 Station House, South Worcestershire: another view of the platform elevation after the completion of conversion work shows clearly the elaborately-carved bargeboards and the decorative 'diapered' brickwork of the main gable

The former booking-hall fireplace took on an impressive 'pillar-like' quality when the wall panels to either side of it were demolished in order to enlarge the new living-room into the former ladies' waiting-room and WC areas (Fig 66). Much of the original internal and external woodwork is pitch-pine which has proved to be very durable, resisting well the rot which could easily have been induced by the earlier long-term lack of maintenance of the highly exposed painted external surfaces of the building.

In the reconstruction of the southern single-storey section, material salvaged from the selective demolitions was used, where possible, to create the new external surfaces with the intention of producing a matching appearance. This policy extended to covering the new roof-slopes with Welsh slates that had been stripped from the dismantled roofs. Somewhat ironically, the slate covering of the central and northern sections of the building was subsequently found to be irreparable and these surfaces have been re-covered with lightweight synthetic slates of 'riven' surface texture, in colours matching the purple and blue-grey bands of the original Welsh slate covering, while 'recycled' slates remain on the newly built southern section (Plates 59 and 60).

The architectural style of the station is akin to the 'simplified Gothic' of many Midland Railway structures but here, either

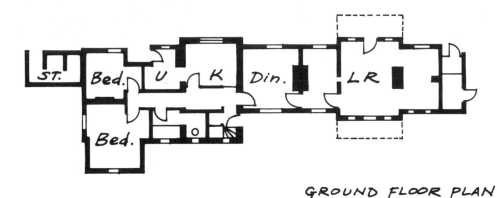

GROUND FLOOR PLAN

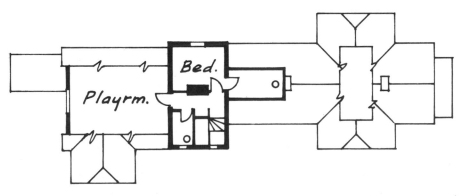

FIRST FLOOR PLAN

0 1 2 3 4 5 m

Fig 66

Plate 61 Station House, South Worcestershire: this view of the restored station and the newly built garage and 'granny-flat' block demonstrates the great care the owners have taken to blend new construction with the retained structures

because of the policy of the Tewkesbury and Malvern Railway, or the preference of architects of the 1860s for rather 'muscular', thick-set, even coarse, detailing, a more than usually elaborate treatment has been adopted, including heavily sculpted barge-boards, stratified and diapered 'poly-chromatic' brickwork, alternating bands of differently coloured roof slates and multi-coloured brickwork, pointed arches capping window openings. Indicative of the great care that has been taken to use forms and materials that harmonise with the original structure in the conversion and recon-struction of the station, is the present owners' adoption of a virtually identical architectural treatment for the new garage and upper-storey 'granny flat' accom-modation that has been erected alongside the main buildings (Plate 61). That this care and recognition of the cultural significance of the station by the owners and their architect Mr H. G. Raggett has been acknowledged by the local authority is evidenced by the inclusion of the restored building in the statutory list of buildings of architectural or historic interest.

Avon House, Harvington, Worcestershire

Some notes on the conversion of the former Harvington station are added as a postscript to this section on the re-use of railway build ings in order to illustrate that sympathetic 'improvements' can be made by quite simple and inexpensive means.

'Avon House', when Harvington railway station, was an intermediate stop on the Evesham and Redditch Railway. The section of line between Evesham, Worcestershire, and Alcester, Warwickshire, was opened for passenger traffic on 17 September 1866, the link to Redditch, Worcestershire, being completed in 1868. From the outset the line was operated by the Midland Railway and although it was not engineered to accom-modate express trains, it was an important route for freight because it allowed goods trains to avoid the notorious Lickey Incline, south of Birmingham. Passenger services on the line were withdrawn in 1963, eight months after buses were substituted for trains between Evesham and Redditch, and

Plate 62 Avon House, Harvington, Worcestershire: an Edwardian view of Harvington station shows the simple, solid station buildings and tidy platform characteristic of Midland Railway policy

Plate 63 Avon House, Harvington, Worcestershire: although considerably changed since its days as a working station, the alterations that have transformed Harvington station into Avon House have been carried out with sensitivity

Plate 64 Avon House, Harvington, Worcestershire: the simple shapes of the old station building are apparent in this rear view; a 'kit' conservatory acts as an attractive foil to the solid, cubical forms of the converted structure

Plate 65 Avon House, Harvington, Worcestershire: the interior of the prefabricated conservatory which also acts as an entrance lobby to the house

freight services were withdrawn soon afterwards.

The present owner of Avon House, David Hutchings, is an architect who is better known as the doyen of the inland waterways restoration movement in Britain. Following his highly successful leadership of the restoration of the Southern Stratford Canal which reopened that waterway between Lapworth and Stratford-upon-Avon in the mid-1960s, he turned his attentions to the opportunity to restore navigation to the upper reaches of the Warwickshire Avon, between Evesham and Stratford. Much needed for the execution of the necessary civil engineering works was an area of vacant land, close to the river, where construction materials could be stored. In his search for a suitable site, David Hutchings came across the recently vacated buildings of Harvington station which were in danger of being rapidly reduced to a ruin by the actions of thieves and vandals. The buildings adjoined a goods yard which, denuded of its sidings, would make an excellent area for the storage of materials as it was only 0.8km (½ mile) away from the river. Angered by the sight of what he regarded as a public asset being left to rot, David Hutchings at once moved into the shell of the station to secure it against further vandalism and set about modifying the building to meet both his own needs and those of the Upper Avon Navigation Trust, because the building was to house the office of that organisation as well as living accommodation for him and his family. This 'direct action' in due course prompted a predictably unsympathetic reaction from British Rail, but after protracted negotiations, the new occupant eventually succeeded in buying the land and buildings following his submission of the highest offer after tenders for the purchase of the property had been invited.

Although care has been taken to conserve the general impression of a station building, a comparison of a view of Harvington station in its prime, before World War I (Plate 62) and now (Plate 63) shows that the present owner has not been afraid to modify and adapt the original structure significantly where this was necessary to cater for new needs. Fortunately, Harvington station was built in a plainer style than the south Worcestershire station described earlier, so that the large, long, flat-roofed dormer granting upper-storey accommodation over the former single-storey 'offices' on the platform elevation and the external metal spiral stair do not mock the simple forms of the 'T'-plan original building. A fitting and comparatively inexpensive enrichment of the entrance elevation has been achieved by erecting a standard 'kit' conservatory in the angle between the original offices and residential wings of the building (Plate 64). This space doubles as a pleasant summer sun-room and a generous glazed entrance hall (Plate 65), the roof textures of the old building being just sufficiently complex, thanks to the alternating bands of plain and 'fish-scale' tiles, to harmonise with the fairly filigree appearance of the 'kit' conservatory.

Service Buildings
Water Supply Structures
The expansion of municipal enterprise in the late nineteenth and early twentieth centuries was engendered by the Local Government Act of 1894 which created rural and urban district councils. The growing needs of enlarging urban and suburban populations could then be satisfied by either private or municipal enterprise. The means of water supply in towns was an early target for criticism and in many places pressure built up for some sort of systematic provision of fresh water. The setting up of a piped water supply in some English towns was approved by charters as early as the fifteenth century, but, generally speaking, springs and wells met the needs of many towns well into the nineteenth century. A Royal Commission of 1843-5 reported on the unsatisfactory and unhygienic nature of water supplies in populous areas. At that time, water mains could be laid only in the main streets. The Public Health Act of 1848 enabled a local authority to provide a water supply. Accordingly, this service has traditionally been provided by a mixture of private companies and local authority undertakings, each usually established by Act of Parliament.

In rural districts, the position was complicated as the total rateable value of many areas was not adequate to finance expenditure on water supply. The Public Health (Water) Act of 1878 stipulated that no new house should be built in a rural area unless it was within reasonable distance of a water supply. It is likely that this requirement contributed to the nucleation of settlements within suburban areas, thus enlarging rate income and making the provision of a comprehensive piped water supply more possible.

Water Tower, The Mythe, Tewkesbury, Gloucestershire

As a small town with a population of only about five thousand, Tewkesbury was a 'late developer' in the field of municipal enterprise. Electric lighting was not installed in its streets until 1909, despite discussion of its merits by the council in the early 1890s. Not surprisingly, therefore, the town looked to a private company to install a modern, piped water supply serving its buildings, and this service commenced in 1889. To guarantee a continuous supply, water had to be stored and this necessitated the building of a water tower and a reservoir on high ground on the outskirts of the town. As Tewkesbury stands at the confluence of the rivers Severn and Avon, suitable sites were limited, but the optimum position proved to be a site located centrally between the two rivers at a place called 'The Mythe' (which means 'between two rivers') on the north side of the town and adjacent to the main Worcester–Tewkesbury highway that is now the A38 trunk road.

The opening of the waterworks was accompanied by great rejoicing, a procession, including a brass band, being led by the bishop from the town centre to the opening ceremony on the site. To preserve the purity of the water at this roadside location, the reservoir was roofed with brickwork vaults overlaid with turf so that it has become a large, flat-topped grassy mound of a type familiar to many Londoners as evidence of the 'underground' reservoirs which help to satisfy the water supply needs of the capital. The lightless subterranean chamber, which

Plate 66 Water Tower, The Mythe, Gloucestershire: the 'neo-Romanesque' water tower with new, tall windows inserted in the formerly under-fenestrated central bay; in the foreground, the iron ventilators of the adjoining underground reservoir can be seen

Fig 67

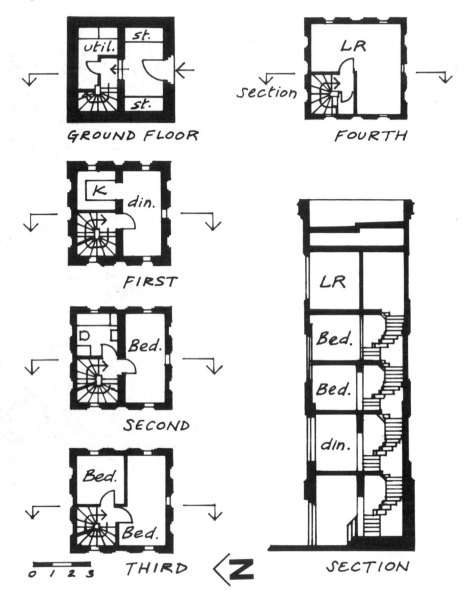

GROUND FLOOR

FOURTH

FIRST

SECOND

THIRD

SECTION

is about 4m (13ft) high internally, is ventilated by Gothic-style cylindrical metal terminals which penetrate the turf of the flat top surface at several points and some of these features can be seen in the general view of the building's entrance elevation (Plate 66). The cuboidal water tower building was constructed from bright red engineering brickwork in a neo-Romanesque round-arched style, with moulded brick or matching terracotta enrichments. A central spine wall supported the weight of the high-level water tank.

The buildings ceased to play a part in supplying fresh water to Tewkesbury in the 1960s, although the water tower continued to fulfil a function as the most suitable elevated site for a local police radio aerial for several subsequent years. In due course, the site was sold at auction and the developer who undertook the conversion purchased the land and buildings for £22,000 in February 1985. The new owner was Martin Wright, a self-employed joinery contractor who recognised that the key to a satisfactory conversion of the water tower into a dwelling lay in the compact planning of the 'spiral', or, more correctly, winding staircase that links the five main levels.

Although the brickwork external walls vary in thickness, being most massive (600mm (2ft) thick) at the base of the building, the internal dimensions of the tower never exceed 4.8 x 4.8m (15½ x 15½ft). Within this area, at most levels, had to be fitted at least one habitable room as well as the staircase. This latter element was condensed into the minimum corner space by making it a continuously winding construction (Fig 67) and the fabrication of this staircase in modular form so that it could be easily manhandled and erected on site very fully tested the skill and ingenuity of the building owner.

The narrowness of the water tower interior posed problems for consideration of the proposal for the granting of some of the necessary official approvals. Several waivers of the Building Regulations had to be applied for and obtained before construction could proceed and the work could be officially accepted. Prominent among requirements which it was difficult to satisfy were standards of fire-resisting construction and means of escape in case of fire. A waiver was necessitated in relation to the latter circumstance because the provision of an alternative means of escape is often required in residential buildings that exceed three storeys in height. In the case of the former condition – ie, standards of fire resistance – it was fortunate for the developer that the consultant structural engineer he had employed was able to persuade the local authority to accept timber construction for the new floors instead of the reinforced concrete that was originally insisted on. However, official acceptance of this change of materials was achieved only at the price of having to install a 30mm (1¼in) thick in situ plaster coating as the ceiling construction below the joists of each new upper floor. Acceptable fire resistance of the staircase enclosure was achieved by installing double-skin plasterboard and an in situ plaster skim coat to either side of framing formed from 75mm (3in) deep timber studs. All doors opening off the stair are of 53mm (2in) thick, one-hour fire-resisting construction, incorporate intumescent strips in the jambs and are self-closing. The staircase itself, which was assembled from pre-

Plate 67 Water Tower, The Mythe, Gloucestershire: because no windows have been inserted in the 'blind' north elevation of the building, many southbound travellers on the A38 are unaware that the water tower has ceased to fulfil its original function

fabricated quadrant-size modules, is largely made from medium-density fibreboard ('MDF').

The policy for the internal reconstruction first required the removal of the high-level water tank. This was sold for scrap and it was originally envisaged that its scrap value would cover the cost of cutting up and removing it. In the event, dismantling and removing the tank from the rather cramped interior resulted in a cost of £300 being incurred. The thick brickwork lateral spine wall, which was 11.5m (38ft) high, was completely demolished above third-floor level and pierced with openings to give access to the staircase and minor rooms on the lower floors. Fitting out then proceeded from the top downwards, with the pre-fabricated stair being installed first in its quadrant sections. The pumps which had propelled water up to the high-level tank had been removed before conversion work commenced, but rather than demolish their solid concrete bases, the developer decided to 'floor over' these projections with a mezzanine level, providing a utility room (Fig 67). The lack of on-site drainage was rectified by installing a 'package' septic tank and the lack of natural light in the interior was corrected by enlarging the few original tiny 'porthole' windows into long, narrow casements, confined in the same way to the decorative, round-headed, recessed panels of the engineering brick elevations (Plate 66). However, no new windows were inserted into the austere, windowless north elevation (Plate 67).

The original lead flat roof surrounded by a parapet was not in need of repair, although a short section of related lead flashing was replaced. The panoramic view of the valleys of the Severn and Avon from this roof terrace, 16.5m (54ft) above the ground, is breathtaking. A practical, indeed necessary, feature which was installed in the resulting five-storey dwelling was an 'entry-phone', giving occupants relaxing in the top-storey living-room the opportunity to refuse entry to unwanted visitors without having to descend and ascend four long flights of stairs.

A local planning policy of 'no infilling' meant that only one dwelling could be created on the water tower/reservoir site, so the developer naturally tackled the structure in which the constructional problems posed would be of the most con-ventional nature – namely, the water tower. Resources were not available to attempt the conversion of the vaulted 'underground' reservoir and, to comply with planning policy, the accommodation provided with-in this structure would have had to be linked with the water tower to produce a single dwelling. In the event, the reservoir, in unmodified form, was sold with the con-verted water tower, its potential as yet unrealised.

Although the site and buildings were purchased in 1985, work on the conversion did not begin until 1986 and was virtually complete by October that year. The de-veloper temporarily suspended his opera-tions as a supplier of joinery to building contractors etc for the duration of the con-version exercise which became his full-time occupation. He estimates that about 15 per cent of his working time was taken up by the manufacture/prefabrication of timber com-ponents in his workshop. The total cost of the conversion work was in the order of £37,000.

In relation to the exercise of forming new openings in formerly imperforate masonry walls – which is a large part of the work in any water tower conversion – it is interesting to note that when this stage of the alterations was reached in the conversion of a high, cubical brick-built water tower at Hunstanton in Norfolk, it was found to be more eco-nomical temporarily to bolt steel channel guides internally alongside the positions of the new window-jambs to accept a circular saw with a large-diameter, diamond-toothed blade which then was used to cut out the greater part of each edge of each new window opening, than it was to form the openings in the conventional way with manual labour and hand-tools. This policy restricted the very labour-intensive hand-tool operation to forming the corners of each opening after the main part of each window head, jambs and sill had been cut with the saw.

Fire Service Buildings

Prominent among the growing municipal services which were being provided at the turn of the century was the town fire brigade. The first organised fire-fighting groups were those employed by the indi-vidual fire insurance companies and these groups were formed early in the eighteenth century. However, by the end of that century it was apparent that, in London at least, a joint effort by the various companies was needed to fight fires efficiently and effectively and in 1826 a single brigade was formed. In 1865, by Act of Parliament, a Metropolitan Fire Brigade was established, paid for by central government, county government and insurance companies. This body was retitled the London Fire Brigade in 1904. The creation of the London County Council in 1888 heralded a massive expansion of municipal enterprise in London and the London Fire Brigade accordingly benefited from the building, on a systematic basis, by the LCC, of many divisional fire stations in the years immediately following the turn of the century. One of the most famous of the 'arts and crafts' style buildings produced by the LCC architects of the time was erected on Euston Road in Central London in 1902 and still serves as a fire station. In 1906 the northern suburb of Highgate also obtained its own LCC fire station, a much smaller structure which nevertheless boasts a more elaborate 'arts and crafts' treatment than the Euston Road building.

Fire Station, North Hill, Highgate, London N6

This fire station was built to accommodate horse-drawn, steam-powered mobile pump appliances and so a neighbouring block on its north side was dedicated to stables. With the introduction of motor vehicle appliances, the need for the stables disappeared and they were converted into a cottage providing additional living accommodation for the resident firemen. The rear part of the main building which housed the appliances also provided a dwelling for the chief fireman and his family.

With the rationalisation of the fire service in the post-war years and the ever-increasing size of the modern appliances, the building ceased to be a suitable base for the fire brigade and became, instead, the local headquarters of the St John's Ambulance Brigade (Plate 68). The owner of the building was by now the London Borough of Haringey which recognised, at the end of the 1970s, the potential of the building for making a contribution to the solution of homelessness locally if it could be converted into dwellings. Accordingly, the architects Timothy Bruce-Dick Associates were commissioned to prepare a design for the conversion and the necessary alterations to the building were completed in the first half of 1981.

The original architect's desire to separate the residential part of the main station building from the appliance bay and mess-

Plate 68　Fire Station, Highgate, London N6: the front elevation of the building before conversion; the high sliding-folding doors of the appliances bay are apparent

rooms had resulted in an internal 'party wall' which crossed the main, square section of the plan in the middle (Fig 68). This arrangement was very helpful to the architect designing the conversion scheme because sound transmission is one of the greatest problems in creating residential accommodation for multiple occupation in formerly unitary spaces. The existence of this solid, massive spine wall was therefore exploited rather than ignored, by siting separate dwellings to either side of it. Perhaps fortunately, the 'greasy pole' and associated hole-in-the-floor via which the firemen gained rapid access to the appliances from their upper-storey mess-room had long gone, so that the ground-floor appliance bay could be satisfactorily converted into the

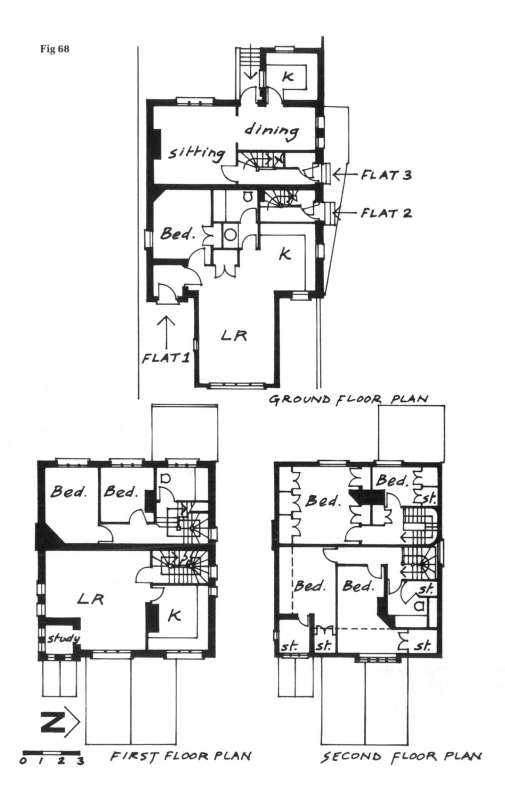

Fig 68

FLAT 3

FLAT 2

FLAT 1

GROUND FLOOR PLAN

FIRST FLOOR PLAN

SECOND FLOOR PLAN

0 1 2 3

Plate 69 Fire Station, Highgate, London N6: the converted building; other than the addition of a new pitched-roof dormer, apparent on the northern roofslope, and the replacement of the engine-bay doors with a large window of similar pattern, little seems to have altered

sitting room of a single-storey one-bedroom flat. The large folding doors which had graced the front elevation of this projection were replaced by an almost equally large window, subdivided into an identical number of small panes in an attempt to retain a sense of the structure's previous use (Plate 69). A private entrance to this flat was formed under a new pitched-roof porch applied to the front of the base of the former hose-drying tower and the remainder of the habitable accommodation of this unit was 'wrapped around' the bathroom/WC and related small utility room which were located at the centre of the plan, backing on to the central spine wall (Fig 68).

This arrangement allowed the existing 'dog-leg' staircase, located in the north-west corner of the front half of the building, to be retained as access to the second dwelling, which is a two-storey two-bedroom unit occupying the front part of the first and second floors. From the large, first-floor, L-shaped sitting room of this maisonette, an upper section of the former hose-drying tower can be reached. This can operate as a small study or a generously sized storage cupboard. Because the building is located in a conservation area, modifications to the exterior had to be fairly modest and incon-spicuous so that it was not possible to replace the wooden louvred panels that had vented this level of the tower with windows. The louvred panels were retained and repainted and weather-resisting glazing was added internally. However, on the level above, which provides the two bedrooms and bathroom of the maisonette, the tower had originally been pierced with windows as well as louvres, so the converted volume provides a more satisfactory space which can be used as a small dressing-room en suite with the main bedroom. To introduce adequate daylight into this space, a new pitched-roof dormer window had to be added to the south-facing roof-slope. A complementary dormer was added to the northern roof-slope to light the second-floor bathroom/WC that was added on this side.

To the rear of the spine wall which divided the main building, it was decided to create one three-storey dwelling. Satis-factory sound insulation between the units in the front part of the block and that to the rear was easily achieved by extending the masonry spine wall upwards to meet the underside of the roof. Within the simple rectangular plan thus formed at second-floor level, two bedrooms and the new top flights of a modified staircase were easily accommodated. On the intermediate level, two further bedrooms and a bathroom/WC were installed and the ground floor pro-vided a small cloakroom/WC adjoining the entrance door, sitting-room, dining-room and kitchen. In all, eleven people can be accommodated in the main building. The adjoining stables block was upgraded to provide a six-person house with a garden and the total cost of the work was £137,000, a significant proportion of which was dedicated to 'invisible' operations such as underpinning, which was needed beneath the west elevation of the building where the ground falls away steeply. The builder, who approached the work with commendable care, was Henry Norris & Son of Hertford.

It should be apparent that few branch fire stations which are still in use but scheduled for closure in the near future are likely to provide such compact and easily converted accommodation as that which was offered by the buildings at Highgate. The demands placed upon these buildings for increasingly large areas of garage space to suit the new appliances mean that most of the small 'village' stations passed out of fire brigade use many years ago and have found new uses as shops, offices, warehouses and garages. However, the pressure of tech-nological change is now affecting the grander city-centre buildings, as is evidenced by the current proposal to con-vert Manchester's giant former central fire station of 1906 into an hotel. Where the creation of new dwellings can play a part in rescuing such monuments of municipal enterprise from the attentions of the demo-lition contractor, it is likely to be as part of a conversion to combined uses, and this development is dealt with in the final chapter of this book.

10 Combined Uses and the Future of Building Conversion

An area of intense activity in the field of building conversion is the adaptation of redundant buildings of formerly unitary function into structures housing two or more separate uses. It is an activity that is fraught with problems because it runs counter to the general policy of local planning authorities that specific buildings or sites should be devoted to readily definable single uses – rather in the manner of the 'zoning' that is practised as a rudimentary form of development control throughout the USA. Planners tend to be suspicious of proposals that involve a mixture of uses because they believe that the boundaries between, say, residential and commercial use can be blurred easily to the advantage of the building owner (for instance, official acceptance of the combination of an office and a dwelling may allow a building owner to evade the statutory responsibilities that must be fulfilled by the occupants of purpose-built offices). To some extent, this lack of flexibility on the part of the planning authorities has resulted from a just and understandable desire to uphold established standards of health and welfare. Nevertheless, and no doubt in deference to demands that the definitions of the planners' 'use classes' should be broadened in an attempt to increase opportunities for employment, a revised 'Use Classes Order' was issued in 1987 which gives official blessing to the blurring of some of the previously distinct boundaries. It is now possible to turn premises classified for 'light industrial' use into offices or premises for research and development without the need to apply to the local planning authority for planning permission because a new 'Business Class' groups these activities together. However, the distinction between residential and industrial/commercial uses remains as clear as ever – there is no blurring of the boundaries that would allow a householder to let his house as offices or vice versa.

To commence this account of the growing interest and activity in the conversion of redundant buildings to a combination of uses, it is appropriate to describe a pioneering scheme which is situated in the current centre of building conversion activity – the London docklands.

New Concordia Wharf, Mill Street, London SE1

This building is a grain warehouse of 1885, situated east of Tower Bridge on the corner of the cul-de-sac St Saviour's Dock on the south bank of the River Thames. St Saviour's Dock was once the outlet of the River Neckinger which was diverted along Jacob Street, Bermondsey, in the seventeenth century to create 'Jacob's Island'. Before the area was redeveloped in the late nineteenth century, it was a notorious slum and it appears in this guise in several of Charles Dickens' novels. A wealthy grain merchant, Seth Taylor, developed the warehouses at New Concordia Wharf. He named the buildings after a town called Concordia near Kansas City, USA, the source of much of the grain that was stored in the warehouses. In 1934 he sold the buildings to the Butler's Wharf Company who undertook not to use the premises for flour or provender milling. Large cranes were added to the dockside elevation in 1937 and the buildings became tea warehouses. Between 1950 and 1979 they were used to store a wide range of products. As well as tea, they housed rubber, paper, film, radios and, finally, computers.

By the end of the 1970s, many of the Victorian warehouses that lined the banks of the Thames east of London Bridge had

Plate 70 New Concordia Wharf, London SE1: in this view from the north bank of the Thames, the building and the inlet of St Saviour's Dock are seen between the tower crane and the old warehouses of the Butler's Wharf Company

lain derelict since the closure of the docks in the mid-1960s. They were mainly owned by property developers who frequently put forward grandiose schemes that would have over-developed the sites of these often large and simple, yet impressive, structures. One scheme after another was dropped because it was either too expensive to execute or was unacceptable to the planners. In September 1979, while looking for more 'interesting' accommodation than premises he had occupied in Fulham and Kensington, a young property developer, Andrew Wadsworth, discovered New Concordia Wharf. It took him over a year to persuade the owner to sell the building, and at the end of 1980, he and his girlfriend moved in and became the sole residents of the 11,000sq m (118,404sq ft) building. By this time, in collaboration with a building contractor, he had formed the Jacob's Island Company in order to undertake property development.

From the outset, the building's new owner wanted to achieve a mixed development which would include as many different uses as possible. He also insisted that the building should be converted to 'shell' stage only to allow lessees to fit out their own spaces. This preference resulted from a period spent in New York where he developed a taste for 'loft living', a policy practised in that city's central Soho district, in which many of the clothes manufacturing 'sweat shops' of the 1900s, constructed largely of cast-iron members framing large open spaces and with no load-bearing walls, have been transformed, often in a haphazard way, into apartments, workshops, offices, studios, restaurants and shops.

In April 1981, planning consent was granted by Southwark Borough Council for a scheme which included 60 flats (of 27 different sizes and shapes), 1,900sq m (20,450sq ft) of workshops/studios, 275sq m (2,900sq ft) of offices, 330sq m (3,550sq ft) of restaurant space, a riverside swimming-pool, boat jetty, games room, communal roof-garden, caretaker's flat, laundry room and basement car park. The London Docklands Development Corporation was set up in September 1981 and in February 1982 the building was listed Grade II . Work on the building's conversion commenced on site in May 1982 and finished in May 1984.

The building was a typical Victorian warehouse, consisting of load-bearing brickwork external walls penetrated by arched windows and loading bays, its internal structure comprising a grid of cruciform-plan cast-iron columns supporting massive timber beams and joists carrying boarded floors. The restoration and conversion of the building has been carried out impeccably under the supervision of the London architects, Pollard Thomas & Edwards. Except for the addition of balconies and a completely new sixth floor, the building must now look almost the same as when it was first brought into use in 1885 (Plate 70).

A thorough examination and analysis of the building's structure by the consultant structural engineer confirmed that the original builder had achieved the intended high load-capacity of almost 1,000kg (2,200lb) per sq m. The only fault found was at the junction of the base-plates of the cast-iron columns with the timber floor beams, where the omission of packing shims had produced an unintended gap, causing lateral stability to be poor. In order not to lose the 'warehouse quality' of exposed timber beams and cast-iron pillars and yet to meet the specified period of fire resistance between storeys, a solution which is simple in principle was adopted. A thin screed of reinforced concrete was cast on top of the floorboards and, in the event of a fire, this membrane will hang from anchors in the walls and the main floor beams after the boarding has burnt away. This in situ concrete coating steps down to meet the top surfaces of the main beams and grips the cast-iron pillars; it is reinforced as an additional longitudinal beam above each main timber beam (Fig 69). Thus, in a fire, the floor structure would become a slender reinforced concrete beam and slab structure. In all other circumstances, the timber structure does all the work.

To prove the suitability of leaving the existing cast-iron columns as main elements of the internal structure with little fire protection, a pillar was tested at the Fire

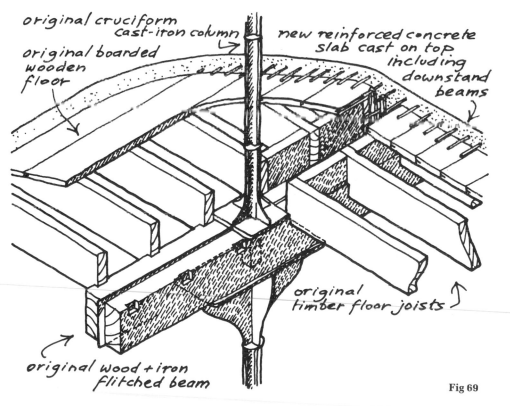

original cruciform cast-iron column

original boarded wooden floor

new reinforced concrete slab cast on top including downstand beams

original timber floor joists

original wood + iron flitched beam

Fig 69

Insurer's Research and Testing Station where it did not suffer cracking when subjected to quenching tests even after one hour's exposure to fire. The iron structures of warehouses are often formed from high-quality castings and a cruciform shape of column helps to reduce concentrated stresses caused by fire or overloading. However, the attitude of the building regulations authority – the Greater London Council – was very conservative. The architects were allowed to retain the cast-iron columns, but only if they were coated with intumescent mastic. This was a 'belt and braces' stipulation because the columns could provide a one-hour period of fire resistance without any fire-resisting coating.

Most of the building's generous load capacity was used up by the additional loads imposed by the concrete floor screed, the sixth-floor penthouses added above the original roof level and the double-skin dividing walls between the flats. Vertical separation of the residential units was achieved by using two separate timber stud walls with three layers of 9mm (^{3}/8in) plasterboard fixed on both sides, finished with a 5mm (^{3}/16in) thick in situ plaster skimcoat. A sound-deadening 75mm (3in) thick glass-fibre quilt was installed in the resulting central cavity, which also houses and protects soil drainage pipes. Despite the all-pervading nature of the new structural measures, at the conclusion of the work the internal structure looked more or less as it did when work commenced. The flat roof over the original top storey was removed and an additional storey was added, using a pitched roll-cap zinc roof-covering on timber joists and boarding, erected on a new steel frame. By omitting sections of the pitched roof, terraces accessible from the flats which occupy this penthouse have been formed (Plate 70).

A large number of waivers and Port of London Authority and London Building Act Section 30 licences were required to retain the building's wood and cast-iron structure, overhanging balconies and cranes. Most of these approvals were received after the building work began and the need for many of these permissions arose from the desire to have mixed uses within one building as well

as from the nature of the existing structure.

The great care taken to conserve and restore characteristic features of the original building extended to relaying the courtyard in salvaged granite setts. All numbering and signs were hand-painted by a signwriter and timber-boarded gates were fitted to the Mill Street entrance to the central courtyard to a design suggested by a 1926 photograph. Replacement windows were made to look exactly like the original frames, down to the decorative rosettes that grace the junctions of glazing bars (although in the new windows these features are formed in plastic rather than cast iron). Various new window openings have been formed below brick arches, matching the original apertures. The brackets supporting the new balconies, as well as all added balustrades and ventilation grilles, were cast in metal in exactly the same way as the nineteenth-century fittings. All internal wall surfaces were cleaned by grit-blasting and, wherever possible, the undersides of the original floor joists and beams have been left exposed. The external brickwork was cleaned and new pointing was carefully coloured to match the weathered original mortar. The very large chimney, marking the entrance to the courtyard, which was the subject of a Dangerous Structure Notice and was about to be demolished when Andrew Wadsworth found the building in 1979, was saved and restored. With a transparent plastic rooflight dome over its mouth, it adds light to the ground-level swimming pool hall. Preservation and restoration of the chimney and other historically noteworthy parts of the building was effected with the assistance of a substantial grant from the Historic Buildings Council.

The building is entered from Mill Street through the cobbled courtyard and at ground level the accommodation consists of a new boat jetty overhanging the river, with public access from the courtyard, a restaurant, swimming-pool, boat-storage room and several workshops/studios/showrooms. The first floor accommodates the office suite of 275sq m (2,960sq ft) with residential 'shells' overlooking St Saviour's Dock and workshops/studios overlooking Mill Street and the courtyard (Fig 70). A similar arrangement applies on the second and third floors.

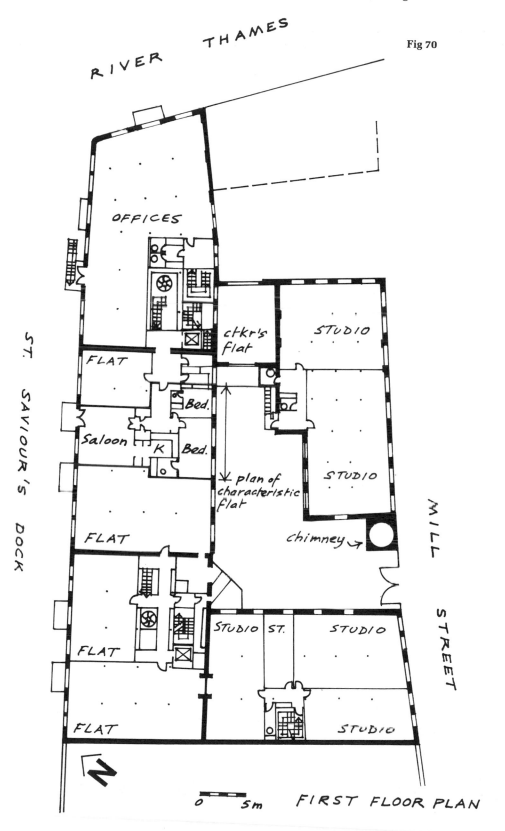

RIVER THAMES

Fig 70

OFFICES

ST. SAVIOUR'S DOCK

FLAT

Saloon

K

Bed.

Bed.

FLAT

FLAT

FLAT

FLAT

ctkr's flat

STUDIO

STUDIO

← plan of characteristic flat

chimney →

STUDIO ST. STUDIO

STUDIO

MILL STREET

N

0   5m

FIRST FLOOR PLAN

Fourth, fifth and sixth floors house only residential shells with balconies or roof terraces. The basement contains car parking, store-rooms, a laundry and a communal games room. The original water tower rises two storeys higher than the rest of the building and has become the home of the owner/developer. In each 'shell' flat, up to four service 'stacks' were provided to give flexibility in siting bathrooms and kitchens, and more than fifty buyers employed a wide range of architects, designers and builders to fit out their units at an additional cost of from £5,000 to £50,000 in every conceivable style. The development received the well earned accolade of a Civic Trust Award in November 1987.

to house female orphans of the Crimean War. Its architect was Major Rhode Hawkins, RE. It is a three-storey Gothic Revival style building of basically symmetrical plan, constructed of yellowish gault brickwork with Bath stone dressings. Its central hall is flanked by two large courtyards, surrounded by enclosed 'cloister' corridors that gave access to the classrooms, administrative offices, etc, (Plate 71, Fig 71). 'Domestic offices' – a laundry, workshops, kitchens and a coal store, were ranged around a third courtyard at the rear of the site and a chapel was included as an independent building to the north of the main blocks.

The complex continued to be used as a children's home until 1914. Throughout

Royal Victoria Patriotic Building, London SW18

The Royal Victoria Patriotic Asylum was erected in 1857-9, at a total cost of £31,337,

Plate 71   Royal Victoria Patriotic Building, London SW18: the main elevations of the converted building with the high-roofed central hall with its lantern seen behind the turreted entrance tower; studio offices occupy the lowest storey whilst flats are located on the first and second floors

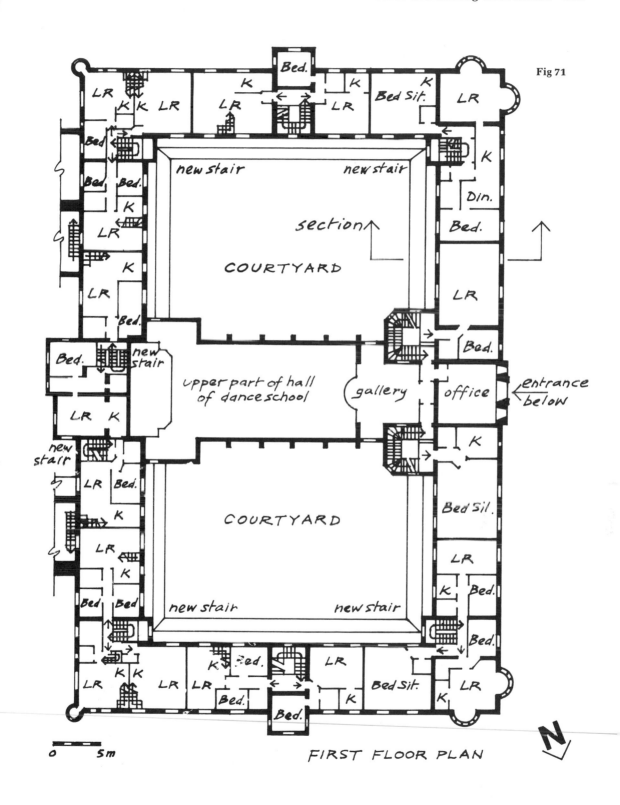

Fig 71

FIRST FLOOR PLAN

0   5m

World War I it served as the Third London General Hospital for the care of the wounded. In the inter-war period the building returned to its original use as an orphanage. During World War II it again saw emergency service when it was used as a debriefing centre by the security services. For this purpose, additional 'temporary' concrete buildings were erected in the main courtyards. These structures remained throughout the period 1945-78 when part of the building was used by the Inner London Education Authority as Spencer Park School. The first and second floors were left empty during this time. With the construction of the new Spencer Park School on an adjacent site, the remainder of the building was gradually emptied. Partial occupation of the building had meant that there were insufficient funds to maintain the structure satisfactorily and this circumstance worsened as the population of the school diminished. After 1978 the building was effectively abandoned, quickly became derelict and was extensively vandalised. As it had been listed Grade II and was well regarded by the Historic Buildings Division of the Greater London Council and the local amenity group, the Wandsworth Society, any proposal by the ILEA to demolish it would have encountered considerable opposition. Obviously, they viewed it as a liability and would probably have been delighted if it had collapsed spontaneously. This almost happened in 1981 when a serious fire destroyed the roof structure of the central hall.

At about that time, the ILEA had invited offers for the purchase of the building, associated with strict conditions relating to its repair and maintenance. Also, the local planning authority, Wandsworth Council, had drawn up a planning brief defining acceptable ways in which the building might be used. It was felt that a renovated building should offer some fairly low-cost housing; if possible, small workshops and small office suites should be provided as a means of generating employment; the main halls (ie, the central hall and the square hall at the south-east corner of the main blocks) should be dedicated to a community use and they should not be divided up; in deference to its status as a listed building, external alterations should be kept to a minimum; all vehicle parking generated by the redevelopment should be accommodated within the site curtilage and any new uses should generate as small an amount of vehicle traffic as possible. This last stipulation was important because access to the building can only be gained via the narrow and sinuous roads of the adjoining council housing estate which, having previously belonged to the GLC, was in the process of being adopted by Wandsworth Council at that time.

From the foregoing account it can be appreciated that by 1980 purchase of the building hardly seemed like a sensible investment and various attempts by the local authority and amenity groups to promote new uses for the building had foundered on the question of finance. In the event, the bid of an entrepreneur and restaurateur, Paul Tutton, to buy the building for the sum of £1, allied to a commitment to undertake certain specified repairs, etc, was accepted. The successful tenderer was required to create new boundaries to the site, to arrest the spread of dry rot and to repair the roofs. The existing freeholder was only prepared to grant a lease to the purchaser pending completion of this work. Following attention to these matters – which represented an expenditure of around £250,000 – the freehold was conveyed to the new owner.

Mr Tutton's brief to his architects, Dickinson, Quarme & Associates, was, first, to stabilise and repair the building to prevent any further decay, and secondly, to convert the entire building into economic use, providing a commercial return on his investment, yet still complying with the local authority's planning brief. Both aspects of the conversion were to be carried out at the minimum cost compatible with the sympathetic re-use of an historic building. The need for extreme economy in funding repairs was encouraged by judgements from a prominent London firm of estate agents and the ILEA Surveyor's and Estates Department that the building had a 'negative value' because this opinion made it virtually impossible to obtain bank finance other than in relatively small tranches of money suitably covered by collateral.

When the condition of the structure which survived to 1981 is described, the scope and difficulty of the work can be fully appreciated. Almost all the lead flashings, valleys and cappings from the roofs of the complex had been stolen; the cast-iron rain-water gutters and downpipes were either blocked, broken or missing; large areas of slating were missing from the roofs; stone dressings were in an advanced state of decay; large areas of the building harboured outbreaks of dry rot; all the services were either defunct, damaged or dangerous and almost every window and its glazing was damaged or broken.

The new owner's response to this long schedule of essential repairs was not to employ a firm of building contractors to undertake the work on his behalf, but instead, to set up his own construction company. He employed a project manager to supervise a small number of skilled in-house staff who executed most of the repairs and alterations. The size of this directly employed workforce varied, but it was usually 8-10 men, consisting of a foreman, a 'ganger', 2 carpenters, a bricklayer and 3-5 labourers. Accepting that the age and dilapidated condition of the building represented nil collateral in the eyes of lenders, the developer's approach was to use his initial capital to obtain loans which would finance renovation of the first sections of the building and then to rely on the project becoming self-financing. This was achieved through the sale of flats on 99-year leases and also from the security granted by gradual letting of the workshops and offices, against which increased borrowings could be made.

The effect of this policy on the rebuilding work was that large sections of the building could not be renovated in an integrated construction process. The work had to be carried out as sales and leases were entered into, and therefore the contract had to be run primarily in accordance with the dictates of cash flow, rather than the logical sequencing of building operations. Thus the flexibility offered by the 'direct labour' system that was adopted was invaluable.

The building owner closely controlled the financial aspects of the project. Financial meetings took place at monthly intervals over a six-year period from 1981. The role of the architect extended to designing the overall scheme, assisting the project manager on budgeting and cost control, experimenting with different building techniques and construction methods in collaboration with the project manager, and providing 'quality control' by being a virtually permanent on-site inspector of the works.

Two main difficulties arose to present greater problems than are normally associated with building works. They were the extremely tight budgetary restraint that was exercised throughout the project and the great difficulty in obtaining 'Means of Escape Consent'. It is the architects' view that until this scheme was promoted, no similarly large building had been converted to house a combination of commercial, light industrial and residential uses. Consequently, it was difficult to apply existing building regulations to the conditions that emerged from a mixture of uses. For example, the regulations forbade the use of means of escape exits by both residential and commercial uses. Even though the architects very ingeniously added six new fire escape staircases of fire-resisting concrete construction within the main blocks, complete separation of the circulation systems could not be achieved without radical – and unacceptable – changes to the anatomy of the building. Hence, only after two years of continuous negotiations with the controlling authority (the GLC) could approvals be obtained for the means of escape proposed for the second-floor maisonettes and for the use of the cloisters as escape routes for both the commercial and residential elements. While these negotiations were proceeding, the owner was advancing the renovation work 'at risk' in order to prevent any further deterioration of the building and to try to minimise the effects of gradually mounting costs. Eventually, in addition to the appropriate approval documents, the necessary waivers and relaxations of the regulations were obtained.

The exercise of securing the shell of the building to facilitate renovation and improvement of the interiors for the range of new uses necessitated a considerable amount of repair and renewal work. The roof had to be thoroughly overhauled, and in some areas entirely re-covered with matching, graded, Lakeland slates. All missing leadwork, including flashings and ridge cappings, was replaced. Many roof trusses were treated with preservative to ward off dry rot attack and were repaired in situ by splicing-in new timber which had also been impregnated with fungicidal fluid. All windows were replaced, repaired or overhauled as necessary. Reglazing alone called for the replacement of approximately six thousand sheets of glass. Most of the internal joinery – doors, door linings, architraves, etc, – was removed and renewed. All internal plasterwork was hacked off on the advice of the dry rot specialist and every brick wall was injected at approximately 300mm (12in) intervals with fungicidal fluid. Suspended floors at ground floor level and complementary wood block finishes on solid floors were removed to eliminate dry rot, and the infected timber lath shuttering of the wrought-iron-framed 'filler joist' floors located at first- and second-floor levels was also removed. The external rainwater disposal system was overhauled and repaired, and missing sections were replaced with fittings of matching pattern. This necessitated work to almost 3km (1¾ miles) of guttering. Most external brickwork surfaces were cleaned and repointed where necessary and plastic repairs were made to badly eroded stonework.

The architects' strategy for re-use of the building was to site offices on the ground floor of the main blocks; to dispose workshops around the rear courtyard; to devote the first and second floors to flats and maisonettes respectively, and to accommodate a dance and drama school in the main halls and their ancillary spaces. It was also their aim to modify the external appearance as little as possible and to confine alterations to the interior. In order to maximise the internal area and to create rooms with ceiling heights appropriate for modern living, mezzanine levels were inserted in the lowest and highest storeys.

Every attempt was made to tailor alterations so that they would be sympathetic to the character of the building. The new 'fire-check' doors occupying all openings within, and leading off from the main cloisters, were purpose-made in neo-Gothic style. Most new windows re-used cast-iron centre-pivot casement frames removed from other sections of the building and were set in 'stone' surrounds formed from 'plastic' stonework. Redundant vent grilles were used to make moulds in which facsimile fittings of aluminium alloy were cast and these fittings were inserted in the external walls in order to vent the voids below the renewed suspended timber ground floor (no underfloor ventilation had been provided in the original building, inviting the onset of dry rot). Other external features that were faithfully reproduced included the elaborate lead finials over dormer windows and the Victorian profiles of the original boundary wall in sections where this element had been demolished or altered.

The ground-floor office 'studios' and workshops were all created as part of the overall conversion scheme, but prospective leaseholders of the flats were offered the choice of purchasing each unit at one of three separate stages of conversion – 'shell', partial conversion or full conversion. Shell conversion included all the work to the common parts (such as shared entry lobbies and staircases), the major internal structural alterations (including the construction of a mezzanine level in the second-floor dwellings) and any alterations to the external shell of each unit, such as the insertion of roof windows and vents. Additionally, each shell unit would be provided with the normal services: soil and waste drainage, electricity and gas supplies.

The partial conversion would include all the above items and also partitions between newly formed rooms, internal doors and associated joinery 'trim' (skirtings and architraves). The basic services would be extended to provide internal plumbing, electrical distribution and central heating. The first partly converted flat was sold in 1982 for what would now be regarded as a nominal sum. Subsequently, demand has rocketed, leading to areas being combined to form larger units with a consequent increase in purchase price. 'Full conversion' included all the features of the partial conversion as well as any additional finishes, such as decorations, wall tiling, specialist joinery and floor surfaces.

This approach gave considerable freedom to leaseholders to determine the exact level of financial commitment they should make at the outset and at later stages, and it gave them the opportunity to 'mould' the interiors of their dwellings to their specific needs and tastes. The majority of leaseholders opted for the partial conversion, adding the finishes later by their own efforts or those of their own subcontractors. Some of the braver leaseholders purchased units converted to 'shell' only and employed their own architects and designers, rather than the developer's architects, to design and monitor the execution of the fitting out of their flats. Consequently, the whole range of contemporary styles in interior design, materials and finishes, is visible within the building.

Exclusive of the expense incurred in restoring the fire-damaged roof of the central hall – the cost of which was met by the building's insurers through a policy which guaranteed the replacement of the old construction with matching new materials and first-quality workmanship – and independent of the cost of work separately commissioned to complete the interiors of the 'shells' and partial-conversion flats, the total cost of the development was around £1.9 million. Eighteen workshops and thirty-one studio offices have been provided, together with twenty-six flats. Because it is a constricted site and parking is not permitted in the rear 'workshop' courtyard, yet the development had to absorb all the operational and residential parking that it generated, to standards laid down by the planning authority, approximately 120 car parking spaces are distributed around the edge of the site and in every accessible corner.

The cross-sectional principle of creating single-storey flats at first-floor level and maisonettes above second-floor level by means of inserting mezzanines is clearly shown in Fig 72. What is less apparent from the drawing is the fact that these mezzanines were introduced at a level at which substantial stone transoms cross the centres of the high 'semi-dormer' windows of the top storey. This arrangement necessitated a waiver of the building regulations because the London Building Acts required a solid masonry panel, at least 900mm (3ft) deep, to separate the windows of the newly formed upper storey from those of the level below. The architects' endeavours to obtain official acceptance of this detail provide just one example of the vast amount of patient negotiation that was needed in order that this ambitious, innovatory and highly complicated project could succeed. The outcome has been the retention and praiseworthy restoration of a characterful building, a boost for local employment opportunities and a contribution to the local supply of housing.

The intention of the owner and his architects was to produce an artistic community where people could both live and work, the description 'artistic' embracing industrial crafts such as joinery manufacture as well as the traditional fine arts. To some degree, this aspiration has been fulfilled – a number of leaseholders occupy both flats and workshops or offices.

The capital now boasts further 'recycled'

Fig 72

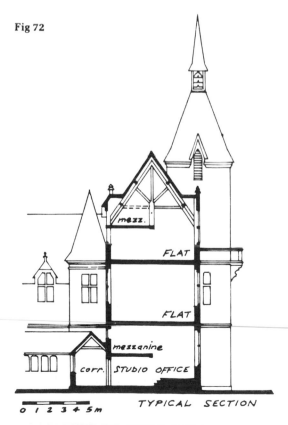

mezz.

FLAT

FLAT

mezzanine

corr. | STUDIO OFFICE

0 1 2 3 4 5m

TYPICAL SECTION

buildings offering opportunities for their occupants to both live and work on the premises and though it allows less intimacy between the commercial and residential elements than is found at the Royal Victoria Patriotic Building, an impressive example of the type is described below.

The Power House, Stamford Brook, London W4

Around the turn of the century 'tramway mania' gripped many British towns and cities. Proof of the practicality of the electric tram-car and the growing demand for cheap public transport to link the fast-expanding outer suburbs with the city centres led to the rapid growth of tramway systems, many of which were developed by municipalities under powers available to them after 1891. However, the development of an electric tramway system in west and south-west London was undertaken by the London United Tramways Company who electrified and extended their existing horse-tram network. To provide the necessary electrical power, they established a generating station at Stamford Brook, West London, in 1901. A very large but simple building housing boilers and turbine-powered generators was designed by the company's engineer, Clifton Robinson, and, no doubt in deference to the feelings of local residents, an architect, William Curtis Green, was employed to design the elevations. Green had previously worked in the office of John Belcher, one of the leading exponents of the neo-Baroque style during the late-Victorian and Edwardian periods, and the adornments he designed for the otherwise basic 'brick box' of the power station reflect his schooling in this architectural style. Probably the piebald arches of alternating voussoirs of red brick and Portland stone, the stone-trimmed 'blind' windows tucked below the giant cornice and the huge 'bull's-eye' apertures in the stratified brick-and-stone parapet owe

Plate 72 The Power House, Stamford Brook, London W4: the entrance elevation of the building during the conversion work, showing the giant scale of this monolithic block; before the scaffolding was dismantled the brickwork and stonework were water-washed to give an 'as new' appearance

more to the British Baroque of Sir Christopher Wren and Nicholas Hawksmoor than they do to continental examples, but, combined with the considerable height and vast bulk of the building, they make a striking contribution to the townscape of this part of London (Plate 72). As built, the power station was complemented by a massive chimney, almost 100m (330ft) high, which acted as the boiler exhaust flue.

London United Tramways' investment in the Stamford Brook complex of power station and adjoining tram depot came to more than £1 million, but barely a year after it was completed, most of the company's shares were bought by the competing Underground Electric Railway Co Ltd, and the importance of the tramway began to diminish in favour of the 'tube'.

The building was a true 'cathedral of technology'. Dominating the 18m (60ft) wide engine room was a 25-ton electrically powered overhead crane, while an upper level of the south end of this space housed a giant and highly ornate switchboard and instrument panel. The boiler and engine-rooms housed the most advanced machinery available. Mechanical stokers fed the boilers from high-level coal storage bunkers and ash was automatically removed by conveyor belt.

In June 1917, in the midst of a legal battle to acquire LUT's Inner City network, the London County Council purchased the power station for £235,000. By August of that year it had been decommissioned, its chimney was demolished and all the equipment was removed. For the next decade its sole use was to operate as an electricity substation, but this function occupied only a small part of the engine room. In 1929 the boiler-room was rented out to Mr. T. Ireby Cape's Theatrical and Film Company as a scenic studio and in 1940 the descent of the building into dereliction accelerated when this space became a store for the tram depot. From 1962 the whole building was used to store surplus bus-shelters. Plainly, London Transport regarded the structure as something of a liability and in 1975 they announced their intention to demolish it. There was an immediate public outcry and demolition was prevented by the building being 'spot-listed' Grade II.

Plate 73 The Power House, Stamford Brook, London W4: a view into the terraces adjoining the flats which are screened by the high rooftop parapet; note the prominence of the retained roof trusses

In 1984, David Clarke, an architect who lives locally, read of London Transport's search for a buyer for the building in one of the district's newspapers and he quickly managed to interest a property developer in the potential of the building for conversion. His proposal was for a mixed development of nineteen maisonettes, a film and recording studio and around 800sq m (8,600sq ft) of offices. Although the great width of the building suggested that the maisonettes should be located just below roof level if the largely imperforate external walls were to remain unaltered (an almost inescapable constraint in the case of a listed building), because the building is such a conspicuous landmark, the planners were equally insistent that its silhouette should not be changed. Thus the maisonettes were 'sleeved' in between the steel-framed roof trusses just below the slopes of the pitched and hipped roofs rather than being allowed to penetrate the roof-slopes. By 'cutting away' sections of the roofs close to the inner face of the perimeter parapet, it was possible to install new glazed walls containing windows and French windows which light the interiors of the maisonettes and link the terraces with bedrooms (Plate 73). The roofs were stripped of their original slate covering and the existing close-boarded sarking was supplemented with additional thermal insulation before the slating was reinstated. As the steelwork supporting the new 'plat-

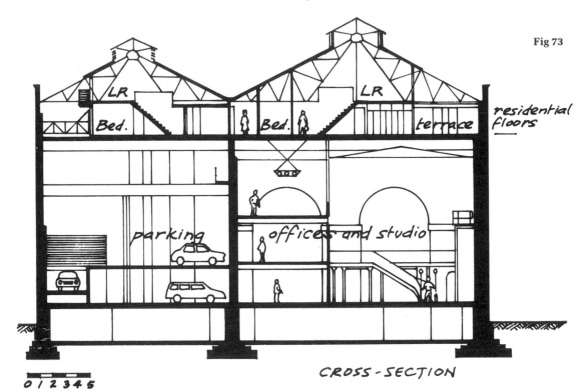

Fig 73

CROSS-SECTION

form floor', off which the maisonettes are built, bears on the external walls at the track level of the former travelling crane, there was room below the bottom chords of the roof trusses to install a single storey of accommodation, with the remainder of the rooms being sited in the roof space (Fig 73). Each maisonette contains an inverted version of the normal domestic arrangement – bedrooms are placed at the lower level, en suite with the external terraces, and living/dining-rooms are located upstairs.

Access to the dwellings was gained via a lift lobby formed in a corner of the old boiler-room, the remainder of which houses two levels of car parking. The ground floor of the original building was raised above external ground level so that a shallow undercroft could accommodate steam mains linking the boilers to the turbines and the main power supply from the generators to the network. This level was retained and therefore short ramps were needed to reconcile the new pedestrian and vehicle entrances with the external ground level.

The benefits of the original huge entrance doors became apparent during the first phase of the conversion work when the

gantry crane was demolished and the new steel beams supporting the lower floor of the maisonettes were installed. Articulated lorries were able to drive right into the building to deliver these large members. A decision to order such components before planning consent was received was something of a calculated risk in the sense that it was a rather controversial application, vehicle access to the site being very constricted, but it turned out to be a gamble that paid off. The building was found to be in excellent condition and had been built very accurately – setting of the new floor levels with laser equipment showed that the brick courses were at precisely the levels anticipated.

The second phase of the conversion was construction of the flats. Planning consent was applied for in October 1984 and was granted in January 1985. Because the steelwork had already been ordered, construction was able to commence in February 1985. Half of the flats were handed over at the end of January 1986 with the other half following in May of that year.

The third phase of the work was the conversion of part of the former engine-room to provide an office suite. This phase was underway in the second half of 1987. The remainder of the space – around 550sq m (5,920 sq ft) in area and 11m high – has been fitted out as a recording studio.

Because a large part of each flat was constructed in the roof trusses zone, many rooms are dominated by large sections of the steel-angle roof trusses (Plate 74). Indeed, except where flats have been confined to the 'corridor-form' dictated by the positions of parallel roof trusses – for instance, at the corners where trusses supporting the roof hip cross the space diagonally – in order to connect rooms and to create convenient accommodation, it has been necessary to remove various braces and struts from the trusses and to install new structural members to replace the 'lost' steelwork. The estate agents who marketed the flats were at first unsure about the suitability of these trusses as prominent features of the interiors, but they had no cause to be worried as all the smaller flats were sold 'off the drawings', well in advance of completion, at prices ranging from £65,000 to £85,000. As with so many of the projects featured in this book, the appeal of 'something different' appeared to be irresistible.

All the flats were sold on 125-year leases and the largest unit, which is at the southwest corner, and which enjoys panoramic views over West and Central London, is 270sq m (2,906sq ft) in area (Fig 74). In order to obtain a clear understanding of how the roof space between the trusses might best be manipulated to create convenient living accommodation, the architect was obliged to make many three-dimensional scale models of the building.

In contrast to the great ingenuity that had to be exercised in threading rooms through the roof trusses, re-use of the upper part of the block-like form of 'The Power House' as the lower floor of the maisonettes was fairly straightforward, and this fact suggests that the similarly simply-shaped office buildings of the post-war period may hold some promise for conversion into dwellings. This notion is corroborated by the suspicion that the 'microprocessor revolution' in acting to reduce the number of clerical jobs, must also reduce the demand for purpose-built offices, leaving redundant the under-serviced and

Plate 74   The Power House, Stamford Brook, London W4: a maisonette interior showing the two living levels and the main role played by a retained roof truss

therefore 'hard-to-let' structures of the 1950s and 1960s. Unfortunately, in the case of speculative office buildings from the office building boom of the 1960s and early 1970s, it is almost invariably found that the desire of the original developers to minimise costs by building only the bare minimum interior volume and cheapening finishes, etc, severely constrains the options for re-use. These buildings are simply too inflexible and poorly constructed to offer the 'spare' space for the inclusion of new finishes or the installation of the multiple services terminals needed in a conversion into dwellings.

More promising may be the more generously constructed bespoke office buildings of the post-war and inter-war periods. A proposal has been made to convert Thames House, the former headquarters of Imperial Chemical Industries, erected in 1928, into 750 luxury apartments, while the former West London Air Terminal of British Airways on Cromwell Road, South Kensington, is being converted into 350 flats. In this latter building, the inability of the 'minimalist' modern movement architecture of the 1960s to accommodate change readily is apparent. The creation of this large number of flats from a former administrative building is only achievable with the complete demolition of the tower block that formed a prominent feature of the original building and its reconstruction as a

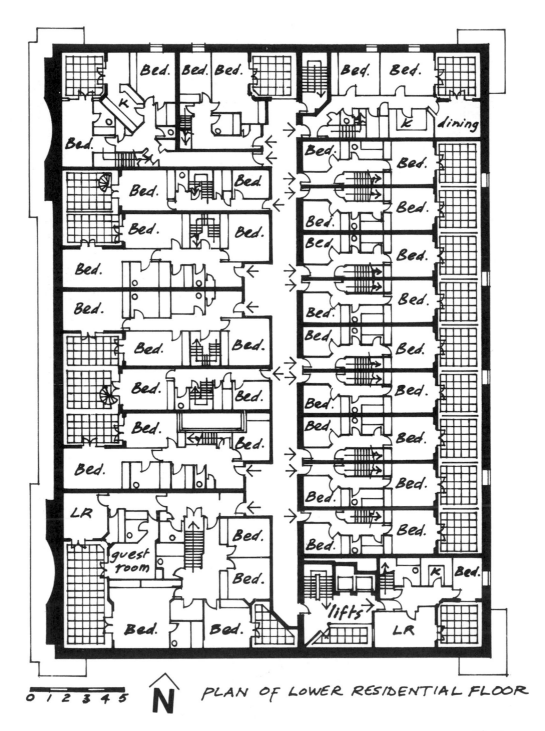

PLAN OF LOWER RESIDENTIAL FLOOR

Fig 74

purpose-designed residential tower. The adjoining eleven-storey 'slab' block of offices offers more opportunities for adaptation and is being reclad and its interiors subdivided to create a significant proportion of the new dwellings (Plate 75).

Most of these projects, being sited in London, owe their existence to the boom of the late 1980s in property prices in south-east England. Yet many other British towns and cities, outside the affluent south, house fine and noteworthy old buildings which continue to stand empty because their conversion into dwellings cannot be made to pay. We have seen how, in the case of Granby House, a former cotton warehouse in central Manchester, a central and local government subsidy in the form of an Urban Development Grant acted to turn a conversion proposal into a viable proposition for its developer and an impressive Edwardian commercial building was saved from dereliction and eventual demolition in consequence. Despite the fact that this pioneering project was followed by further schemes in which even larger city-centre warehouses have been re-used for housing, many old buildings in central Manchester, as well as the giant mills and warehouses of

Plate 75 The increasing size of building-conversion projects; the former West London Air Terminal is being re-clad and restructured to provide 350 flats

a multitude of other northern towns, continue to decay for want of imaginative proposals for their re-use, or, more likely, the finance to realise these proposals.

An example of such a building is provided by Victoria Mills, Skipton, North Yorkshire, a Grade II listed former woollen mill of 1849 which stands close to the town centre on the north bank of the Leeds and Liverpool Canal at Belmont Wharf (Plate 76). This twin-gabled stone structure has stood empty and been deteriorating for many years since it ceased to be used as a warehouse. It was a somewhat unwelcome legacy for the young owner who inherited it in the early 1980s because he became responsible for an apparently unusable, decaying building of possibly 'negative' value which, owing to its listed building status, he was effectively unable to demolish. Its attractive canalside location suggested that it could be converted to domestic use and, accordingly, a planning application for change of use to flats was submitted to the

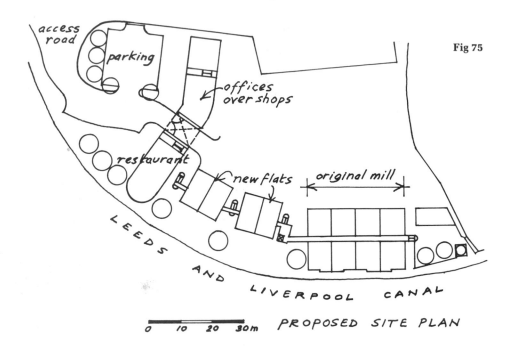

PROPOSED SITE PLAN

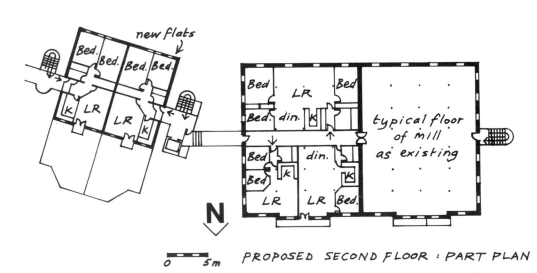

PROPOSED SECOND FLOOR : PART PLAN

local district council. Because the building adjoins a factory, the council had zoned the area for industrial use and, despite the fact that it had not been used for manufacturing purposes for forty years, in 1983 they rejected the change-of-use application. The hapless and impecunious owner then turned to the only course left to him – an application for Listed Building Consent to demolish the structure. This was also refused and in consequence of the owner's

appeal against this decision, a public inquiry was held. At this inquiry, the Secretary of State's inspector expressed his support for the building's conversion to residential use and, accordingly, the owner's architect, John Wharton, produced a revised scheme proposing the re-use of the building as twenty-six flats, a shop and a showroom, which then received Listed Building Consent.

It would be comforting to be able to report

that the survival of Victoria Mills – the best piece of industrial architecture in Skipton – has been assured. Unfortunately, this would be overstating the case. Because Skipton is not London docklands and home buyers are not prepared to pay, say, £50,000 for a 'shell' flat in part of an old warehouse when a well-appointed stone-built three-bedroom terrace house can be bought locally for considerably less, the viability of the conversion and upgrading of Victoria Mills needs to be secured by redevelopment of adjacent land as new housing, shops and offices (Fig 75). This proposal involves the loss of no noteworthy buildings because, apart from one or two decaying properties of domestic scale, such as a builder's yard, the greater part of this adjoining site (which provides the only route to the nearest road) is vacant land. Since the granting of planning permission for this mixed development, the possibility of its implementation has receded because the North Yorkshire County Council, as owner of one or two of the premises that abut the 'land-locked' Victoria Mills site on the west side, has sold freeholds to sitting tenants, thus reducing the opportunity to 'assemble' a site which will allow an integrated and viable development.

The case of Victoria Mills indicates clearly how projects involving the conversion to domestic use of former commercial or industrial premises in even picturesque northern towns, which show only a marginal profit in investment terms, can founder on a detail. This is in clear contrast to the great time and trouble that developers would take to remove much greater obstacles standing in the way of realisation of an equivalent scheme in central London. In the current climate of great enthusiasm for the re-use of redundant buildings, the pursuit of official acceptance of combining different uses in one building, the identification of

Plate 76 Victoria Mills, Skipton, North Yorkshire: many such handsome and impressive commercial buildings of provincial towns and cities which might be saved through conversion into dwellings continue to stand empty and decaying for want of viable schemes for their adaptation

uses that can be made, with ingenuity, to co exist happily and the clever tailoring of redundant buildings to these combinations of uses are sure to be increasing interests of architects and developers. It is to be hoped that, over the coming years, the enterprise stemming from this enthusiasm will do as much to save many of the aged but handsome religious and secular buildings of Britain's provincial towns and cities as it is currently doing for those of the capital.

Useful Addresses

Advisory Board for Redundant Churches
(Anglian churches only)
Fielden House
Little College Street
LONDON SW1P 3SH
Tel 071 222 9603

The Ancient Monuments Society
St Andrew's By The Wardrobe
Queen Victoria Street
LONDON EC4 V 5DE
Tel 071 236 3934

Architectual Heritage Fund
17 Carlton House Terrace
LONDON SW1Y 5AW
Tel 071 930 0914

British Constructional Steelwork
   Association Ltd
29 Old Queen Street
LONDON SW1
Tel 071 222 2254

British Rail Property Board
274 Bishopsgate
LONDON EC2M 4XQ
Tel 071 247 5444

Building Employers Confederation
82 New Cavendish Street
LONDON W1
Tel 071 580 5588

Civic Trust
17 Carlton House Terrace
LONDON SW1Y 5AW
Tel 071 930 0914

Civic Trust for the North West
The Enviromental Institute
Greaves School
Bolton Road
Swinton
MANCHESTER M27 2UX·
Tel 061 794 9314

Department of the Environment
(City Grant enquiries)

Regional Offices:
Eastern Regional Office
Department of the Environment
Room 416B
Charles House
375 Kensington High Street
LONDON W14 8QH
Tel 071 605 9000 Ext 9150

East Midlands Regional Office
Department of the Environment
Room 205
Cranbrook House
Cranbrook Street
NOTTINGHAM NG1 1EY
Tel 0602 476121 Ext 468

Greater London Regional Office
Department of the Environment
Room 2602A
Millbank Tower
21-24 Millbank
LONDON SW1P 4QU
Tel 071 211 6144

Merseyside Task Force
Department of the Environment
Graeme House
Derby Square
LIVERPOOL L2 7SU
Tel 051 227 4111 Ext 506

Northern Regional Office
Department of the Environment
Room 703
Wellbar House
.Gallowgate
NEWCASTLE UPON TYNE NE1 4TD
Tel 091 232 7575 Ext 2566

North West Regional Office
Department of the Environment
Room 1107
Sunley Tower
Piccadilly Plaza
MANCHESTER M1 4BE
Tel 061 832 9111 Ext 2346

South East Regional Office
Department of the Environment
Room 548B
Charles House
375 Kensington High Street
LONDON W14 8QH
Tel 071 605 9080

South West Regional Office
Department of the Environment
Room 306
Tollgate House
Houlton Street
BRISTOL BS2 9DJ
Tel 0272 218431

West Midlands Regional Office
Department of the Enviroment
Five Ways Tower
Frederick Road
Edgbaston
BIRMINGHAM B15 1SJ
TEL 021 631 4141 EXT 2541

Yorkshire and Humberside Regional Office
Department of the Environment
Room 1001
City House
New Station Street
LEEDS LS1 4JH
Tel 0532 438232 Ext 2440

Grant Aid for Historic Buildings

Department of the Environment of
Northern Ireland
Historic Monuments and Buildings Branch
23 Castle Place
BELFAST BT1 1FY
Tel 0232 230560

English Heritage (Historic Buildings and
    Monuments Commission)
25 Savile Row
LONDON W1X 2BT
Tel 071 734 6010

Historic Buildings and Monuments
    Commission (London Division)
Chesham House
30 Warwick Street
LONDON W1R 6AB
Tel 071 734 8144

Scottish Development Department
Historic Buildings Division
20 Brandon Street
EDINBURGH EH3 5RA
Tel 031 556 8400

Welsh Office
Conservation and Land Division
New Crown Building
Cathays Park
CARDIFF CF1 3NQ
Tel 0222 465511

The Georgian Group
37 Spital Square
LONDON E1 6DY
Tel 071 377 1722

The Historic Buildings Company
PO Box 150
CHOBHAM
Surrey GU24 8JD
Tel 099 05 7983

Housing Corporation
149 Tottenham Court Road
LONDON W1P 0BN
Tel 071 387 9466
(also various regional offices)

Institution of Structual Engineers
11 Upper Belgrave Street
LONDON SW1
Tel 071 235 4535

National Federation of Housing Associations
175 Gray's Inn Road
LONDON WC1X 8UP
Tel 071 833 1811

Registry of Friendly Societies
15 Great Marlborough Street
LONDON W1
Tel 071 437 9992

Royal Institute of British Architects
66 Portland Place
LONDON W1N 4AD
Tel 071 580 5533

The Royal Institution of Chartered
    Surveyors
12 Great George Street
LONDON SW1
Tel 071 222 7000

Royal Town Planning Institute
26 Portland Place
LONDON W1N 4BE
Tel 071 636 9107

Society for the Protection of Ancient
    Buildings
37 Spital Square
LONDON E1 6DY
Tel 071 377 1644

The Victorian Society
1 Priory Gardens
LONDON W4 1TT
Tel 081 994 1019

Further Reading

Maintenance and Repair of Old Buildings

How To Restore and Improve Your Victorian House Johnson, Alan (David & Charles, 1991)
Old Stone Buildings; Buying, Extending, Renovating Harrison, J. A. C. (David & Charles, 1981)
The Care of Old Buildings Today Insall, Donald (Architectural Press, 1972)
The House Restorer's Guide Lander, Hugh (David & Charles, 1986)
The Repair and Maintenance of Houses Melville, Ian, and Gordon, Ian (*Estates Gazette*, 1972)

Re-use of Old Buildings

Adaptive Reuse; Issues and Case Studies in Building Preservation (American) Austin, R. (Van Nostrand Reinhold, 1988)
Bright Future; The Re-use of Industrial Buildings, Binney, Marcus and Machin, Francis (SAVE, 1990)
Re-architecture; Old Buildings New Uses, Cantacuzino, S. (Thames & Hudson, 1989)
Rehabilitation and Re-use of Old Buildings Highfield, David (E. & F.N. Spon, 1987)
Restoring Old Buildings for Contemporary Uses (American) Shopsin, W.C. (Watson Guptill, 1987)
Re-using Redundant Buildings; Good Practice in Urban Regeneration URBED (HMSO, 1987)
Saving Old Buildings Cantacuzino, S. and Brandt, S. (Architectural Press, 1980)
The Refurbishment of Commercial and Industrial Buildings Marsh, Paul (Construction Press, 1983)

New Uses for Old Churches

Change and Decay; The Future of Our Churches Binney, Marcus, and Burman, Peter (Studio Vista, 1977)
Churches: A Question of Conversion Powell, Ken, and de la Hey, Celia (SAVE, 1987)
New Life for Old Churches Anon (HMSO 1977)

Index